Children and their accidents

Children and their accidents

JG Avery MD, FFPHM, DTM&H

Formerly Director of Public Health, South Warwickshire
Health Authority, Warwick

and

RH Jackson OBE, MC, FRCP

President, Child Accident Prevention Trust,
London

Edward Arnold
A division of Hodder & Stoughton
LONDON   MELBOURNE   AUCKLAND

© 1993 J. G. Avery and R. H. Jackson

First published in Great Britain 1993

British Library Cataloguing in Publication Data

Avery, J. Gordon
  Children and their accidents
  I. Title   II. Jackson, R. Hugh
  618.92

  ISBN 0–340–37001–7

Whilst the advice and information in this book is believed to be true and accurate at the date of going to press, neither the author nor the publisher can accept any legal responsibility or liability for any errors or omissions that may be made.

Typeset in 10/12 pt Times Roman by Anneset, Weston-super-Mare, Avon. Printed and bound in Great Britain for Edward Arnold, a division of Hodder and Stoughton Limited, Mill Road, Dunton Green, Sevenoaks, Kent TN13 2YA by St. Edmundsbury Press, Bury St. Edmunds, Suffolk and Hartnolls Ltd., Bodmin, Cornwall.

CONTENTS

Foreword   vii

Preface   ix

1 Introduction – the greatest killer of all   1

2 Why do children have accidents?   5

3 Road traffic and other transport accidents   18

4 Accidents in the home   43

5 Accidents at school and at play   71

6 Sports and leisure accidents   85

7 Accidents at work including on the farm;
    natural and man-made disasters   106

8 Non-accidental injuries   115

9 What can we do to prevent children's accidents?   125

10 Who is responsible?   156

11 The need for evaluation **170**

12 Where do we go from here? **176**

Useful addresses **186**

Bibliography **195**

Index **206**

FOREWORD

Accidents to children are common. They cause a lot of pain and distress and they make considerable demands on the Health Services. Many, though not all, can be avoided. The purpose of the authors is to present to anyone who is concerned, the facts relating to the accidents, what injuries result and what we can do about them. Although both authors are doctors, it is written for anybody. Medical information is kept to a minimum, just enough to recognise the nature of the injury and apply simple remedies and no more.

The book is timely because it is the declared objective of the UK Government to reduce the death rate from accidents in childhood by 33% in the next 15 years. We must all hope that that will be achieved and that it will be accompanied by a similar fall in all injuries whether serious or trivial. This book is an excellent introduction and resource for anyone involved in this initiative.

Accidents take many forms and occur in many situations. It is possible because of the clear presentation and structure of the book to dip into it and learn, say, about drowning accidents in children with epilepsy. But many I believe would benefit by reading it from cover to cover. It is well written and peppered with facts and sound advice. The reader must be warned that it is the authors view that whoever we are, we all have opportunities and the responsibility to take steps to reduce accidents in childhood. And they do not hesitate in telling us what we should do, whether we are parents, teachers, doctors, drivers, etc.

If you were not aware before you open the book it will quickly become obvious to you that the authors are considerable authorities of long experience. I hope and believe that all their hard work preparing this text and framing their advice will itself make a considerable contribution to preventing childhood accidents, and that many families in the future should be grateful, but happily they will not know it!

David Hull
President
British Paediatric Association

PREFACE

This book on childhood accidents is being launched at a most opportune time, since the United Kingdom government intends to make accident prevention one of the main thrusts for health improvements in the 1990s. The book has taken several years in its gestation.

From the time when the authors first started to think about putting their experiences in Childhood Accident Prevention into print there have been some very major changes in the United Kingdom. There have been changes in international affairs, in society and in health service management. There have been major advances in technology and quite profound changes in attitudes towards accident prevention and safety.

There is no doubt that parents and children are far more aware of safety than they were a decade ago. They practise safety in the home, in the car and on bicycles, at school and at leisure. They have access to safer homes and playgrounds and safer products. But we have still a long way to go. Nobody can be satisfied until we have made further progress in reducing the heavy toll of deaths and injuries to children.

In order to expedite the production of this book the authors asked Jane Bishop to edit their original material. As a mother of two young children and a former Editor of RoSPA's *Safety Education*, Assistant Editor of their *Care on the Road* and a writer and editor of books and articles on safety, health and education she was well placed to lend her knowledge and assistance.

Whilst the responsibility for any inaccuracies and inconsistencies must rest entirely with the authors they wish to extend their most grateful thanks to Jane Bishop for the diligence she has shown in arranging the material in its current format, seeking out source material, and checking facts. It would not have been possible to launch the book at this time had it not been for her enthusiasm and dedication to getting the task completed.

1

INTRODUCTION – THE GREATEST KILLER OF ALL

Accidents are of sufficient importance to the health of our children to merit considerably greater attention than they have attracted in the past. In many of the more developed countries accidents are now the biggest killer of children and young people beyond 1 year of age. In developing countries they are still of great importance even if overshadowed by infectious diseases and malnutrition.

In Britain today:

- Nearly half of all the deaths of children aged 10–15 years of age are due to accidents
- Three children die as a result of an accident **every day**
- 120 000 children are admitted to hospital after an accident every year
- Every year one in five children requires hospital or family doctor treatment for an accident

Minor accidents are generally accepted as an inevitable and necessary part of the growing-up process of children. They will often learn important lessons from the experience. They do not need, however, to sustain some of the very serious accidents that are still too common: very many of these accidents have a known cause and can be prevented.

Children experiencing accidents is nothing new. Throughout history in all societies children have come to grief in different ways, depending on the local customs and hazards. In the past children have been far more exposed to accidents than at present: consider the plight of children working in coalmines and living in the world of sordid tenements during the industrial revolution, and the daily hazards and dangers associated with this existence.

Nevertheless today's sophisticated society brings its own dangers, and accidents still predominate amongst young children (Figure 1.1). Many accidents are eminently predictable and occur with monotonous regularity. At certain stages of development and for given types of environments children will experience specific types of accidents. Many of these are quite trivial and of no great consequence; but enough are of sufficient severity to merit attention.

Table 1.1   Leading causes of death by age. England and Wales, 1987

| Age | Leading causes of death (Rates per million population) | | | Total no. of deaths |
	1st	2nd	3rd	
4 weeks– 1 year old	Signs, symptoms and ill-defined conditions **2040**	Congenital anomalies **739**	Respiratory disease **443**	**2824**
1–4 years old	ACCIDENTS **101**	Congenital anomalies **89**	Diseases of the nervous system **47**	**1067**
5–14 years old	ACCIDENTS **71**	Cancer **37**	Congenital anomalies **19**	**1196**
15–44 years old	Cancer **219**	ACCIDENTS **106**	Suicide **81**	**19 010**
45–64 years old	Cancer **3196**	Heart diseases **2817**	Cerebrovascular diseases **505**	**88 819**
65 years old and over	Heart diseases **19 018**	Cancer **12 842**	Cerebrovascular diseases **8029**	**462 406**

Source: OPCS. Deaths by cause. Quarterly Monitors DH2 88/3, London: OPCS, 1988.

Nearly 25 years ago Professor Ross Mitchell said:

> 'It is strange that a society that professes to care for its children and spends great fortunes on the study of leukaemia and congenital malformations virtually ignores the greatest killer of all – accidental injury.'

Some 10 years later Professor Donald Court, in his important report on child health, said:

> 'The greatest single need in medicine in the next 25 years is to give **prevention** the degree of scientific and educational attention that has been given in the last 25 years to treatment.'

Professor Court emphasized this need in his conclusions to the first ever major conference on children's accidents in Britain in Newcastle-upon-Tyne in 1976 saying:

> 'The main requirements for prevention in this field is for a change of behaviour on the part of parents, professionals and children . . .

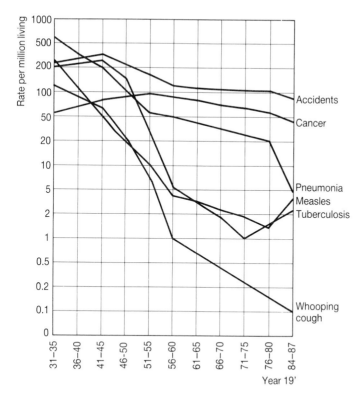

Figure 1.1 Mortality rates from selected causes for children aged 1–4 years, England and Wales 1931–1987. Rates per million population. Source: OPCS. Deaths by cause. Quarterly Monitors DH2 88/3, 1988.

nevertheless we must protect the young child and teach the older child to protect himself.'

The problem of preventing child accidents is exemplified by the Swedish psychologist Stina Sandels who noted in the mid-1970s:

'Traffic is the most complicated environment a child can experience' and *'In the end adults are always to blame for traffic accidents involving children.'*

The truth of these comments is self-evident.

What has been done?

The many improvements that have taken place in Europe, the United States, Australia, New Zealand and many other countries have helped to make the world a safer place in which children can live. Professor Ragnar Berfenstam of Uppsala, Sweden has noted that children:

'Have the rights to a safe environment, and somebody stronger than the children must guarantee them this right.'

There have been significant improvements in the urban environment, in housing, in playgrounds and in product safety. There has also been enlightened legislation in the field of toy safety, flammability of nightdresses, child-resistant containers for medicines and household chemicals and in systematic approaches to 'education for survival'.

Finally in its recent Green Paper 'The Health of the Nation', the United Kingdom Department of Health has looked at strategic plans for the future of the National Health Service, with particular emphasis on the prevention of ill health. It is gratifying to note that accident prevention is included among the 12 main target areas for special emphasis in this important document.

There is still much to be done, however. Society must ensure that children can:

- Move freely around their own homes without falling down stairs, cutting themselves on glass or tipping boiling kettles over themselves
- Go out into the street without being knocked down
- Go to playgrounds that are designed with safety as a priority
- Play and ride their bicycles with reasonable standards of safety

This and much more must be achieved before parents can be satisfied that they are bringing up their children in a reasonably safe environment. This environment should be one in which it is safe to explore and have fun – without the need of parents to be over-protective – and an environment in which children can learn to avoid major hazards in order to deal with similar hazards in their teenage years and adulthood, and in turn to pass on their knowledge of preventive safety to their own children.

In this book the main accidents experienced by children in Britain today have been highlighted, as well as some aspects of accidents to children in other countries. Particular attention has been paid to those areas meriting greater remedial measures, for example products that could be improved, how the environment could be changed, who needs to be taught and about what and who has the responsibility for this education. Finally, those people who have the responsibility to carry out these remedies have been identified.

The future

In the coming years a better understanding of the problems of childhood accidents and major improvements to avoid such accidents must develop. Preventive medicine is the main thrust of the National Health Service for the future and accident prevention should warrant a top position in its priorities.

Hopefully all those who read this book will only experience minor disasters with their own children or with the children in their care, and that they will pass on the lessons learned to as many people as possible. If the word can be spread widely enough there will no longer be the need to ask 'why did it happen?' nearly as often as we do at present.

2

WHY DO CHILDREN HAVE ACCIDENTS?

Before considering the types of accidents in which children are involved and analysing ways to prevent them we must look at why children have accidents in the first place. Any child may experience an accident but the sex, age and stage of development of the child are of crucial importance in their likelihood of encountering one.

Sex

Boys are more likely than girls to have accidents, as shown in Figure 2.1. This fact has been proved by virtually all studies. The only age at which this is not the case is in the first year of life. From about 9 months onwards boys are involved in more accidents than girls. More boys are involved in fatal accidents, more are admitted into hospital because of accidents and more visit Accident and Emergency departments for treatment.

This does not necessarily imply that boys have more accidents because of their sex, but maybe that they are exposed to more situations in which an accident is possible. For example, boys have more cycle accidents than girls but this may be entirely explained by the fact that boys ride their bicycles more frequently than girls do. It does not mean that they are inherently less able or safe on the road.

Children under 9 months experience the same proportion of accidents between the sexes. At that age the carer is responsible for the child's actions rather than the child itself, and so the exposure to risk is equal. After this age boys are more likely to have accidents of all types – amongst the few exceptions are clothing-related burns and horse-riding accidents in which girls are more frequently involved.

It is difficult to quantify exactly how much a child's sex has a bearing on his or her accident involvement, but the studies are so consistent in all countries and across all social groupings that one must accept that boys are much more likely to be involved. This is probably related to boys being exposed to more risk and to their innate level of physical activity and aggressiveness. To what extent this is genetically determined or culturally imbued by parents' and society's expectations of boyish vigour remains open to debate.

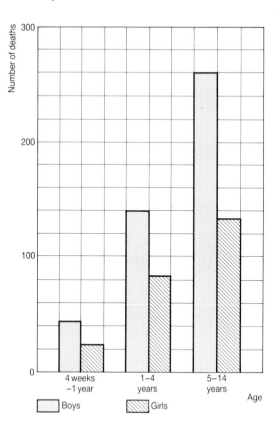

Figure 2.1 Fatalities by age and sex, England and Wales 1987. Source: OPCS. Deaths by cause. Quartely Monitors Series DH2.

Age

Accidents are the most common cause of death among toddlers and older children; accidents contribute to nearly half of all deaths for children aged 10–15 and this group are nearly twice as likely to attend hospital as a result of an accident than children in the 1–4-year-old age group.

Local studies in various parts of the United Kingdom have shown that attendances by children at hospital following accidents rise steadily with age. In each age group the boys outnumber girls by a ratio of 3:2.

In the infant (0–1 year of age) and toddler (1–4 years of age) groups the majority of accidents occur in the home. A very small proportion occur on the road and during sports and leisure activities.

In the school age groups the older the child becomes the more likely the accident will be due to sports and leisure activities. A proportion will occur during school activities, mostly on the playground or during organized sports or gymnastics. Road traffic accidents steadily increase with age. Analysis of Accident and Emergency department attendances and admissions to hospital has its limitations in measuring the true incidence of accidents by age, one

Table 2.1 Deaths from all causes and accidental deaths by age, 1990

Cause of deaths	4 weeks–1 year	1–4 years	5–14 years	Total
Injury and poisoning	90	246	423	749
Infections	100	76	36	212
Neoplasms	26	87	257	370
Endocrine, nutritional and metabolic	45	36	44	125
Nervous system	132	118	120	370
Circulatory system	41	48	46	135
Respiratory system	207	82	48	337
Digestive system	29	20	16	65
Genitourinary system	15	8	4	27
Congenital abnormalities	367	222	90	679
Other symptoms and ill-defined conditions	1071	49	42	1162
All causes	2343	1027	1121	4491

Source: OPCS. Deaths by cause. 1990 Registrations DH2 91/2 Table 2.

reason being that it misses out all the general practitioner attendances. These may account for between 25–33 per cent of all childhood accidents in rural areas though they are not nearly so significant in cities and towns.

A more reliable measure of the true incidence of accidents is from the cohort studies using a valid sample of the population as a whole. In the '1000 Family Study' in Newcastle-upon-Tyne, for example, the largest number of accidents in the 0–5-year-old age group occurred to children in the 2–3-year-old age group. Accident rates in the first 5 years of the study were:

Year 1	0.066
Year 2	0.255
Year 3	0.223
Year 4	0.138
Year 5	0.182
Years 5–15	0.085

per child/year

During the study the accident rate was 864 per 1000 children at risk over a 5-year period. The national cohort study found a rate of 607 per 1000 children at risk.

Table 2.2   Fatal accidents by type. England and Wales, 1987

Transport accidents		
vehicle occupants	80	
pedestrians	214	
pedal cyclists	63	
other	24	
Total		381
Home accidents		
burns and scalds	89	
suffocation	33	
drowning	20	
falls	11	
poisoning	7	
other causes	37	
Total		197
Other locations		
drowning	27	
falls	21	
other causes	62	
Total		110
All accidents		688

Source: OPCS. Deaths by accidents and violence. Quarterly Monitors DH4 Series. London: OPCS, 1988.

Social and geographical factors

Social class I	Professional
Social class II	Managerial
Social class III	Skilled Manual (M)/ Non Manual (NM)
Social class IV	Partly Skilled
Social class V	Unskilled

As classified by the Registrar General according to the occupation of the main provider within the family.

Social class is the single most relevant factor in accidents in childhood. Variations between social classes are greater in childhood accidents than for any other 'disease' or for any other age group. Children in social class V are five times more likely to be killed in an accident than children of social class I (Figure 2.2). This compares with the risk being twice as likely for all forms of

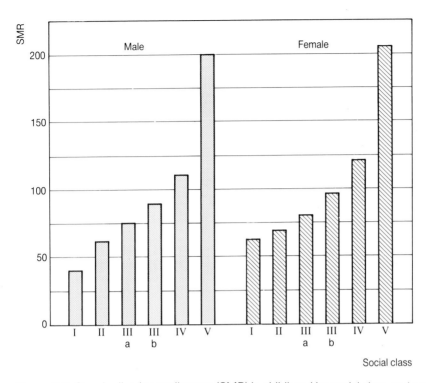

Figure 2.2 Standardized mortality rate (SMR) in childhood by social class and sex for accidents, poisoning and violence 1970–72. Source: OPCS, 1978.

death. These differences are emphasized even more strongly in certain classes of accidents where socially deprived children are even more at risk. Boys in social class V are:

- Seven times more likely to be killed in pedestrian road accidents
- Fifteen times more likely to be killed in accidental death by fire
- Nine times more likely to drown

} than those in social class I

One type of accident that is more equally distributed through the social classes is poisoning. This is probably because as many dangerous substances are available in better-off households as in poorer ones.

The social class gradient is more marked in the younger age group and least marked amongst older children. The geographical distribution of deaths from accidents in childhood (Figure 2.3) confirms the social class gradients. Children from the north and the west of England are more likely to die from an accident than children from the south and east. Children in the most socially deprived inner city areas of Birmingham, Manchester and London have a five to six times greater likelihood of death from an accident than

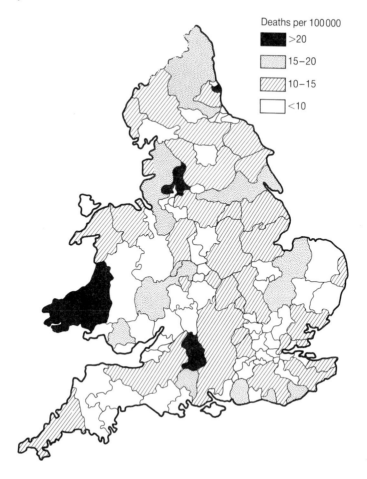

Deaths per 100 000

■ >20

15–20

10–15

<10

Figure 2.3 Death rates from children's accidents (0–14 years) by Health District in England and Wales, 1975–1979.

children from the well-off commuter belt areas around London and from the rural areas of southern England and the Midlands.

Environmental factors

The greatly increased accident mortality of children in social classes IV and V cannot be fully separated from the poor quality of housing in which they live. Working class children live in a far more dangerous environment than middle class children. Children living in poor quality housing are more at risk from fire and burns because their homes are more likely to contain flammable materials, the occupants are more likely to be smokers and other houses (with a similar risk) are close together.

Hazards in the near environment of these children include busy streets, derelict slum housing, deserted canals, mineshafts, factories, railway lines and rubbish tips. The absence of safe play areas for socially deprived children in Salford, for example, was found to be a contributing factor in a much higher incidence of pedestrian fatalities in the 1970s.

The '1000 Family Study' in Newcastle-upon-Tyne noted that there were less accidents in social classes II and III, and that significantly more accidents occurred in conditions of overcrowding, poor quality housing and where there were poor mothercraft skills. Families who are socially deprived are also less likely to use specific safety devices such as car safety seats. They may also use older and less well-maintained vehicles, which put the children further at risk. These families are often unresponsive to education and publicity, and special provision will probably be necessary to encourage safe practices.

Other factors that must be considered are the domestic circumstances of the child including the mental state of the parents (in particular the mother), poor health in the family, shortage of money and marital tensions, which can all cause the parents to take less care of the children and for the child to behave in such a way as to lead to the likelihood of increased numbers of accidents.

Stages of development

Early years

During the first year of life babies have accidents which are not their fault. The types of accidents they are involved in include falls, scalds and car accident injuries; together with choking or inhalation, which is often beyond the control of the adult.

With the onset of crawling and walking towards the end of the child's first year of life the situation changes rapidly as the child sets out to explore the environment and all its hazards.

Firstly the child is exposed to risks around the home. The accidents in which they are mainly involved include poisonings, scalds, minor falls, abrasions and lacerations. Parents and carers are still responsible for safety at all times and must seek to protect the child by providing fireguards, stairgates (both top and bottom), car seats, electrical socket covers, locks on medicine cabinets, under-sink cupboards and child-resistant containers. Toddlers cannot 'learn by their mistakes' and parents must not rely on training or education, only protection, at this stage.

Even experienced parents are surprised at how quickly an immobile baby becomes an active toddler. Last week the baby could not follow you into the kitchen, this week as you turn from the oven with a scalding plate in your hands he is sitting inches behind you; last week you ran upstairs alone, this week he's on the fourth step before you've realized he can move that far, that quickly.

As mobility begins the child refines his ability quickly and without warning. Parents of under twos must try to stay one step ahead in the provision of safety before the child tests the system!

School days

As the child grows his strength and capacity increase, as does his range of activities. Accidents in the home start to diminish and those on the road, playground and at school increase. New skills and activities such as crossing the road or riding a bicycle bring with them increased risk (the same pattern is repeated as teenagers start to ride motorcycles or drive cars). Up to 11 and 12 years of age (and often beyond) impulsive and unreliable behaviour is characteristic, and environmental protection is therefore of great importance, particularly in the prevention of road accidents. Road safety training is obviously necessary for this age group but its effectiveness is not easy to assess, as however much the children are taught and trained their behaviour is never totally reliable.

The need for play is paramount for this age group. It is much more than a way to pass the time. It provides opportunities to find out about colour, texture and form, to learn new skills and refine old ones. It's a chance to socialize and mix with ones peers and to learn about relationships and interactions. Because of the explorative and investigative nature of play it holds many risks. Even young children cannot be totally supervised all of the time and for older children it is important that they are given the scope to play alone with their friends. The chance of accidents at play for the school-age child is therefore increased.

As adolescence approaches more formal sporting activities may begin and further exposure to risk is inevitable. This is the age of testing oneself and learning to take risks, which must be encouraged up to a point. High-risk activities, for example, rock-climbing, canoeing, boating and orienteering must clearly be supervised at all times.

Adolescents often model their behaviour on a peer or on a real or perceived 'hero' and this is an important factor in accidents. It is also relevant in the development of anti-social or self-destructive behaviour such as solvent-abuse or drug-taking. Self-training and taking responsibility are important here, as is the encouragement of appropriate role models – but legislation to protect the young adult also has a part to play.

Attitudes

Children from social classes IV and V are at further risk because the parents are more likely to have a fatalistic attitude towards the child's safety, probably because they feel they have little control over their own lives.

These parents are also often impervious to safety education, especially if it is put to them by middle class professionals who have little knowledge and even less understanding of their specific problems. Children from this background are further at risk because their parents may put a high value on physical activity and risk taking.

Overall, these children may have little supervision, a lack of order and planning in their lives, low resources and parents with high stress factors who perhaps cannot cope with their own lives.

Children with a disadvantaged background:

- Live in a more hazardous environment
- Have low supervision levels
- Engage in more dangerous and risky activities
- Have parents who have a casual attitude to safety
- Have parents who have little money to spend on safety provision
- Have parents who are resistant to intervention measures to improve safety whether these are by persuasion, coercion or legislation

Behaviour

The British Births Survey of infants born in Great Britain in one week in 1970 includes a report on child behaviour and accidental injury in the 11 966 pre-school children who were examined. Parents were asked to report all injuries that had occurred in the first 5 years of life. It was found that aggressive behaviour was associated with all accidental injuries after adjustments for social class, crowding, mother's psychological distress, age, marital status and the child's sex. Over-activity was also associated with injuries not resulting in hospitalization after the same adjustments had been made. Children who scored highly in behavioural tests to ascertain aggression and overactivity were nearly twice as likely (1.9 times to be exact) to sustain injuries requiring hospitalization than those scoring low marks on the same tests.

The '1000 Family Study' carried out in Newcastle-upon-Tyne in the 1960s and 1970s followed a group of children from 0–15 years of age. Accidents occurring in school years correlated significantly with the mother's ability to cope with the family. This was particularly so for those accidents in which the child could not be held responsible for the incident. Less intelligent children were more likely to have accidents whereas children of above average ability in initiative, physical agility and in powers of concentration had fewer than expected accidents.

The increased liability to accidents in lower socio-economic groups may be more related to the environmental components than to behaviour. Children from these groups are more likely to live in sub-standard housing and to play in more dangerous places. Both aspects must be borne in mind in devising prevention programmes. The younger child's ability to perceive danger increases with age but children from higher socio-economic groups are more able to identify danger than those from lower groups.

Sight and sound

The child's development of sight and hearing play an important role in their propensity to accidents. Many parents over-estimate their child's ability to cope alone – for example in crossing a road. Because the child is sensible and seems to have absorbed the principles of the Green Cross Code, they may allow a child of 6 years old to walk to school alone. Research has shown that a child's visual field is simply not developed enough at that age to reliably assess traffic safely.

The development of the visual function is not completed until about 16 years of age. The peripheral vision of children is different from adults. 6 year olds, for example, cannot see traffic out of the corner of the eye as adults can. 5 year olds can see changes in direction away from them more clearly than when objects are coming towards them; their eyes have difficulty in accommodating from distant vision to close-up vision. Although a 5 year old may look at an approaching car he may not have 'registered' it or even realized that it is moving. Even adults sometimes have difficulty in judging speed and distance, and for children it is further restricted by their lack of physical development.

In the same way the development of the hearing function is important when we rely on 'looking and listening' to cross roads safely. Small children with normal hearing levels can mistake the direction of sound and consider it to be coming from a different or even the opposite direction. The implications of both these aspects of development are very important in traffic safety. Allied to these is the relationship between the physical stage of development and the use to which the child puts his or her skills.

Handicapped children

It is often assumed that handicapped children are at greater risk from accidents than other children. In hospital, handicapped children are always having minor bumps and grazes. On the other hand the parents of a handicapped child are likely to be very attentive in caring for their child and may restrict the child's exposure to hazardous situations and activities. Some specific handicaps increase the risk of accidents. For example:

- *Down's Syndrome* children can experience atlanto-axial instability that may result in dislocation of the neck and can cause paralysis. To help prevent this a single x-ray of the child's neck can be taken when the child is going to start travelling in a car without a neck support. If the x-ray shows the child to be at risk they should be provided with a head support when travelling by car and should also avoid vigorous sport.

- *Epileptic children* are at special risk of drowning (a four times greater chance), burns and scalds and falls. They are especially at risk when swimming, cycling and riding because an attack could result in loss of control. It is advisable to give these children as much freedom as possible whilst ensuring that all appropriate safety equipment (e.g., a helmet) is used and close supervision is undertaken.

A Danish study carried out on mentally handicapped children in a hospital over a 3-year period found handicapped children to be three times more likely than other children to experience accidents. The greater the degree of handicap the greater the accident incidence and severity.

Records are seldom kept to correlate which disabilities people have when they experience which accidents. It is therefore not possible to show what significance there is, if any, of physical disability in causing or contributing to an accident.

Other medical conditions

Children with brittle bone disease, *fragilitas osseum*, do not necessarily experience more accidents but they are certainly more likely to suffer injury as a result of any incident in which they are involved. Children with this condition have a marked propensity to break bones even with the slightest trauma. There is no easy cure; therefore these children must be kept in a protected and safe environment until their bones are fully formed.

Obese children may find themselves at an advantage when it comes to accidents. Firstly the amount of subcutaneous fat in obese females may protect them from extremes of cold and accidental hypothermia. Secondly their lack of mobility may restrict their involvement in dangerous activities. A study in the United States in the late 1960s, however, found that fat boys aged over 2 years old experienced significantly more burns than thin boys. The study suggested that fat boys were more mischievous or less dexterous and too slow to avoid an accident or its serious effects.

Ethnic minorities

The special circumstances and situations of immigrants to a country may render them more likely to have accidents. Many of the problems have more to do with their socio-economic circumstances rather than any genetic or racial susceptibility.

Ethnic minorities in Britain include immigrants from the new Common-wealth, Pakistan, Afro-Carribean as well as newer groups such as Vietnamese, Filipinos, Arabs and Turks. In addition, long established groups such as gypsies, the Chinese and Cypriots exist.

The special health problems of these groups are not always understood and little reliable information is available about their accident rates. One study in 1983 looked at the mortality rates of immigrants to England and Wales who died between 1970–78. It showed that overall, all immigrant groups experienced a higher mortality from accidents and violence as well as higher perinatal mortality rates than the rest of the population. Studies in the United States have also shown higher mortality rates amongst immigrants than in the indigenous population.

Factors thought to affect this are changed diet, increased tendency to smoke, urbanization and the general effects of migration that may all directly or indirectly have effects on childhood accidents. On a more positive note, the increased family size of Asian and West Indian groups can be a help in preventing accidents as the young children are likely to benefit from more than one carer at any given time. Ethnic minorities are more likely to be involved in specific kinds of accidents. For example:

- *Pedestrians* – A recent study of pedestrian accidents to children in Birmingham by Lawson showed an excess of Asian children in both the 0–4 and 5–9-year-old age groups.
- *Children in cars* – Asian families often travel long distances to visit friends and relations in overloaded cars. Children often sit unrestrained on the laps of parents in the front seats or are packed in, unrestrained, in the rear. Many Asian children have been killed or injured for this reason and this constitutes as extra risk compared with the general population.
- *House fires* – Because many Asian and West Indian families live in poor quality inner city housing they are highly susceptible to house fires. The use of open paraffin stoves that may be easily tipped over adds to this likelihood. An additional fire hazard is the danger of Asian girls wearing highly flammable saris and nightdresses.
- *Lead poisoning* – A well-recognized hazard in Asian children is of lead poisoning from the use of Surma, an eye make-up, which has a high lead level. This is often imported from the Indian sub-continent.
    Ethnic minorities living in inner city areas may also encounter the hazard of old houses with paint containing lead, which children may take in by chewing or licking.

Overall ethnic minorities may:

- Be slow to adapt to a new cultural environment
- Lack awareness of hazards in the new culture
- Have a low usage rate of safety equipment (i.e., child car safety seats, seat belts)
- Live in poor quality, high-risk housing
- Use dangerous household items (such as paraffin burners) not generally used by other groups
- Have a fatalistic approach to life
- Travel with too many people in a car (because of larger family groups).

Risk and accident proneness

Every day we take risks. When we cross the road the risks are obvious but even when we sleep at night we could be at risk from a house fire. We can never eliminate all risk but we can do much to reduce it.

Sometimes we increase risk by failing to foresee the consequences of our actions, for example, by judging the measure to be too expensive financially or by deciding that we do not wish to be overprotective. Many people think accidents will never happen to them and they therefore fail to reduce the risks they take. Even when we have identified a risk we are inclined to treat the problem symptomatically. We encourage the wearing of seat belts to reduce the severity of injury in a car accident instead of eliminating from our roads dangerous or drunken drivers who cause the accidents.

Acceptable risk is the amount of risk a person is prepared to take when undertaking a specific activity. This may not be objectively calculated but is more likely to be a subjective judgement taken by the person concerned.

The risk of death varies according to modes of transport, for example, travelling by car is 20 times more hazardous than travelling by air and 600 times more dangerous than travelling by rail. These figures only relate to death while undertaking the activity; calculating the risk of injury is far more difficult.

The risks we take may lead to our involvement in accidents. If we have many accidents we may be said to be 'accident prone'. Yet, somebody who has more than his share of accidents may simply have an inability to judge the risk attached to an activity, or he may be prepared to accept risk that other people would not. The use of the term 'accident prone' implies that a person has a particular combination of personality traits inherent in his or her make-up that render him more likely to have an accident. Were accidents totally random events there would be some people in the scale of random distribution who would have more accidents than others. Conversely some people would have less than their fair share. This raises the question of where the cut-off point is drawn in such a random distribution curve. Above a certain point a person may be labelled accident prone, below it they may be regarded as being within normal limits. Some studies have been carried out to identify whether it is possible for a certain range of personality traits to be responsible for a person's accident level. All have concluded that it is not possible to apply the same criteria when assessing children's accident levels.

There is a distinction between accident liability and accident proneness. Liability is related to environmental factors, which may change from time to time, proneness to personality factors, which will also vary according to an individual's ability to cope with stress, which in turn will affect his risk factor.

It is a combination of social background, sex, age, developmental stage and personality that will render an individual more at risk from an increased frequency of accidents.

3

ROAD TRAFFIC AND OTHER TRANSPORT ACCIDENTS

Road Traffic Accidents

Roads are potentially dangerous places; particularly so for young children who may have little or no road sense. Ultimately children's safety on the road is the responsibility of an adult, either the parents or guardian of the child, car drivers or other road users.

Children often use the roads as pedestrians, cyclists or as passengers in cars, coaches, buses etc., and in all these modes they experience accidents. Figures 3.1 and 3.2 show the serious child casualty rates by activity and age and by activity and sex.

Pedestrian accidents

Pedestrian accidents represent the single biggest accidental killer of children in Britain. Each year 250–300 children are killed, and between 6000 and 7000 children are seriously injured as a result of pedestrian accidents. In all, between 20 000 and 25 000 children annually go to hospital having been involved in pedestrian accidents.

Pedestrian accidents represent about a quarter of all childhood accidental deaths per year in the United Kingdom, which has one of the highest pedestrian accident rates in Europe (Figure 3.3).

Trends

During the 1930s there were well over 1000 child deaths each year from pedestrian accidents; today there are some 300. However, the fall in deaths has not been consistent. During the late 1950s and early 1960s children's deaths as pedestrians were either rising or remaining static. From 1972 onwards there has been a fall, particularly so since the mid-1980s both in the number of children killed and the number taken to hospital after pedestrian accidents. Two main reasons for this are; the introduction in 1967 of the drink–drive laws and the breathalyser, and in 1971 the intensive efforts made by road safety educators with the introduction of the Green Cross Code.

Overall deaths and casualties to children of all age groups have fallen since the early 1970s. The age group giving most cause for concern, however, is the 10–14 year olds who seem to have been impervious to road safety education and are now almost as much at risk as the younger children in the 5–9-year-old age bracket. Future road safety training needs to take account

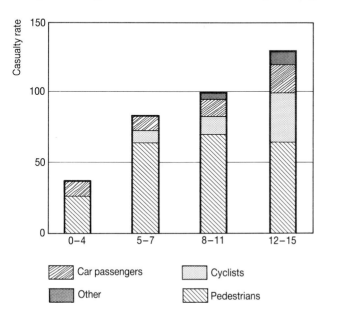

Figure 3.1
Serious child casualty rates by age and activity (killed and seriously injured per 100 000 population).◆

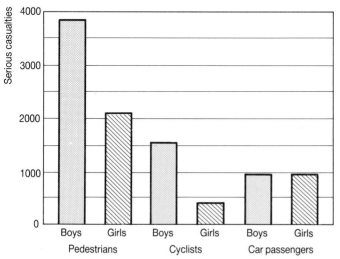

Figure 3.2
Serious child casualties by sex and activity. ◆

◆ *Children and Roads: A Safer Way*, Department of Transport, 1990.

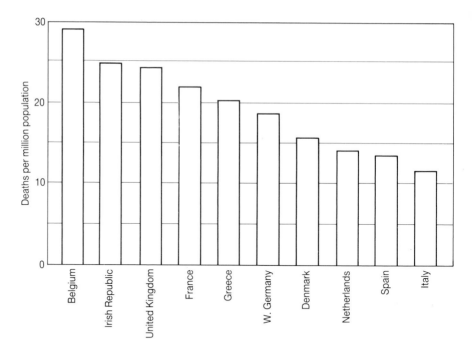

Figure 3.3 Child pedestrians killed in Europe. *Children and Roads: A Safer Way,* Department of Transport, 1990.

of this physically active, often rebellious age group who experience greater freedom and less supervision than younger children, and therefore are more exposed to risk.

Who has pedestrian accidents?

In all age groups males experience more pedestrian accidents (except over 60s) and the most marked difference is in the 5–9-year-old age group where twice as many boys as girls are involved.

All age groups of children are affected starting from the age of one, when toddlers venture out and about, often attended by older children. Children just starting primary school are the most 'at-risk' age group and as they mature the numbers drop. Even throughout the teenage years, however, when many adolescents ride bicycles or motorcycles, pedestrian accidents still occur. During the secondary school years children are more prone to showing off for their friends and acting impulsively, and this raises the accident figures for pedestrians. The abuse of alcohol, drugs and solvents is another risk during the later teenage years. Children from deprived homes are also more likely to be involved in pedestrian accidents, when compared with children from professional homes. Boys from social class V have eight times more chance of sustaining a fatal accident as a pedestrian compared with boys from social class I. The ratio for girls is 5:1.

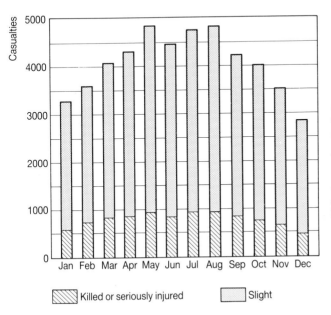

Figure 3.4 Child road casualties by month, 1990. Source: Department of Transport [1990]. *Child casualties in road accidents.* Accident Fact Sheet No 5.

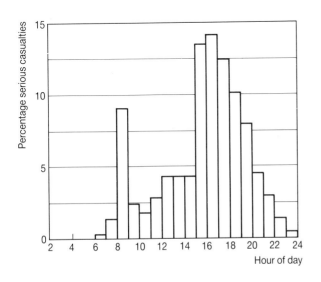

Figure 3.5 Serious child casualties by time of day. *Children and Roads: A Safer Way*, Department of Transport, 1990.

When do pedestrian accidents occur?

Amongst children in the United Kingdom accidents are at their lowest during December and January. From the start of the year they rise steadily to reach a plateau between May and August with only a slight reduction in June (Figure 3.4).

The initial increase in early Spring is associated with the introduction of British Summer Time (usually late March), which, combined with the milder weather, gives children an extra hour to 'play out' in the evenings. The peak times for children's pedestrian accidents are between Monday and Friday 3pm to 6pm (particularly on Fridays) (Figure 3.5). Lesser peaks also occur between 8am and 9am Monday to Friday and between 11am and 6pm on Saturdays.

Clearly the most vulnerable period for children is the journey home from school, between 4pm and 5pm on school days. During this time children may loiter on the way home or play in the streets. During the winter months, especially, this can be a hazardous time with children out after 4pm (in the dark). Overall, around 30 per cent of all children's pedestrian accidents happen when they are journeying to and from school.

Where do pedestrian accidents occur?

Well over 95 per cent of child pedestrian road traffic accidents occur in urban areas. Around two-thirds of these urban accidents happen in ordinary residential streets, often with parked cars down both sides and where vehicles are driven in excess of the 30mph speed limits.

Less than 5 per cent occur on rural main roads with fast moving traffic, and very few occur on country lanes or in villages. Very rarely a child is killed on a dual carriageway or motorway where pedestrians should not, in any case, venture. Child pedestrian road traffic accidents often occur near junctions and crossings – around 60 per cent of these occur within a quarter of a mile of the child's home (Figure 3.6).

Accident analysis from 1984 showed that over 90 per cent of all child pedestrian road traffic accidents occurred when the child was crossing the road. One-third of these occurred when the child was masked by a stationary vehicle (particularly where younger children are involved) and around 12 per cent occurred when the child was on or within 50 m of a pedestrian crossing. In 1984, 25 children were killed and 702 seriously injured on or within 50 m of a pedestrian crossing. Figures for accidents near or on crossings have fluctuated quite considerably during the 10-year period from 1978–87 and there is little sign of improvement in the number of children injured or killed in this way.

Improvements can be made to pelican crossings to make them safer for users, these include:

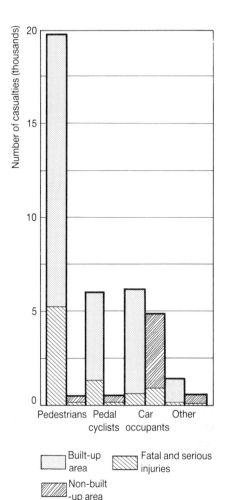

Figure 3.6 Child casualty severity by location. Source: Parliamentary Advisory Council for Transport Safety [PACTS]. *Road accidents in focus*, **4**, *Children.*

- Quicker response from the 'green man' once the button has been activated
- Increased crossing time with the green man (to help the old, disabled, children, parents with prams or pushchairs and walking children)
- Infra-red sensors to detect the presence and movement of pedestrians to enact the green man, and to re-activate the green light for drivers as soon as all pedestrians have passed safely across the road

The number and sitings of pedestrian crossings are another cause for concern. In France, for example, crossings are set up every 100 m but widely abused. In Britain they are only set up after extensive traffic–pedestrian surveys and when the number of accidents justify the measures.

Local highway authorities have considerable discretionary powers over the installation of crossings. Local public pressure can do much to achieve crossing facilities where local authorities are resisting.

How do pedestrian accidents occur?

The main reason for pedestrian accidents is that children are being relied upon to manage the road environment alone, at far too early an age. Parents grossly overestimate their child's ability on the road. Research carried out in the early 1970s in Britain by Sadler found that 50 per cent of mothers questioned thought their 5-year-old child capable of crossing a road unaided. In fact the youngest a child can safely cross a road alone is around 8–9 years old.

In the same study an alarming 19 per cent of mothers of 3 year olds and 13 per cent of mothers of 2 year olds also thought their child could safely cross a road alone.

Observations of children crossing the road have shown that they are just not capable of safely computing all the information from a complex road environment together with the speed and distance of approaching traffic. In desperation they will dash out when one side of the road is clear on the assumption (or hope) that the other side is also clear. Indeed, most child pedestrian accidents happen when a child dashes out into the road and the driver later says 'I just didn't see him'. The child may have been playing in the street and might be distracted by a friend or be pursuing a ball. Alternatively he may have been crossing the road, hesitantly or impulsively. The driver is most likely, though not always, to be a young, male car driver, driving too fast for the conditions. Overall, over 80 per cent of child pedestrian accidents involve saloon car drivers, 10 per cent involve motorcycles and 10 per cent other vehicles. Parental responsibility is clearly important here, though failure to supervise a child or teach him or her the correct road-crossing procedure cannot be held responsible for all pedestrian accidents: excessive speed on the part of the car driver is probably equally important.

An added complication is when a child perceives a pedestrian crossing as a totally safe haven for getting across a road. Unfortunately, this is not always the case as drivers may fail to stop altogether or will impatiently hurry pedestrians across a road. Occasionally a child may be knocked down while walking along a road and three-fifths of pre-school child casualties occur when the child is playing in the street.

The socio-economic differences found relate mostly to exposure. Children from less privileged homes are more likely to be playing out in the street (lack of private gardens) and are more likely to live nearer dangerous roads, which they have to cross to go to school, shops and playgrounds. Observations of childrens' activities in the street confirm that boys play out in the street twice as much as girls. The exposure of boys and girls to traffic on journeys to and from school remain the same, yet nevertheless boys still have more accidents than girls on these journeys. Whether or not an adult is present doesn't always have a bearing either, as up to one third of all child pedestrian accidents happen when an adult or a supervisory older child is present.

Behaviour near the roads is the key difference between boys and girls. Boys tend to act in a more reckless, impulsive and adventurous way than girls. They are more likely to dash ahead or loiter behind at critical times when a road is to be crossed, than do girls. Overall, girls exercise more care and attention themselves near the road, and also are more likely to stay close to their parent or carer.

Methods of actually crossing the road are surprisingly similar; there are only marginal differences in boys and girls behaviour. Girls are more likely to stop on the kerb and look up and down the road before crossing, boys tend to look more as they approach the kerb and whilst crossing.

Most behavioural observations have shown that boys and girls develop in a similar way in their ability to perceive a problem, judge a situation and make the final decision to cross the road. They both scan the environment, estimate speed and distance of oncoming traffic and process the information in similar ways. Yet, girls are safer on the roads and the one area where they score better than boys is in reaction time. These have been measured on computer-simulated road crossings and girls have been consistently better than boys with the more complex tests. This suggests that boys may find it more difficult than girls to make accurate decisions and judgements in more complex traffic situations.

Filmed records of children crossing roads have also shown that boys adopt an adult-like strategy for crossing roads earlier than girls do, and as they do not have the ability to make the same judgements as adults this may be seen as a negative development.

Swedish researcher Stina Sandels maintains that adults are always responsible for child pedestrian accidents. She claims that even if a child dashes out into the road adults are still responsible for:

- Supervising the child in the first place
- Driving with due care and attention (particularly in built-up areas)
- Creating and regulating (i.e., maintaining sufficiently low speed limits, perhaps 20mph on residential roads) the environment to ensure child-safety

In Scandinavian countries, northern Europe and Japan large reductions in child pedestrian accidents have been made by recreating the residential environment, drastically reducing speed limits and by providing adequate play facilities for children. Britain has improved its figures dramatically in the last decade but our record is still one of the worst in Europe – there is still much to be done.

Injuries sustained

Pedestrian accidents are more likely than any other to result in death. Injuries sustained are caused by:

- Direct impact with the hard surface of the motor vehicle
- Being flipped up and onto the bonnet or windscreen
- Being dragged along under the vehicle
- Being flipped sideways onto the road or pavement or onto a roadside object or into the path of another vehicle

Head injuries and/or multiple internal injuries are often the cause of immediate death. Typical injuries sustained are:

- Head injury with skull fracture and internal bleeding
- Multiple fractures of pelvis and/or spine
- Injuries to abdominal and chest organs
- Fracture of femur or tibia and/or fibula
- Road burns and grazes
- Deep lacerations, contusions and sprains in any part of the body
- Joint effusions especially of the knee
- Superficial grazes and lacerations

The outcome of a pedestrian road traffic accident is often more serious than for any other form of accident. The main permanent disabilities following childhood pedestrian accidents are (in order of priority):

- Brain damage including epilepsy
- Loss of limb or deformity of limb
- Spinal injury with paraplegia

Local studies indicate that around 5–10 per cent of children admitted to hospital following pedestrian road traffic accidents will experience some form of disability.

Reducing pedestrian accidents

For many years the main emphasis on reducing child pedestrian accidents was to teach young children how to cross the road by 'kerb drill' and the 'Green Cross Code'. In the last few years, however, it has become recognized that because of the aspects of child development mentioned above, not too much reliance should be placed on teaching behaviour by rote. Instead education is more likely to be effective once the child is capable of appreciating and understanding what is being taught – at about 7 or 8 years of age. The emphasis has therefore shifted somewhat to making the world itself a safer place by traffic-calming measures such as road humps (sleeping policeman), chicanes, road narrowing or road throttles. In addition 20mph speed zones are now being introduced.

Emphasis too has been placed on the responsibility of the driver to be much more aware of children and to anticipate that they will behave as children, that is, impulsively and unpredictably. The Autumn 1991 campaign of the Department of Transport centred around speed reduction, pointing out that when a car going at 40mph hits a child the chances are very high that the child will be killed; at 30mph the chance is 50 per cent and at 20mph only one in 20 will be killed.

Examples of other responsibilities which can be taken by all those affected include:

Children can:

- Learn the correct procedures for crossing the road, as taught to them at the roadside by their parents or road safety teachers
- Use pedestrian crossings, footbridges and underpasses
- Remember when walking where there are no pavements to – face oncoming traffic; walk in single file; wear bright reflective/fluorescent clothing)
- Only cross at pelican crossings when the green man shows
- Act sensibly in and around the road

Parents can:

- Set their children a good example when they cross the road, and actively teach their children themselves how to cross the road
- Not let children under 8 years old (and only then when they are capable) cross the road alone
- Make sure their child knows the Green Cross Code (although total reliance should not be placed on it)
- Enrol a young child in the Tufty Club (Royal Society for the Prevention of Accidents) or similar traffic club
- Discourage children from playing in the road and reinforce the idea of roads being dangerous places designed for vehicles not people

Teachers can:

- Invite safety groups into playgroups and reception classes to provide practice at safe road crossing
- Ensure all children are exposed to a Planned Programme of Education for Health (PPEH), which includes a component on survival on the roads
- Ensure that all children are accompanied by an adult or responsible older child especially when travelling to and from school
- Set a good example when crossing the road

Vehicle drivers can:

- Always be on the look out for children, particularly near schools, near playgrounds, by ice cream vans, where children are playing
- Reduce their speed in all residential areas
- Keep within speed limits and slow down near schools, shops, playgrounds or where children are playing
- Anticipate unexpected and impulsive behaviour on the part of children
- Give way to pedestrians at road junctions

Vehicle manufacturers can:

- design and produce pedestrian friendly cars with recessed windscreen wipers and windscreens, no frontal bonnet protrusions, sloping bonnets, rubber collapsible bumpers and bonnets to limit injury in the event of impact.

Local authorities can:

- Recognize the pedestrian as a prime user of towns and in residential areas
- Redesign and rebuild the urban environment to make 'living' streets that favour pedestrians and cyclists (e.g., the Dutch Woonerf system)
- Provide 'sleeping policemen' or other methods of slowing down traffic if living streets cannot be introduced
- Pedestrianize shopping precincts in town centres
- Make adequate provision for pedestrian crossings including wider use of guard rails and longer, more frequent crossing times at controlled crossings
- Ensure that there are enough stimulating but safe playgrounds and play areas for children so as to reduce the necessity for them to play on the streets
- Site crossings at key sites near schools, playgrounds and shops
- Set up 'safe way to school' projects where pedestrians and cyclists have priority at pre- and post-school times
- When planning new residential estates provide walkways and cycleways. Ensure that children do not have to cross busy roads to access facilities such as shops, schools and playgrounds
- Provide by-passes and urban roads or motorways to keep heavy or through traffic away from residential areas
- Set up traffic clubs for pre-school children to encourage early development of road safety skills

Cycle accidents

Each year approximately 90 children are killed following cycle accidents on Britain's roads. Many more are seriously injured or at least attend hospital Accident and Emergency departments because of cycle accidents. Precise figures are not available for injuries, however, because statistics rely on returns of 'Police Stats 19' records that only cover accidents involving other road vehicles. That is, any accidents involving a cycle and another road vehicle are recorded, but those involving two cycles or solo accidents when a child falls off his own bike are missed out. It is estimated that only about 20 per cent of cycle accidents are reported to the police. Overall, an estimated 1000 children are admitted to hospital each year and as many as 150 000 visit hospital for treatment following cycle accidents.

Who has cycle accidents?

Boys in the 10–14-year-old age group are the children most likely to have cycle accidents. The ratio of boys to girls in all groups is 5:1 for all cycle accidents and 9:1 for fatal accidents. The increased usage of their cycles by boys accounts for this discrepancy. (See Figures 3.1 and 3.2).

Overall, trends for all cycle accidents show a decline, although numbers indicate that there has been an increase for boys in the 10–14-year-old age group since the early 1980s. If babies and toddlers are involved in cycle accidents it is usually when they are travelling as passengers on the back of their parents' cycles. Children as young as 3 years old are sometimes allowed out on the road on their bicycles and by the time children are 7 or 8 years old many are riding around even though they have neither the training or the skills to cope with the dangerous road environment.

By the ages of 9 and 10 years old many children, usually boys, are riding bicycles both to and from school as well as for recreation. It is vital that any child riding on the road has taken and passed a cycling proficiency scheme (operated by RoSPA, or a similar scheme). The minimum age a child should ride on the road is 9 years old.

When do cycle accidents happen?

Bicycle accidents happen all year around but are far more prevalent in the summer months than the winter ones. Local studies show that from April to September childhood attendances for cycle accidents are around five times greater than for October to March. The peak months for children's bicycle accidents are June, July and August. The peak time of the day for bicycle accidents covering all ages is Friday afternoon between 4pm and 6pm. Similar, but lower peaks are recorded at this time of day on Monday through Thursday. The other major peak is between 7am and 9am on weekday mornings. These peaks are clearly associated with the times of journeying to and from school. Saturdays and Sundays show a more even distribution around the middle of the day, relating to recreational cycling. Throughout the winter cycle accidents are fairly evenly spread although there is a slight rise in the darker months of November, December or January.

Where do cycle accidents happen?

Most (about 65 per cent) children's cycle accidents occur in solo riding on the road – they usually involve the child losing control of the bike. In around 10 per cent of children's cycle accidents another vehicle is involved, very often a car. These occur typically in a residential road but also often on a main road in a town, and are far more likely to happen in an urban road than in a rural area. The vast majority occur within half a mile of the child's home. Other cycle accidents, which are not road traffic accidents, may happen in the driveway of a child's own house, in a playground area or a playing field.

How do cycle accidents happen?

Factors that concern cycle accidents include:

- *State of the bicycle* – Poor maintenance of bicycle brakes and tyres contributes to between 5–10 per cent of all cycle accidents. The design of the bicycle itself can also lead to problems especially in the case of 'Chopper' bikes with high handlebars causing instability and thus lack of handling; different wheel sizes causing differing centrifugal force on the wheels; elongated saddles encouraging more than one rider to travel at a time (illegal); rounded front of saddle so that the rider can easily slip onto the gear change lever and damage the genital area; seat over rear wheel. In addition, BMX design bicycles have a steering column capable of 360° turn that can cause damage to the abdomen and genitalia.

  Bicycles of the wrong size can lead to accidents, therefore care should be taken to choose a suitable size bicycle for the size of the child. The American Acadamy of Pediatrics gives the following guidelines:

  - The child should be able to place the balls of both feet on the ground when sitting on the saddle with his or her hands on the handlebars
  - Straddling the centre crossbar should be possible with both feet on the ground; there should be about one inch clearance between the crotch and the bar
  - The handlebars should be within easy reach
- *Competence of the rider* – Lack of basic training for the type of bicycle being ridden is the main cause for concern as far as the rider's ability. Other problems include: failure to appreciate hazards through poor judgement, over confidence and inexperience; distractions by friends; riding with a friend on either the handle bars or saddle; showing off to friends; doing stunts and racing each other.
- *Conspicuity of the rider* – Motorists often report after an accident with a cyclist 'I just didn't see him'. Making sure you can be seen by other riders is therefore of prime importance for all cyclists; particularly in overcast conditions, at dusk and during rain, cyclists must ensure that they wear brightly coloured clothing with fluorescent (by night) or luminous (by day) additions such as Sam Browne belts, armbands or tabards. In addition, lights must be used on bicycles at night or in rainy darkness and reflectors should in any case be fitted. **Be safe – be seen.**
- *Hazards on the road* – An estimated 80 per cent of all cycle accidents officially designated as 'road traffic accidents' involve motorcars, 15 per cent involve motorcycles and 5 per cent involve other vehicles. The drivers of these vehicles are not always aware of the vulnerability, or sometimes the existence, of cycle riders on the roads. Other physical hazards for

cyclists include: road junctions, with an estimated 75 per cent of cycle road traffic accidents involving a right turn; bends in the road; potholes; ditches and drains; hills; motorists coming out of side roads; parked cars; roundabouts; or the cyclist coming from side roads or pavements into main roads. Finally, adverse weather conditions especially rain, fog and ice greatly increase the risk of a cyclist having an accident.

Injuries sustained

The injuries sustained by children in bicycling accidents are often quite serious. This is because the speed of the bicycle contrasts with the speed of the 'other' vehicle involved in any collision. In addition, the cyclist may travel some distance after impact before coming to a stop.

Amongst young cyclist fatalities, most will be due to head injuries, which indicates the importance of wearing cycle helmets. Serious injuries will usually involve:

- Head and facial injuries
- Limb fractures
- Severe lacerations and grazes

Facial injuries are often severe grazes, nose fractures and loss of teeth. Limb fractures are most likely to be wrists, hands, elbows and less commonly the tibia or fibula and the femur. Some seriously injured children suffer long-term disability with intellectual impairment, epilepsy or personality changes. Sometimes injuries result in permanent paralysis of limbs or the trunk. Serious facial injuries may leave scars and disfigurement.

Many cycling injures are made worse by lack of use of safety equipment in particular approved headgear and protective clothing.

Reducing cycling accidents

The bicycle is potentially hazardous and often used in the hands of inexperienced, untrained riders on busy roads. Many courses of action can be taken.

Parents can:

- Provide all necessary safety equipment including British Standards Institute approved cycle helmets and highly visible clothing
- Not let children on the road alone until at least age 9
- Accompany the child on the road until the child is fully competent
- Ensure their child takes the Cycling Proficiency Test or participates in the 'Cycleway Scheme'
- Provide a BSI approved bicycle suitable for the age, size and the development of the child
- Make sure that the brakes are working, the tyres properly inflated and that the handle bars and saddle are correctly adjusted

Children can:

- Wear BSI approved protective headgear (cycle helmet) properly adjusted and done up at all times when out on their bike
- Learn to ride properly by taking the National Cycling Proficiency training and test (RoSPA) – one must be at least 9 years old to take this test
- Learn the rules of the road as they affect cyclists
- Look after their bicycle and keep it regularly maintained especially brakes, tyres, lights and reflectors, adjustment of handlebars and saddle
- Keep off main roads and very busy roads
- Avoid making risky right turns across major roads wherever possible by planning their route
- Make sure they can hear other traffic – **never** wear a Walkman when cycling

Drivers can:

- Be aware of cyclists and their needs especially near schools, playgrounds, sports centres, shops and road junctions
- Look out for cyclists before opening their car door and allow plenty of space for cyclists when overtaking them

Schools can:

- Ensure all cyclists are trained
- Arrange training where necessary
- Inspect bicycles for standards of maintenance and use of safety equipment
- Ensure that cycle safety is covered in school through the use of the Cycleway Road Safety Education Pack (RoSPA see page 192)
- Encourage the use of safety equipment such as helmets, reflective clothing i.e., tabards or belts
- Consider making it a school rule that all cyclists must use safety equipment
- Consider the bulk purchase of cycle helmets, which can then be sold at a cheaper rate to the children

Local authorities can:

- Recognize the needs of cyclists by providing cycleways and other facilities
- Include the needs of cyclists in future developments
- Provide off-road cycling facilities where there is a local demand

Police can:

- Enforce the laws concerning bicycle lighting and braking

Retailers can:

- Advise parents and children on correct type and size of bicycle for the age and stage of development of the child
- Issue safety pamphlets with each purchase
- Keep adequate stocks of safety equipment especially helmets and be able to advise purchasers on suitability and fit

Manufacturers can:

- Ensure that their products meet the requirements of all safety standards – BSI where necessary.

Government can:

- Consider making the use of cycle helmets compulsory as has been done in Australia, for example. Because about 80 per cent of child cycle deaths fatalities are due to head injuries and because the death rate would be reduced by about 70 per cent if helmets were worn all the time, legislation making their use compulsory would be the most effective single measure to reduce mortality
- Declare a national strategy or campaign to improve cycle safety
- Coordinate work of all government departments with an influence on cycle safety
- Develop a transport policy that encourages a wider use of off-road cycling facilities and use of cycle helmets by all age groups

Children as car occupants

Each year in Britain about 100 children are killed as a result of car accidents in which they are passengers. Additionally 1800 children are seriously injured and 9000 receive slight injuries from accidents as car occupants.

With improved driving standards we might assume that many of these accidents could be prevented, and certainly with increased use of safety restraints many of the deaths could be avoided and injuries minimized.

Accidents to children as vehicle passengers are a good example of where diligent application of known safety measures can produce a large dividend in reduction of death, serious injury and disability.

Children can obviously be involved in an accident at any age from birth onwards. The number of deaths to children as car occupants is on a par with those of cyclists (approximately one in six of all road traffic accidents) and well below pedestrian accident figures. In other countries, however, child-car-occupant accidents assume a higher proportion making up as many as one in three of all fatal road traffic accidents.

Who has car-occupant accidents?

Both sexes are equally at risk in cars. Although there are no specific published statistics of accident involvement by social class, some local studies have indicated that all groups are at risk. Children from higher social classes are involved because their parents use cars more frequently; those from lower classes because they are more likely to have less safe cars and less likely to use safety seats or seat belts.

How are children injured?

The vast majority of children injured as car occupants are travelling as passengers, although a few may be driving the cars themselves illegally. Occasionally children may be in stationary cars that are hit by other cars; they may be in a car set in motion by the release of the brakes (possibly by the children themselves). As a passenger the child can be a victim of bad or drunken driving, or 'joy-riding'.

The effects of the accident may be compounded by failure to use safety restraints. At worst children can be thrown out of the car, increasing the risk of death or serious injury by five times. If the child is allowed to climb about in the car, stand up or otherwise distract the driver the problem is further amplified.

Bad vehicle design, for example rigid steering wheels, protruding mirrors and non-laminated windscreens all increase the passenger damage. The advent of childproof locks on doors has solved the dilemma of children opening the car door whilst the vehicle is in motion. Adults carrying a child on their lap without a seat belt or with a seat belt around both adult and child contribute further to the risk of injury. In this case the child acts as a cushion decreasing the injury to the adult by absorbing the impact, but the child itself may sustain serious abdominal injury.

As many as a third of all accidents to children in cars occur in cars driven by somebody other than their parent or guardian. Notable amongst these situations is the notorious 'school run' where several children are crammed into one vehicle and not restrained adequately.

Injuries sustained

Injuries to children in cars are often very serious. Along with pedestrian accidents and burns they constitute the most severe injuries to children.

The main types of injuries received by children in car accidents are:

- Head injuries
- Internal bleeding
- Internal chest injuries
- Abdominal injuries

- Spinal fractures
- Pelvic fractures
- Fractures of the femur

Less serious injuries include:

- Limb injuries (often fractures of the leg)
- Whiplash injuries of the neck
- Facial cuts and lacerations

If the child is thrown from the car the most likely injuries are:

- Head injuries
- Spinal damage
- Internal injuries
- Limb fractures
- Multiple injuries because of the increased risk of being run over by other vehicles

Most children injured will recover well, about 5 per cent are left with disabilities, the most common forms of which are:

- Brain damage with intellectual impairment, epilepsy or paralysis
- Limb deformity
- Disfiguring scarring
- Spinal injury

The long-term psychological or personality changes in children following car accidents have not been researched but could well be underestimated.

Preventing accidents to children as car occupants

Preventing accidents happening in the first place is the obvious solution to reducing injury and fatality. Almost the entire responsibility for these accidents rests with the parent or guardian, many of whom fail to realize how vulnerable children are in the car. As one medical specialist observed 'you wouldn't put your best china loose on the back seat', yet so many parents think they can carry their children this way.

The basic accident prevention methods are:

- Do not drink and drive
- Keep to a reasonable speed in relation to the prevailing conditions
- Do not drive when tired or taking drugs
- During long journeys break every 2–3 hours
- Keep your distance from the vehicle in front
- Overtake only when it is safe to do so

Use of restraints

Ideally the aim is to reduce the number of accidents happening. But the use of child restraints is very important in preventing or reducing injury in the event of an accident. Studies have shown that the correct use of occupant restraints could reduce the risk of serious injury by between 40–70 per cent and fatalities by between 50–90 per cent.

By using restraints we aim to prevent the child from either being thrown out of the vehicle or striking any hard objects in the rapid deceleration period following impact.

Many different types of restraint are available, and it is important that the right one is used for the size and weight of the child. The first important factor to consider is that a child is **not** a miniature adult. The comparative weight of the head in relation to the body is greater and is therefore vulnerable in the event of impact. The child's skeleton is also less well developed; the shoulders and pelvis in particular are at risk as they are not sufficiently well formed to take the heavy loads sustained in a car accident. The relatively soft bony structure of the rib cage also makes the internal organs vulnerable to injury. The best restraint is one which distributes the impact force over as wide an area as possible. The majority of impacts are frontal and most children sit facing forward, so that when the car stops suddenly the child will continue to travel forwards. An effective restraint will limit this movement.

Experiments in Sweden have shown that movement of the head on impact is reduced when a child is in a rear facing seat. Rear facing seats are now available for children from birth to 20lbs in weight and are secured by an adult lap and diagonal belt. Some local authorities, health authorities, voluntary or commercial agencies have set up hire or buy schemes to make these more widely available to parents.

Another consideration must be how easy it is to fit and use safety devices. If parents are to be encouraged to use them they must be widely available, sensibly priced and easy to fit and use. Having bought and fitted a suitable device it is then vital that it is used correctly and during every trip. A recent article in the *British Medical Journal* has drawn attention to the dangers to the child if the belt is not used correctly. Innovations in recent years mean that the market place now provides a wide range of suitable restraints for children from birth up until the age at which they can use adult devices. Some examples with relevant age group and weight restrictions are shown in Table 3.1.

Car manufacturers in the United Kingdom have had (since 1981) to ensure that all new cars have anchorage points of a standard type, which enable parents to fit child seats quickly and easily.

For families with up to three children it is fairly easy to provide adequate safety seating using the three rear seating positions. For larger families the only safe answer is to use a vehicle with three rows of seating such as a family estate, space cruiser or a minibus. Some manufacturers allow for extra seating at the rear of an estate car by providing rear facing seats. This is acceptable, provided seat belts are used, and any weight restrictions are adhered to. The rear cargo area of an estate car is not a safe place to travel unrestrained. It is designed as a 'crumple zone' to take the force of an impact and anybody travelling here unrestrained would be crushed or catapulted backwards through the rear windscreen.

The law and children in cars

A summary of the current position (UK 1992) is:

- All front seat passengers must wear seat belts – apart from a few rare exceptions, in old cars or for medical reasons
- All rear seat passengers must wear seat belts where fitted (all cars manufactured or sold since 1 October 1986 must be fitted with rear belts)
- All children under 14 must use a seat belt, child seat or harness where fitted and available
- A child under 1 year of age in the front passenger seat of a car must use an approved child restraint

Table 3.1 The best types of car safety device for children of different ages

Age (weight) of child	Type of device	Where fitted
0–6–9 months (up to 10 kg or 22 lbs)	Infant carrier* (BS AU 202) Carry cot in carry cot straps (BS AU 186 a)	Front or rear seat (Rearward facing) Rear seat placed sideways
6–9 months – 4 years (10–18 kg or 22–40 lbs)	Child safety seat* • with 4 point fitting (BS 3254) • or with 2 point fitting using adult lap belt (BS AU 185)	Front or rear seat (forward facing)
Young child 4–9 years (18–36 kg or 60–80 lbs)	Booster seat with adult seat belt or 4 point harness (BS 3254) – booster seat	Front or rear seat
Older child 10 years or above	Standard adult seat belt (with take off adjustment) if available	Front or rear seat

* Some two-way child safety seats cover the period from infancy to 4 years (BU AU 202 + BS 3254)
Note: More precise details to meet the requirements of your child may be found in manufacturer's brochures or from local road safety units or hire schemes.

What can one do?

Parents can:

- Above all **drive safely**
- Provide a suitable restraint for their child's age and weight
- Make sure the device is BSI approved, correctly fitted and adjusted
- Insist that their child uses the restraint whenever they travel
- Make sure their child is always restrained in other people's cars and always restrain other children in their own car
- Provide books and games or story tapes to occupy the children on long journeys
- Avoid leaving children alone in cars

Car manufacturers can:

- Design cars that are passenger friendly and have interiors that are safe for all users
- Ensure that pre-drilled anchorage points are available, accessible and easy to use for parents fitting child safety seats

Traders can:

- Make staff aware of the different devices available and of their correct use
- Be prepared to demonstrate and fit safety devices

Health authorities and road safety units can:

- Set up educational programmes to encourage use of child safety devices (in parent craft classes and antenatal clinics)
- Set up hire schemes for baby car seats ideally based at maternity units

Other road accidents

Every year between five and ten children are killed, and a further 300–500 are admitted to hospital because of road accidents involving vehicles such as buses and coaches, heavy goods vehicles, motorcycles and taxis. As many as 2000–2500 children visit Accident and Emergency departments each year as a result of this type of accident. Again boys are more often involved than girls, and although all ages of children are represented the largest proportion is in the 10–14-year-old age group.

Currently holders of an ordinary passenger car driving licence may drive a minibus of up to 7.5 tonnes in weight without taking any further test. There are proposals from the European commission for drivers to take a second test and to fulfil higher medical standards if they wish to drive a minibus with more than 8 passengers and weighing more than 3.5 tonnes. These regulations are still being debated but will obviously have wide implications for schools, hospitals and sports clubs who use minibuses.

Drivers of vehicles carrying school children have a particular responsibility, which may not always be easy to fulfil, for example, when children behave badly. Local Education Authorities and organizations using minibuses should pay careful attention to the suitability and capability of drivers of these vehicles. Written guidelines should be available detailing the responsibility for the running and use of such vehicles.

Children travelling on buses or coaches are currently at risk as there is no provision for seatbelts in these vehicles. For teachers supervising school trips it must be difficult enough keeping young children seated at all times. Legislation currently requires the driving seat and the front passenger seats to be fitted with seatbelts, but the decision to wear them is not compulsory. Fitting seatbelts to the other seats on buses and coaches is very difficult.

In the future we must look at ways of providing seatbelts for all seats on public service vehicles to provide safety for all passengers, but particularly vulnerable children.

Ideally children should not travel in heavy goods vehicles, but the attraction to travel, perhaps with a parent or a friend is obvious. The statistical risk of injury travelling in a lorry is actually very much lower than in an ordinary passenger car, but nevertheless the practice should be discouraged particularly when dangerous goods are being carried. In rural areas an additional form of transport and a potentially dangerous one is the tractor, although it is illegal for a child under 13 to travel on one.

Increasing public concern about motorcycle safety has resulted in a number of measures being taken by national government and by the motorcycle industry. These include:

- Issue of a free Bike Fax personal organizer with all new provisional motor cycle licence holders by motorcycle dealers. This gives advice on choosing the right machine, training and skills necessary, and how to dress safely and conspicuously
- Compulsory basic training for all new riders
- Compulsory accompanied motorcycle test with an examiner travelling with the rider either on another motorcycle or in a car giving directions by radio link
- Banning learner riders from carrying pillion passengers
- Restriction of newly licenced riders to motorcycles of less than 400cc capacity, progressing to the possibility of riding larger machines after 2 years riding experience
- Restriction of provisional licences to 1 year with extensions only where the rider has either booked a test and failed it, or booked it but not taken it
- Car driver licence holders only permitted provisional motorcycle licences after completion of basic training

As 70 per cent of all motorcycle casualties sustain leg injury there is a strong case for the provision of a leg guard on motorcycles. Both the industry and many motorcycle enthusiasts are, however, resistant to the use of these.

Overall, the importance of the Government's Traffic Policy cannot be ignored. Encouragement of the use of rail transport both for long distance passenger and goods transport, of light rail and bus transport for commuters and inner city transport and of safer cycle transport would undoubtedly reduce the number of road accidents.

Other Transport Accidents

Railway accidents

Accidents on or around railways for children amount to between ten and 20 fatalities each year and an estimated 100–200 admissions to hospital. Boys aged 10 years and over are most likely to sustain this kind of accident. The majority of these incidents occur on public railways but a few occur on private leisure or industrial railways. They occur throughout the the year but more frequently in the summer months. (See Table 3.2).

Table 3.2 Casualties amongst child trespassers (under 15 years of age) on railways in Great Britain, 1989, by accident type

	Injuries			
Type of accident*	Fatal	Major	Minor**	Total
Movement	5	2	1	8
Non-movement	3	11	3	17
Total Child Casualties	8	13	4	25

* A 'movement' accident involves rolling stock whereas a 'non-movement' accident may involve electrified lines or falls and so on.
** Minor injuries would be rarely reported.

How do railway accidents happen?

Travelling by train is the safest form of regular transport and accidents are more likely to be concerned with trespass or misadventure than straightforward collision. Accidents on railways result from several causes, these include:

- Being hit by a train (including being on a level crossing)
- Falling from a moving train

- Falling from a train at a platform
- Falling or tripping on a platform or on or near railway lines
- Being a passenger in a train collision
- Leaning out of a window on a moving train
- Contact with live wires or rails
- Acts of vandalism and trespass

Injuries sustained

The injuries sustained by children in railway accidents are often fatal or very serious, especially when the child has fallen from a train or been hit by one. Apart from head injuries and cuts and lacerations, the major injuries sustained are internal chest and abdominal injuries and fractures and amputations of limbs. Electrocutions on railway lines are invariably fatal – in rare cases involving overhead wires the child may be thrown clear, and will survive with severe burns or spinal injuries. Many of the serious railway injuries result in permanent disability ranging from brain damage or paraplegia to loss of limbs and physical deformity.

Reducing railway accidents

Keeping children away from railways, except as passengers from stations, is the key to preventing this kind of accident. In many places access to railway lines is all too easy for children, especially where vandalized fences allow children to enter railway lines. Older boys, in particular, find a great attraction and challenge in venturing onto lines. With peer pressure they may then take part in stunts such as running across lines in front of approaching trains or simply become distracted and forget to take care. In addition, children sometimes place objects on the line or drop objects from bridges onto lines both of which are highly dangerous activities.

Railways have a legal responsibility to maintain fences around their property. Members of the public should alert the railway authorities if they know of any broken or defective fencing.

In some urban areas, 'Q Trains' patrol alerting the police when children are trespassing on railway lines. Parents and schools can also help by informing children of the dangers associated with railways and preventing them playing near them. The relatively rare occurance of collisions at railway crossings between cars and trains can be reduced further by using photographic evidence of drivers trying to beat the trains. In future drivers 'jumping the light' will be open to prosecution.

Air and sea accidents

Children are occasionally involved in air and sea accidents either on scheduled commercial flights and voyages or in sporting and leisure activities.These are relatively rare events, which are often fatal.

Drowning at sea is covered on page 92. Other accidents at sea involve drifting out on rubber inflatables, fire and explosion on motor yachts and cuts and abrasions on sailing dinghies and canoes.

Accidents on scheduled air flights are very rare – this is the safest mode of travelling per mile travelled – even charter flights and small plane private flights are relatively safe. Less safe are microlight gliders and hang gliders, though children rarely use these.

Preventing air and sea accidents

Safety in air travel rests with the civil aviation authority maintaining high standards of airworthiness, pilot licensing and fitness, careful control of aircraft flights and attention to adverse weather conditions. People using private aircraft rely on safety standards set by their organizations and clubs.

Current safety requirements mean that passengers must be able to leave passenger aircraft in the event of an emergency – i.e., fire – through 50 per cent of the exits within 90 seconds.

As a result of the Manchester runway disaster, the Civil Aviation Authority has suggested the following improvements:

- Removal of seat obstruction to exits
- Clearly marked routes to exits
- Fitting of water sprinklers (spray or mist systems)
- Toxicity tests for cabin materials

The use of smoke hoods recommended by some researchers has so far been rejected by the Civil Aviation Authority.

The safe carriage of children by aircraft has still not been fully resolved. There are no provisions of requirements for children beyond the standard passenger safety lap belt. Many airlines provide an extension for young children sitting on their parents laps to be strapped onto their seat belt, and some now provide car safety seats. Neither arrangement is satisfactory. Research is underway at the Oklohoma Institute, United States and at the Cranfield Institute, United Kingdom to design better, preferably rear-facing seats for children in aircraft.

The more varying circumstances of sea travel requires a wider range of safety measures including rule of the road, attention to weather changes and skill in handling craft. Parents must ensure that their children use any appropriate safety devices (i.e., life jackets) and that all safety rules are considered.

4

ACCIDENTS IN THE HOME

During the early years of life the home is where small children learn about the world around them. It is also the place where they experience their first accidents.

There are innumerable types of accidents in the home for the child to encounter, ranging from falls, burns, scalds, cutting or piercing accidents, suffocation, inhalation, electrocution and accidents involving baby or child equipment, as well as the child's own toys. Table 4.1 gives the HASS data on children's home accidents for 1988.

Falls

At least half of all domestic accidents to young children involve falls; about 20 children die each year in England and Wales as a result of a fall in the home.

The younger the child involved the greater the chance of the fall being a major cause of injury. Of course all children experience falls of some kind as a natural part of the growth and explorative process. However, when falls are more serious – from great heights or onto hard surfaces where bone damage or head injuries may occur – there is cause for some concern. Overall, we must make sure that children do not fall from great heights, that if they do fall it is onto an absorbent or soft surface and that the child's environment, especially in the home, is modified to make falls less serious.

Who falls?

Falls occur at all ages and stages of childhood although toddlers are most at risk. The peak age occurrence for falls is between 0 and 4 years old with boys outnumbering girls in a ratio of 3:2.

Children of manual workers, social class V, are ten times more likely than children from social class I to have fatal accidents involving falls.

Table 4.1   Home accidents: types of accidents by age and sex

Type of accident	Age (Years)			
	0–4		5–14	
	Male	Female	Male	Female
Falls				
— from stairs	1 420	1 205	640	734
— from ladder	23	20	33	18
— from building	132	65	138	70
— between two levels	2 703	1 964	1 365	1 038
— on same level	2 588	1 733	1 395	1 175
— other	1 705	1 262	844	681
Animal/insect bite	324	285	535	498
Cutting/piercing	865	585	1 549	924
Struck				
— by object/person	2 695	1 876	2 870	2 006
— by falling object	351	212	285	233
Burning				
— from controlled heat source	1 045	843	303	275
— involving uncontrolled fire	22	20	16	16
Foreign body	1 011	867	466	369
Poisoning from inhalation/ ingestion	1 101	858	112	73
Suffocation/choking	1	1	1	0
Explosion	14	8	26	14
Electric current	10	6	9	5
Radiation	5	2	2	5
Over exertion	123	178	44	53
Drowning	3	4	0	0
Other	342	368	270	351
Unknown	1 071	783	964	790
Total	17 554	13 145	11 867	9 328
National Estimate (000s)	325	243	220	173

Source: Home Accidents Surveillance System, 1988 data, UK.

Typical falls of all types to children by age

Age	Falls
0–1	• From baby bouncers
	• From beds or tables
	• Down stairs (possibly using baby walkers)
	• From prams; shopping trolleys in supermarkets
1–4	• Down stairs
	• Out of windows
	• Off balconies
	• Off tables or other furniture
5–9	• From bicycles
	• From playground equipment
	• From horses
	• From climbing frames/fences or trees
10–14	• As for 5–9 year olds
	• During organized sport
	• During adventurous play i.e., climbing, ice-skating, roller skating, skate boarding

When do they fall?

Falls occur all year round but twice as many occur in the summer months. Another marked increase is shown during snowy or icy weather because the young, like the old, are particularly susceptible to these conditions. Fractures to the arm or wrist increase as the result of falls during icy weather. In addition, children are more likely to engage in ice-skating, tobogganing or outdoor play in the snow and this too will increase the number of falls.

Where do they fall?

Babies experience falls largely in the home and these occur when a baby bouncer or cradle is placed on top of a table, or when the child itself is placed on a raised surface i.e., table, bed or pram.

Toddlers learning to climb may have a lack of awareness of risk, poorly developed coordination and lack of fear, which together adds to the likelihood of falls. Many of these are very trivial but where stairs, window ledges or balconies are involved the consequences may be more serious. Other falls involving toddlers occur in the street or playground.

As well as accidents in the home, school children encounter the playground and its associated risks, as well as organized sports and more adventurous play. Later, older children develop these activities further and may be involved in more risky activities such as hang gliding, BMX-cycling or horse riding. Falls on building sites are an important problem. Safety here is covered by the Health and Safety at Work Act, but adolescents unfortunately find building sites attractive places for adventurous play. 34 children died because of falls in 1990.

Injuries sustained

Most falls will result in bruises or minor cuts. More serious falls, however, can cause broken limbs or head injuries, which could result in permanent disability.

In general, the younger the child the more likely they are to sustain head and upper limb injuries; older children are more prone to leg injuries.

The major injuries sustained are:

- Head injuries
- Limb fractures – usually the forearm
- Contusions, cuts, abrasions and grazes
- Fracture of the collar bone

Less frequent injuries are:

- Internal injuries of the chest or abdomen (e.g., ruptured spleen)
- Fracture of the spine

Preventing falls

Many falls at home are preventable by taking steps to provide a safe environment.

Parents can:

- Never leave a baby unattended where they could fall, i.e., from any raised surface, particularly in a baby bouncer
- Not let a child go onto a roof top or outside balcony unless it is safely fenced in and remember not to leave anything onto which a child could climb
- Keep babies or young toddlers in a playpen when they are not being closely supervised
- Fit barriers to bunk beds or ensure the bunk beds are up to British Standards Institute (BSI) standard
- Fit BSI approved stair gates at the top and the bottom of stairs, also use these across a doorway to keep a young child from a particular room, e.g., the kitchen
- Beware of open plan stairs with young children: either fill in risers or supervise the child on the stairs

- Fit childproof window latches or latches that limit the width that the window can open
- Avoid leaving furniture where it could encourage a child to climb onto cupboards or window sills
- Avoid the use of baby walkers (see page 66)
- Beware of horizontal bannisters and balcony railings
- Use reins or a harness on babies in the pram or pushchair, highchair and supermarket trolley
- Take care when carrying a baby in a papoose not to fall
- Teach older children to take risks sensibly and to use safety equipment where appropriate
- Keep children away from building sites, quarries and industrial premises

Children can:

- Beware of the dangers of climbing, particularly up trees, walls and cliffs

Teachers can:

- Discourage excessive aggression on the playground and sportsfield
- Teach children to fall correctly in gymnastics and sport

Local Authorities or Housing Departments can:

- Provide basic items of safety equipment (stair gates, window locks) as part of total house rental scheme

Local Authority Social Services Department, District Health Authority or voluntary bodies can:

- Establish loan schemes for safety equipment, particularly for the the use of socially deprived families.

Local Authorities and amenities and recreation departments can:

- Ensure that no playground equipment has a free-fall height of more than 2.5 m and that it meets BSI standards
- Provide suitable soft landing surfaces under and around playground equipment

Architects or Planners and Builders can:

- Consider the needs of children in all developments
- Provide in-built safety features in homes as a priority of the design
- Design homes in accordance with the 'Guidelines on Child Safety in Housing', Child Accident Prevention Trust

Burns and scalds

Burns and scalds are second to road accidents as the most common cause of accidental death for children in Britain with about 100 child fatalities each year.

Today there are far less burns accidents than in the slum housing days of the mid-19th century but nevertheless the injuries sustained through such accidents can be horrific and distressful. Table 4.2 shows that house fires are the commonest cause of deaths in home accidents.

Who is scalded or burned?

Burns and scalds are more likely in babies and toddlers than older children. The peak age for scalds is between 1 and 2 years old; for burns between 1 and 4 years old. The commonest way for a baby to sustain a scald is to be put into too hot bath water (over 54C), for a young toddler it is spilling a hot drink over its face and shoulders. The next most common cause is for a toddler to pull the flex of a kettle and spill scalding water onto him or herself. These two types of incident account for about half of all scalds in toddlers in Britain. Other accidents include spilling hot fluids from teapots, jugs or hot fat from chip pans. Toddlers are also susceptible to contact burns from open fires, radiators, gas fires and hot objects such as irons that have been unplugged and left to cool, or from the surface of a very hot oven.

Where older children are concerned, boys are more likely than girls to be burned, particularly in accidents involving bonfires, firework, explosions, burning petroleum products and accidents where clothing catches fire.

Children of any age may be caught in house fires, but younger children are more likely to have difficulty escaping – the peak age for involvement in house fires is between 1 and 3 years old, with girls slightly more likely to die in house fires.

Occasionally children are involved in car fires, perhaps where the child has been playing with matches or a cigarette lighter; these incidents can be compounded if the car seat covers are inflammable. Older children may also be caught in fires in unusual situations, for example on farms, at industrial premises or disused buildings. A small number of burns in older children may also be caused by chemicals (acids and alkalis), electricity, lightning and radiation.

Products involved

Fires in homes in Britain leading to child fatalities are often caused by matches or other igniting materials such as unstubbed cigarettes (33 per cent), space heating appliances (33 per cent) or other products including cooking appliances, electrical wiring and naked lights (34 per cent). The type of material first ignited is often upholstery, bedding and furnishings.

Risk factors

Specific factors can contribute greatly to the likelihood of children sustaining burns accidents. An important overall risk factor is the social class of the parents. In deaths and injuries from burns social class differences are more

Table 4.2   Home accidents: deaths by age and sex and type of accident

Type of accident	Age (Years)			
	0–4		5–14	
	Male	Female	Male	Female
Falls				
— from stairs	1	0	0	0
— from ladder	0	0	0	0
— from building	6	5	0	1
— between two levels	3	0	1	0
— on same level	0	0	0	0
— other	2	0	1	0
Cutting/piercing	0	2	0	0
Struck				
— by object/person	2	1	2	0
— by falling object	1	0	2	1
Burning				
— from controlled heat source	2	5	1	1
— involving uncontrolled fire	43	23	10	3
Foreign body	23	11	3	7
Poisoning from inhalation/ ingestion	4	3	4	5
Suffocation/choking	8	5	18	1
Explosion	0	0	0	0
Electric current	3	2	0	1
Drowning	18	4	0	1
Other	0	0	0	0
Unknown	0	0	0	0
Total	116	61	42	21

Source: Home Accident Deaths Data (HADD), 1985, E & W.

marked than for other forms of childhood accidents. Boys from a working class background are 15 times more likely to suffer fatal burns than are boys from professional backgrounds.

The following factors can contribute to accidents involving burns:

- *Parents* – stress; low income; one-parent family; unemployment; careless-ness; smokers; young and inexperienced; lack of supervision (or leaving older children to supervise younger siblings).
- *Child* – emotional disturbance (especially in boys); hyperactivity; playing with matches or fire.
- *The environment* – untidy and disorganized home; open fires, electric radiators or gas heaters; easy access to kitchen appliances (kettle, oven, gas rings, hot irons); poor equipment of lack of safety devices; overcrowding in high density housing; poor quality housing; homeless families accommodation.

Injuries sustained

Scalds most often involve the face and neck, chest, arms, buttocks and lower legs. Burns may affect any part of the body depending on the cause, and if clothing is involved a large part of the trunk and chest may be affected.

Depending on how the burn was sustained and the immediate first aid treatment undertaken, a wide spectrum of long-term healing can be seen from complete healing to permanent deep scarring and contractures.

One normally associates burns with damage to the skin but other body tissues are also affected, for example the mouth, throat or gullet can be affected by hot fluids and chemicals. Air passages can be affected by fumes and hot air, and the eyes may be burned by hot objects, chemicals or radiation.

In addition to disfigurement, which may result particularly around the face or the breasts of girls, the development of unsightly, hard bands of skin called keloids can result from burn accidents.

Preventing burns and scalds

As there are many factors involved in children sustaining burns and scalds, so are there many measures that can be taken by parents, manufacturers and authorities to reduce the chances of this type of accident. Improvements in kitchen designs, changes in heating arrangements and the removal of inflammable nightdresses from the market have already reduced the number of incidents.

Further improvements can be made by educating and training parents, teachers and the children themselves about the hazards of hot fluids and fire heat. Children as young as 2 and 3 years old can begin to learn about these dangers and from about the age of 7 to 8 years old we can expect children to take some responsibility for themselves.

Parents can:

- Install smoke detectors in the home
- Install fireguards and spark guards on open fires and fireguards on electric fires
- Consider keeping a small toddler in a playpen in the kitchen while cooking
- Use coiled kettle flexes or cordless kettles so as to avoid flexes hanging over the edge of a work surface
- Turn pan handles away from the front of a cooker
- Consider having a fire blanket in the kitchen
- Dispose carefully of all smoking materials (or not smoke)
- Do not allow children to play with matches
- Buy flame resistant or inflammable clothing
- Teach toddlers about the dangers of hot fluids, hot objects, fire and flames
- Teach older children about other hazards such as matches, bonfires, fireworks, chemicals, explosives and smoking materials
- Keep children away from bonfires
- Never use petrol, paraffin or oil on a bonfire
- Store inflammable products away from the reach of children
- Be fully aware of fire escape procedures
- Always put cold water in the bath first, and never under any circumstances leave the baby alone in the bath.

Teachers can:

- Follow the plan outlined in Chapter 9, on safety education in schools
- Pay particular attention to the problems of burns and scalds during chemistry and domestic science lessons
- Use topical issues as they arise to teach children, i.e., when there is a fire nearby or when fireworks are on sale

Health professionals or social workers can:

- Follow the plan outlined above for a general approach to accident prevention in the home
- Advise parents about hiring or purchasing smoke alarms or fireguards and other safety equipment
- Ensure that all parents and guardians are aware of ways of evacuating homes in the event of fire, putting fires out and calling for help, as well as the correct procedure for first aid for burns

Government and local authorities can:

- Enact local or national laws directed towards reducing burns and scalds e.g., design and construction of electric kettles with coiled flexes, installation of fire alarms with smoke detectors, flammability of household furniture, control of temperature of water from hot water taps
- Discontinue VAT from bona fide safety equipment
- Ensure compliance with the Housing (Means of Escape from Fire in Houses of Multiple Occupation) Order (1981) for all local authority and voluntary agency children's homes and for houses in multiple occupation

Car manufacturers can:

- Install cigarette lighters only when requested (not as standard fittings) and ensure that these can only be operated when the ignition is on
- Site petrol tanks in position of least vulnerability
- Fit non-flammable upholstery

House designers and builders can:

- Improve layouts of kitchens to limit hazardous areas e.g., avoid 'island' cooking units and install a work surface on either side of the cooker. Ensure that the cooker–sink–fridge triangle is free of obstruction
- Use flame-proof materials wherever possible
- Install central heating
- Install hot water heating systems with thermostat regulated to a maximum of 54°C

House fires

House fires are the commonest cause of death from fire, though often the actual cause of death is from suffocation (carbon monoxide poisoning) rather than from the burns.The effects of house fires are often devastating; ideally we should aim to prevent them occurring. This is not always possible but it is still feasible to limit the effects and reduce the damage. The main aims must be to:

- Reduce the source of ignition – by restricting smoking; disposing carefully of smoking materials; using hot water radiators for central heating; screening space heater and coal fires to control sparking; replacing old electrical wiring systems and improving plugs and fuses; having better control and screening of chip pans; ensuring correct storage of petroleum spirit and other flammable materials.
- Reduce the amount and flammability of materials – by introducing non-flammable materials, i.e., under the Nightdress (Safety) Regulations 1967 whereby materials used for children's nightdress must comply with flammability tests to British Standard 2963, and under the new regulations

governing the flammability of foam-filled furniture – the Furniture and Furnishings (Safety) Regulations 1988 and Amendment Regulations 1989.

- Protect people from fire and flames – by the use of fireguards.
- Restrict spread of fire; by using fire-resistant doors in homes; fitting fire extinguishers and or fire blankets in kitchens.
- Encourage the evacuation of the house as soon as possible by installing early warning systems particularly smoke alarms and detectors, now widely available at 'Do It Yourself' stores and simple to fit.
- Ensure adequate means of escape – by providing emergency exits and fire escapes particularly in buildings such as nursing homes, children's homes, boarding schools and houses in multiple occupation; by advising people to leave the building immediately on discovery of a fire. Fire brigades recommend evacuating the home, closing all doors and leaving quickly and without panic. Fire prevention officers will always be prepared to give advice, e.g., where to site smoke detectors.

Under the Children and Young Person's Act, 1933 ammended 1952, a person over 15 years old must not leave a child under 12 years old alone in a room containing an open fire or unprotected heater. The person can be prosecuted if the child is thereby seriously injured or killed.

Child abuse and burns

Burns and scalds in children may be a sign of child abuse, some studies suggesting that one in five abused children may show signs of being burned or scalded. The specific signs of such abuse are:

- Cigarette stub burns on arms, legs or face
- Linear hot poker burns on buttocks
- Glove and stocking distribution burns and scalds on legs and buttocks from a too hot bath

Poisoning

Relatively few children die as a result of poisoning, although some 15 000 children are admitted to hospital each year because they have ingested a foreign substance. The number of fatalities as a result of a poisoning has been greatly reduced over the past years, mainly due to the wider use of child-resistant containers, blister packs for drugs, child-resistant containers for household chemicals and also increased parental vigilance in ensuring that children cannot get at dangerous substances. Thankfully in most cases today the child recovers completely, and yet all poisoning is preventable and it is, therefore, vital to teach parents and other carers how to keep children away from potentially poisonous substances.

The most dangerous substances and those that are most likely to be fatal are: antidepressants, tranquillizers, analgesics, lead and corrosives.

The most commonly taken poisons are: turpentine, paraffin, salicylates, paracetamol, bleach, iron, tranquillizers and antidepressants.

Plants and animals only rarely cause serious poisonings in Britain today.

Who is poisoned, where and when?

Children aged between 1 and 4 years old, especially the 2 and 3 year olds, are most likely to be accidentally poisoned, and again, boys more frequently than girls. There is a slight rise in the 5–9-year-old age group with incidents such as eating poisonous berries from the garden or drinking poisonous substances stored in sheds or garages. The next increase by age is with teenage girls when attempted suicides with overdoses may be seen as 'cries for help'. Adolescents may also experiment with alcohol or indulge in glue or aerosol sniffing (butane is particularly dangerous) and may be introduced to other drugs at some parties.

Poisoning occurs all year round but there is an increase of incidence in the summer months compared with the winter months. Incidents are also more likely to occur in the mornings. Times of parental stress and family disruption are one of the most important factors affecting the likelihood of a child poisoning occurring.

One study of children under 5 years of age who had taken poisonous substances showed that in 84 per cent of cases the poison had been taken at home, in 14 per cent at grandparents' homes, and in many cases the medicines taken had been prescribed for the mother. Often the mother was depressed or pregnant or there were marital problems. Another study indicated that poisonings were more likely to occur in a home with three or more children.

Other findings show that factors surrounding a poisoning include:

- Serious illness in the family in past month
- Pregnancy
- Recent house move
- One parent away
- Anxiety or depression in the parents

In addition children who are hyperactive or particularly inquisitive were also more likely to ingest poisons. The conclusions were that poisoning often represents abnormal behaviour by a child in an unhappy and disordered home, rather than the ready availability of poisons. In many cases the child merely samples the substance while the parent is momentarily distracted by, for example, the front door, the telephone or by another child. This is particularly true of young children who have a lack of taste discrimination and may try things that an older child would reject on the grounds of taste.

Results of studies on social class distribution for poisonings are controversial. Some show a slight increase for social class V but others have shown a higher incidence in class I and lower in class IV and V, others have shown no class difference.

Main causes of childhood poisonings

The child:

- Explorative nature of this vulnerable age group
- Lack of taste discrimination
- Ease of access to medicines, household products
- Siblings may dare or provoke younger child

The parent:

- Parent taking drugs for illness
- Stress and unemployment
- Carelessness in storage of substances
- Distraction
- Deliberate child abuse (rare cases)

Injuries sustained

In many cases of childhood poisoning the child will sample a product and spit out the majority of it immediately, perhaps swallowing a very small amount. Sometimes it is apparent that more has been taken and that medical attention is required. If so the child must be taken to hospital immediately. The consequences of high doses of certain toxic products may be:

- Brain damage
- Renal failure
- Liver failure
- Corrosive burns

The severity will naturally depend on the amount taken, the age of the child and the substance taken. Certain products may be dangerous even in relatively small doses i.e., digoxin, quinine or tricyclic antidepressants; sympathomimetics; aspirin and paracetamol (to a lesser extent but relevant because of the very wide usage). The most dangerous household products include caustic soda, strong acids, antifreeze, soldering flux and dishwasher fluids or powders, and aerosols containing butane.

Preventing poisoning

In theory if children were segregated at all times from dangerous substances accidental poisoning would simply not occur. In practice useful devices to keep children away from dangerous substances are child-resistant containers and child-resistant catches for cupboards, which can be very effective deterrents.

The following steps can all help to provide this idyllic environment:-

Parents can:

- Ensure that tablets etc. obtained from the chemist are in child-resistant containers or blister packs
- Close child-resistant containers tightly after use
- Ensure that all medicines are kept in a medicine cupboard or cabinet, secured by a child-resistant catch at all times
- Dispose of unwanted drugs down the toilet
- Keep all household products in a cupboard with child-resistant locks on
- Be especially careful when visiting grandparents homes or other child-free homes where dangerous substances may be more readily available
- Keep all chemicals in their original containers, which should be child-resistance containers and which can be easily identified, e.g., weed killer, rat poisons
- Keep garden and other chemicals in a locked cupboard
- Try to prevent children from eating toxic plants or their fruits and seeds

Manufacturers and traders must by law:

- Put certain toxic household products in child resistant containers
- Mark toxic medicines with warning labels or signs

    They could also:

- Change the colour and shape of drugs that look like sweets (i.e., colourful 'Smartie' type tablets).
- Be alert if teenagers buying excessive quantities of butane, e.g. lighter fuel or aerosols

Pharmacists must:

- Dispense tablets in child-resistant containers or strip packs as a professional requirement unless requested by the user

Health professionals can:

- Prescribe drugs only in small quantities at a time
- Advise patients with young children about the dangers of drugs and how to store them
- Refer children with suspected poisoning from a harmful drug or a household substance to hospital immediately. If the health professional is in doubt about the toxicity of any particular drug or substance, advice can be obtained from the National Poison Information Services in London, Edinburgh, Cardiff, Dublin or Belfast or from local poison centres in Birmingham, Leeds and Newcastle-upon-Tyne (full details are given on

page 191). In hospital the child can be kept under observation until it is clear whether a significant quantity of the harmful substance has been taken, or not. If so the child can then be admitted

- Beware of the dangers of delayed symptoms after taking certain drugs (i.e. paracetamol)
- Use waiting rooms at doctors' surgeries and hospitals to publicise information on preventing poisonings

Local authorities can:

- Avoid cultivation of toxic plants near schools, public playgrounds or sports fields
- Organize the collection and disposal of unwanted household drugs

Teachers can:

- Teach children how to recognize toxic plants
- Teach children about toxic drugs and household products and how to store them safely

Cutting and piercing accidents

Childhood deaths from cutting and piercing accidents are relatively few – two or three each year – yet more than 1000 children are admitted to hospital each year, and as many as 20 000 attend Accident and Emergency departments because of injuries sustained through this type of accident.
Most of these (600 or more hospital admissions, 15 000 Accident and Emergency visits) are caused by accidents involving glass.

Such commodities – glass, sharp knives and tin cans are present all around us and so all age groups are vulnerable to possible accidents particularly around the home. Where ordinary annealed glass, as opposed to toughened, laminated or glass covered with a safety film, is used in doors and low windows, the risk is increased. Accidents involving children putting their arms through annealed glass or running straight into it occur. Other accidents occur when young children trip and fall while carrying a glass or bottle. Knives and sharpened garden equipment left lying around the home make up other cutting and piercing accidents, as do open tin cans and shattered glass windscreens and windows in cars.

Types of injuries

The majority of injuries sustained are lacerations to all parts of the limbs, but especially to the hand, and of varying degrees of severity. The jagged nature of broken glass may cause severe lacerations and severing or tearing of muscles, nerves and blood vessels.

The common sites for glass injuries are:

- Hand, wrist or arm after putting the limb through the pane of a window or door
- Feet and legs after walking into or through glass doors in patio windows
- Face from any shattered glass
- Trunk and chest (these may include penetrating injuries involving internal organs)
- Eye, e.g., from exploded carbonated drinks bottles
- Mouth or gullet, e.g., from a broken thermometer

The majority of these injuries will recover fully although sometimes disfiguring scarring may be left. Very severe scarring may require plastic surgery at a later date, and, in particular, psychological problems may follow severe facial scarring. Rarely, a piercing injury may cause severe internal injuries with loss of function of a kidney or the spleen. The outcome of a nerve or tendon injury will depend on the success of the repair and re-establishment of nerve pathways or tendon fibres. A severe injury to a major artery may result in exsanguination and death.

Preventing cutting and piercing incidents

Ideally we should aim to keep children away from jagged fragments of glass or other cutting tools. By safe storage of all such equipment in the home and garden, parents can greatly reduce the likelihood of such injuries. A wider use of safety glass around the home is, however, the most important requirement for children's safety. This can be either laminated or toughened glass (BS 6262).

At present there are no legal requirements that specify the use of safety glass in new buildings, however codes of practice amongst architects and builders generally mean that any expanse of glass below a height of 1 m or in a door will be safety glass.

In older buildings, the following actions can be taken:

Parents can:

- Remove glass hazards by ensuring that only safety glass has been used in low level glazing or in a door. If this is not possible rolls of safety film are available that can be fitted over ordinary glass and that will ensure that in the event of a fall the glass would not break in to sharp pieces
- Stick brightly coloured stickers or tape onto low level glass sections so that the child is aware of the glass
- Place obstacles by glass so the child is deterred from going too close
- If all these measures fail or are not possible board up low level glass

Manufacturers and builders can:

- Use safety glass for: all glass doors, internal glazed areas, fixed panes in doors, all windows within 800 mm of the floor, shower and glass panels, patio doors

Local authority housing departments can:

- Ensure that safety glass is used in new housing and conversions

Motor manufacturers and traders can:

- Fit laminated glass to car windscreens

Milk suppliers or dairies can:

- Replace milk bottles with biodegradable cartons

Government could:

- Ensure that changes in the Building Regulations include regulations relating to the installation of safety glazing in doors and low level windows

Suffocation and strangulation

There are about 50 instances of child suffocation in the United Kingdom each year and they arise from a wide variety of circumstances. Babies and toddlers are most likely to be involved in accidents at home whereas older children are more likely to be injured during an exploration in a forbidden location.

In cases of suffocation the child will suddenly find him or herself in a dangerous situation that can only be relieved if the person finding them knows what to do. Babies and toddlers may suffocate from bed clothes, nightclothing or plastic bags (boys and girls of this age are equally affected). Older children, predominantly boys, may suffocate as a result of exploring tunnels, workings or from venturing into dangerous areas such as grain silos and sand pits. An additional hazard for boys of this age, in particular, is suffocation from a plastic bag while glue-sniffing.

Domestic accidents may occur during the summer and winter months, and at any hour of the day or night. Those occurring out-and-about are more likely in the summer months. Young children are obviously at risk when materials such as plastic bags are left lying around the home, and when these children are left with time on their hands and unsupervised.

Causes of suffocation

The most likely causes are:

- Putting a plastic bag or sack over the head
- Collapse of sand, grain or earth smothering the head
- Baby being left alone with feeding bottle propped up in its mouth
- Small baby smothering in a pillow, blanket or duvet
- Having all air cut off (or replaced by a toxic gas) in a confined space, i.e., disused refrigerator or in a barn

In addition the entry of air into the lungs may be obstructed by hanging, strangulation and throttling.

- *Hanging* – is pressure on the outside of the neck by suspension of the body from a noose. This may occur in children where older boys are playing with rope nooses in trees or lofts.
- *Strangulation* – is the constriction of the outside of the neck by a ligature or other rope-like agent but without suspension. This may occur in babies or toddlers in a cot or pram when a scarf, neck tie or lace in a garment has been pulled tight by becoming caught in something. Baby clothes in Britain must not have pull-ties at the neck of coats or anoraks but parents should beware of buying such items of clothing abroad where clothes may not be so safely manufactured.
- *Throttling* – is from a deliberate assault with a squeezing of the victim's throat to cut off the air supply.

In all these cases lack of oxygen will occur in 3–4 minutes, brain damage and even death within 4–5 minutes. The outcome of this kind of accident is either a complete recovery if the child is found in time, or death.

Preventing suffocation accidents

Although there are a wide variety of causes of suffocation in children there are some steps that can be taken to prevent dangerous circumstances arising.

Parents can:

- Ensure that plastic bags are not left lying around
- Never leave a baby feeding from a bottle propped up
- Make sure there are no jagged edges on cots and prams where clothing could get caught
- Avoid using low-mesh clothing or items with cords or ribbons on babies or clothing such as anoraks and T shirts with ties around the neck with all children
- Avoid using a pillow with a baby

- Make sure the baby cannot snuggle down in a sleeping bag or bedclothes
- Ensure that a baby nest is made to British Standard
- Only use dummies manufactured to British Standard and check them regularly to ensure the teat is secure
- Warn older children of the dangers of plastic bags and of playing in dangerous places where subsidence could occur, or playing with ropes and strings (especially around the neck)

Children can:

- Take care when playing with ropes and swings in trees and lofts
- Keep away from sand and gravel pits
- Keep away from old mine workings or tunnels that may collapse
- Be aware of the dangers of playing in barns with heavy bales of straw
- Recognize dangers of tunnelling in sand pits, sand dunes or the seashore

Manufacturers can:

- Put air holes in plastic bags (other than for food use where bags will need to be air tight)

Local authorities can:

- Ensure that all rubbish tips with items such as disused refrigerators are inaccessible to the public

Inhalation and ingestion

Between 50 and 60 children die each year in the United Kingdom as a result of inhalation or ingestion. Inhalation – choking – occurs when an object is taken into the windpipe and causes an obstruction. Ingestion is when a foreign body is taken into the gullet or stomach.

Choking is the single largest cause of accidental death for children under 1 year of age and occurs when a foreign body is inhaled and the child coughs and splutters trying to cough it up. If the item sticks in the upper airways this is an immediate and dangerous threat.

Ingestion, on the other hand, is not usually such a big threat even when potentially poisonous items such as small batteries (watch-type 'button' batteries) are swallowed. These will usually pass harmlessly through the child without any danger. Rarely, surgery is required to remove the item, if it remains impacted in the oesophagus or elsewhere in the alimentary canal.

Inhalation is most likely between the ages of 6 months and 3 years old when the child puts every new thing in his or her mouth. The types of item most likely to be inhaled include: small bits of food – especially peanuts or peas; sweets; marbles; buttons; small toys or parts of toys; safety pins or uninflated balloons. In older children some deaths have been reported in school children who have inhaled the top of felt-tip pens, possibly by trying to pull the top off with their teeth. As a result of research, safety-pen tops have now been designed to allow air to be breathed through or around their outside, and have been introduced into schools throughout the United Kingdom to meet a special British Standard. Ingestion more often involves coins, small toys or 'button' batteries. Most of these items will pass through the body in between 1 and 7 days.

Unlike poisoning and burn accidents, inhalation or ingestion accidents do not have any association with stress or other adverse social or environmental conditions.

Prevention of inhalation or ingestion

The prevention of choking-type accidents is most relevant between the 6-month- and 4-year-old age group. As children of this age cannot discriminate for themselves, the onus is on the parents to eliminate potentially dangerous items from the child's environment as far as possible.

Parents can:

- Ensure that a baby's dummy meets the British Standard 5329 for dummies, with holes in the flange that allow air through if the dummy gets inhaled into the back of the throat
- Avoid leaving small items lying around the home. In particular, beware of detachable toy parts and ensure that toys belonging to older children are kept safely stored away from under-threes. A Choke Hazard Tester is available from Early Learning Centre mail order that parents can use to test toys or other small items for the suitability for young children
- Pay attention to manufacturers advice on age-suitability of toys. Small toys will often say 'unsuitable for children under 3 years of age because of small parts'
- Never give peanuts to children under the age of 7 years
- Disallow children to run around with toys in their mouths
- Discourage playing when eating food
- Make sure not to leave uninflated balloons lying around
- Check that felt-tip pen tops meet the current safety standards

Manufacturers and retailers can:

- Restrict the manufacture and sale of toys for children under 3 years old that fail to pass the BSI tests for small objects

Special care should be taken with children with specific impaired airway protective reflexes, such as those with neurological conditions, for example, muscular dystrophy or Friedrich's ataxia or children on anticonvulsant or antidepressant medications.

Electrocution

Electrocution, like drowning, is an all-or-nothing event. Either the child makes a full recovery or dies. On average two to three children die in the United Kingdom each year as a result of electrocution. Although the wide range of electrical fittings and apparatus would appear to make the potential for electrocution quite high, the high standard of manufacture and the use of safety devices makes it a relatively rare occurrence.

Inquisitive toddlers sticking items in house electric sockets and adventurous boys aged between 10 and 14 years of age straying onto electric railway lines or climbing pylons are the most likely groups to encounter electrocutions.

Other potentially dangerous sources around the home are faulty appliances such as electric kettles or (for older children) using electrical appliances, for example, hairdryers or cassette players in a bathroom. Outside the home overhead cables (particularly when flying kites or models) can be a source of danger, as can electricity sub-stations.

Lightning is a natural source of electricity that is responsible for one or two deaths each year in the United Kingdom (to all age groups) and is usually encountered during summer thunder storms.

The passage of electricity through the body may cause instant death by interrupting the normal rhythm of the heart (fibrillation), in addition the source may cause burns at the point of entry. Circuit breakers (see below) prevent electrocution by cutting off the current before fibrillation occurs, and are thus the most important preventive measure.

Products involved in electrocution

Outside:

- Electricity sub-stations
- Pylons
- Live electric rails
- Overhead electric wires including railways

Domestically:

- Electrical apparatus (kettles, fires, lawn mowers, power tools)
- Plug fittings, electricity sockets
- Radios, record players, videos, televisions, hairdryers

Preventing electrocution

Sometimes specific buildings regulations protect people from electrocution, for example, in Britain electrical power points cannot be fitted in bathrooms, except especially adapted shaver sockets. Other measures must be taken by individuals, mostly parents, to protect children from danger.

Parents can:

- Ensure that circuit breakers are installed when they buy a new house or when old houses are rewired
- Rewire faulty appliances and plugs, replace or re-insulate frayed or exposed wires
- Avoid overloading sockets
- Use childproof safety socket covers in all domestic sockets from babyhood to discourage playing with the open socket
- Switch off kettles at wall sockets before filling
- Avoid the use of electrical apparatus when standing on a wet floor or with wet hands
- Unplug all electrical appliances before carrying out work
- Fit residual current circuit breakers to electrical drills, and all garden equipment i.e., lawn mowers and strimmers, which cut off the current in the event of a fault
- Wear rubber boots when using electrical appliances outdoors
- Keep children well away from lawn mowers, strimmers etc.
- Do not use electrical appliances outside when it is wet
- Forbid children to go near electric railway lines, sub-stations, near pylons or electric wires
- Take care when flying kites or model aircraft not to become entangled in electric wires

The Electricity Board advises children not to:

- Enter an electricity sub-station after a ball or toy has been thrown in accidentally
- Throw objects at overhead lines
- Climb pylons
- Fly kites or model aircraft, go fishing (fishing rods are excellent conductors of electricity) or move the mast of sailing boats near overhead lines

Staff from the Electricity Board may be willing to visit schools or other groups to show videos and talk to children about the potential dangers of electricity.

Toys

Toys of all forms give hours of pleasure to children. Yet, unfortunately, accidents do happen. Figures collected by the Home Accident Surveillance Survey show that toys are implicated only rarely in childhood accidents and children between the ages of 9 months and 4 years old are most often involved, followed by children aged from 5–9 years old.

Older children are less often involved in accidents with toys, but are more likely to be involved with DIY accidents when they are model-making or helping parents.

Toy Safety in the United Kingdom is now ensured by the Toy (Safety) Regulations 1989, which came into force on January 1 1990. These regulations state that children's toys supplied in the United Kingdom, including imports, must **either** be made wholly to the British Standard 5665 (or to equivalent standards in other EC countries) **or** be made to a prototype approved by an independent body and carry the EC mark and other information. These regulations do not apply to toys supplied before January 1990 and certain goods such as Christmas decorations are excluded. Trading Standards Officers are always on the lookout for faulty toys and violations of safety standards and parents who suspect a toy on the market can contact their nearest Trading Standards Officer direct (under Consumer Services in the telephone directory).

Potentially dangerous toys or items

Some types of toy are implicated more often than others in accidents, as are some items (not strictly speaking toys) with which children may come into contact. Parents and carers should check for the following toys in particular, and supervise their use where necessary:

- Fireworks, especially bangers and rockets
- Small Christmas tree decorations
- All toys working from mains electricity
- Plastic toy-wrappings
- Any small metal or plastic part of a toy (take care with children under 3 years old)
- Pencils in mouths
- Marbles and small balls
- Toy dolls and Teddy Bears with loose limbs, heads or eye attachments
- Guns or air rifles
- Mini motorcycles
- Tricycles and bicycles
- Home playground equipment – climbing frames, swings and slides
- Bows and arrows
- Catapults
- Inflammable toys (particularly soft toys and dressing-up outfits. These should all satisfy British Standard flammability tests)
- Painted toys (lead paint may be used)
- Toys with springs (inside or out)

Another danger is where children copy the actions of a character on Television, e.g., Superman, Batman and think they can put on a cloak and fly. Parents must warn children of the dangers and supervise their activities if necessary.

Preventing accidents involving toys

By following these procedures governing the use of toys children can be well protected from possible danger.

Parents can:

- Check for British Standard 5665, or the British Toy and Hobby Manufacturers Association symbol (the lion in a triangle) on all toys
- Never buy cheap imported toys
- Buy from reliable traders
- Supervise play where necessary
- Match the toy to the age of the child
- Alert Trading Standards Officers of potentially dangerous toys on the market

Manufacturers can:

- Construct toys to BS 5665 or to their Trade Association standards
- Mark age limits of toys clearly

In addition to BS 5665, toys are also governed by the Consumer Safety Act 1978 (Toys' Safety) that covers safety aspects including levels of toxic paints in toys; the Food Imitation (Safety) Regulations 1985 bans the sale of small toys and novelties deliberately designed to imitate food (including scented erasers).

Other accidents in the home

Additional safety hazards for children around the home include some types of nursery furniture or equipment, particularly that used with babies.

These are some of the hazards encountered:

- *Baby Walkers* – These are devices used by parents of children in the age group 5–12 months old and accidents involve both boys and girls. Around 2500 babies are seen each year in hospital because of these accidents, which indicates a very dangerous hazard. The most common form of incident involves the child 'cruising' around in the walker, falling against furniture or a fire or down stairs. Head injuries and facial lacerations may occur, fingers and hands may also be crushed or cut or the child may be burnt. The increased mobility afforded by the device may also lead a young baby towards other hazards such as the cooker. Walkers of an inferior design can tip over and may be easily moved to a dangerous location such as the top of a flight of stairs. No evidence exists that these appliances help babies to learn to walk and the best remedy against such accidents is to reject the baby walker as an aid to child development.

- *Baby Bouncers* – Another hazard for young babies is when a parent places a baby bouncer on a raised surface with the child strapped in. Even a young baby can cause a bouncer to move and it is then easy for the device to fall to the ground: bouncers should only be used on the floor where they cannot fall.
- *Nursery Furniture* – Modern designs of nursery furniture have greatly improved safety features, nevertheless some problems remain, notably with the bars of cots where a child may get a limb trapped or sharp fittings or protrusions where clothing may get caught up and cause strangulation of the child.

Children may also trap fingers in doors; slip on floors or slip in the bath; get mouth injuries from pens, pencils and needles. Outside the home the collapse of wrongly erected pushchairs and garden furniture can cause cuts and contusions to limbs. Drowning in the bath is discussed in Chapter 6.

Preventing these accidents

Improved design and use of safety equipment would obviously improve the risk of danger to children around the home. Safe storage of hazardous items and eternal vigilance by parents are other measures that help to create a safe environment for the child.

Practical guidelines established by the Child Accident Prevention Trust for architects, designers and builders would greatly improve safety in new homes if applied throughout all new buildings. In Australia the Child Accident Prevention Foundation and the Housebuilders Council have pioneered the idea of 'kid safe' houses, which illustrate the ideal environment for a child. Purchasers may visit these designs to stimulate improvements in their own homes. Free leaflets on nursery furniture and safety devices (**Keep Your Baby Safe** and **Keep Them Safe**) have been published by the Child Accident Prevention Trust. They give advice about what is available and the British Standards that apply to them. They can be obtained from local child health clinics or health visitors.

Sudden infant death syndrome (SIDS)

The sudden infant death syndrome (cot death) is the commonest cause of death in infants in the United Kingdom between the age of 4 weeks and 1 year. The definition of cot death, or sudden infant death syndrome, has been defined in the United States as:

The sudden death of any infant that is unexpected from the history and where a thorough postmortem fails to demonstrate an adequate cause of death.

The problem of the SIDS is by no means solved. A small proportion of babies who die unexpectedly are found on postmortem to have had an illness or abnormality that provides a full explanation for the death (and therefore can not officially be described as belonging to the SIDS). Others in retrospect have had some minor symptoms such as snuffles or a cough that might have indicated the presence of an infection. The question of overheating from too many bedclothes was first raised many years ago, but more recently this has been coupled with the baby's sleeping position in that a significantly increased likelihood of SIDS has been associated with the baby being nursed prone, together with excessive bedding. The Department of Health recently mounted an educational campaign to persuade parents to allow their babies to sleep supine, as a result of the mounting evidence of the dangers of babies sleeping prone.

Trends

There has been an increase in the number of cot deaths in recent years but this is probably due to reclassification by the World Health Organization in 1979 to recognize the condition of SIDS together with a greater awareness by doctors.

From 1971 there has been a steady fall in both still births and early neonatal death rates. The post perinatal (1 week – 1 year old) and post neonatal (1 month – 1 year old) rates have remained relatively static especially since the mid-1970s. However, there is no doubt that the rate is now falling.

The rate for deaths registered as SIDS in England and Wales rose during the 1970s and 1980s. This trend may now be expected to fall since the introduction of the campaign to encourage parents to place their babies on their backs to sleep.

Who suffers cot deaths?

Overall cot deaths are responsible for just under half of all deaths in the 4-weeks- to 1-year-old age group. That is, each year around 1 in 500 of all babies die suddenly and unexpectedly before reaching the age of 2 years old. This gives a total each year of around 1500 deaths, with a peak incidence at between 2 and 4 months old.

Typically, an apparently healthy baby will be put to bed at night and next morning will be discovered dead in the cot by the parent. Boys suffer more cot deaths than girls but other factors also influence the likelihood of this incident.

Risk Factors:

- Baby sleeping prone
- Young mother
- Mother smokes
- High number or short interval between previous pregnancies
- Urinary infection in pregnancy
- Short labour
- Low birth weight
- Bottle-fed baby
- Prematurity, especially if baby has many non-specific symptoms
- Age between 2–5 months old
- Second twin (four times risk)
- Sibling to a previous cot death (ten times the risk)
- OB/AB blood group in mother
- Poor socio-economic circumstances

Parents who feel their baby is at risk can use apnoea monitors or other similar devices that can alert them of any disturbance of breathing or heart rate that may result in a cot death. These devices can be a source of comfort to parents but deaths have occurred even while a baby is being monitored and they are not the final answer to the problem. Whenever a cot death has occurred, a postmortem should be carried out by a paediatric pathologist if possible. This not only helps towards a better understanding of the problem but may also provide information to reassure the parents. The coroner must be informed and an inquest may be needed. The police may also need to make enquiries, which will naturally distress the parents.

Parents who lose a baby through cot death may need sympathetic medical, emotional and practical help; they will also need to be reassured that the death is not their fault. Nationally, the Foundation for the Study of Infant Death carries out research and acts as an agency offering considerable support to parents who have lost a baby.

Preventing cot deaths

- Put babies to sleep on their backs or on their side supported from behind by a rolled up blanket
- Do not overheat the baby with too many bedclothes
- Keep a special watch on babies who are at risk according to the above listing
- Child health doctors should work closely with general practitioners and health visitors in follow-up and care of at-risk babies
- Hold a case conference on all SIDS deaths, to include detailed postmortems

- Educate mothers and relatives to be alert to symptoms and signs of illness in babies, infants and toddlers and to call doctors or visit surgery if in any doubt about possible illness in the child
- Monitor at-risk babies by making more frequent health visitor visits i.e., at least once every fortnight in the first 3 months and monthly in the second 3 months
- Keep careful growth and weight charts
- Provide practical support for babies at risk by:
    – installing an apnoea alarm or similar device
    – putting baby to sleep in same room as parents

5

ACCIDENTS AT SCHOOL AND AT PLAY

Accidents at school

During term time school children spend a good proportion of their time at school and clearly there is plenty of scope here for accidents to happen.

Overall less than five children are killed as the result of accidents on school premises each year, but between 10 000–15 000 experience injury requiring admission to hospital and 150 000–200 000 visit outpatients as a result of injuries sustained at school. (See Table 5.1).

In total, accidents in school account for 10–15 per cent of all childrens' accidents and these vary widely from the very trivial to the fatal. Schools' abilities to cope with accidents vary widely too from those with resident nurses to those with only the very basic first-aid knowledge available. Some schools will report every minor injury to the local hospital, just to be on the safe side, whereas others will be able to deal with much more serious incidents themselves.

Schools can reduce the likelihood of accidents happening by ensuring that children receive thorough accident prevention and safety education training. In addition, schools should consider providing basic first-aid and resuscitation training to pupils. Currently most children do not have the benefit of this

Table 5.1 Injuries at place of education, by area and age-group, percentages and UK estimates for 1988

Education area	< 5 years old	5–14 years old	15 years or above	All ages	UK estimate
Creche/nursery	84%	12%	4%	100%	11 000
School/college building	2%	73%	24%	100%	135 000
School/college grounds	4%	85%	11%	100%	149 000
All education areas	6%	77%	17%	100%	295 000

Source: Based on sample hospital data (LASS 1988). This is the first complete year under LASS so trend data is not available.

training although some national medical and safety organizations are making efforts to make such schemes available to interested schools.

Who has school accidents?

Potentially all school children can be involved in an accident but the child most likely to be involved is a boy aged between 10–14 years old.

Local surveys have shown that approximately one child in 50 will experience an accident at school requiring medical attention each year. Amongst younger children, boys and girls are almost equally involved but as the ages increase boys are far more likely to be represented. After the age of 15 the number of accidents at school diminish.

One Australian study noted that girls experienced more accidents at primary school than did boys. This is contradictory to all other studies, in which boys always had more accidents than girls. One explanation for this was that whereas boys shrugged off the less serious incidents girls were less tolerant and more likely to seek attention for even the most minor injury.

No information is available on social class distribution of school accidents and little is known about ethnic distribution, or whether children with certain personalities or with handicaps are more or less involved.

When do school accidents occur?

Local surveys have shown that the most likely time for accidents at school is the start of a new school term – in particular the beginning of the new school year in September. The explanation is a new environment, new friends and new games and activities, therefore the children are more prone to accidents. A lack of training and fitness could account for the spate of sporting accidents at the start of each new season. A small, but significant, proportion of accidents occur when the child is travelling to school, either as a cyclist or a pedestrian, but unless these actually occur on school premises they would be classified under road traffic accidents (see Chapter 3). The peak times for accidents throughout the school day are at the three break times.

Where do school accidents occur?

The school playground accounts for 40–50 per cent of all accidents at school even though only 15 per cent of pupil time is spent in the playground. Similarly 25–35 per cent of school accidents happen on the sporting fields or in the school gymnasium, even though only 10 per cent of pupil time is spent in these places. Although the rest of the school day is spent in the classroom only 15–35 per cent of accidents take place here.

How do school accidents occur?

Most school accidents are every day falls and collisions associated with the impulsiveness and energy of young children. As most school playgrounds are concrete or asphalt even minor falls can result in nasty cuts and abrasions. Some of these accidents occur on playground apparatus and these too can be exacerbated by the hard surface onto which the child falls and also by the height and design of the equipment. Sometimes the design of the equipment is itself responsible for the accident. An increase in violence in the playground is of great concern. The normal competitive skirmishes that take place in every school playground are of course a normal part of growing up. However, bullying and organized gang fighting appear to be an increasing occurrence in the school playground in comparison to society at large, in which overall violence is increasing.

In a detailed survey over a 4-year period in East Sussex, researchers noted that the number of playground accidents increased as well as those associated with fighting and assault.

On the sports field many accidents (particularly in contact sports, i.e. soccer, rugby) are due to lack of fitness or training, especially at the beginning of the season, and these are covered in detail in Chapter 6. Within the school buildings accidents are most likely to occur from slammed doors, slippery floors or running in corridors. Injuries are likely to be trapped fingers, banged heads and sometimes cuts from broken glass. High-risk areas in school are obviously science laboratories, workshops and home economics kitchens. The use of any powered equipment, dangerous chemicals, heat sources or laboratory animals always provide potential for accidents. The strict application in schools of the Health and Safety at Work Act 1974 has made accidents of this type relatively rare, however.

Overall:

- Around half of all schools accidents involve falls
- One in five collisions
- One in eight being hit by moving or falling objects
- One in 15 in laboratories or workshops

Injuries sustained in school accidents

Most school accidents as we have seen are trivial. Cuts, bruises, minor abrasions or contusions are the commonest result. However, around 4–5 per cent of all incidents require medical attention either by a general practitioner or the local Accident and Emergency department.

The commonest of these more serious injuries sustained in school are:

- Fractures of the arm and shoulder (including clavicle)

- Abrasion of the head or face
- Fractures of the leg

Because most of the injuries sustained are minor, treatment rarely requires time off school. Some head injuries or leg fractures may require up to one or even two terms off school for hospital treatment and convalescence. A school phobia or truancy is a rare outcome of an accident at school and is most likely following an assault on the child by his or her peers.

Reducing school accidents

As the number of school accidents is increasing – although many other categories are falling – preventive measures are obviously required. As the school acts *in loco parentis* while the children are at school, the headteacher has a responsibility to see that the children in the school do not come to any harm. However, other agencies also have responsibilities.

The Department of Education can:

- Set up a simple standardized surveillance system for the collection of national data on school accidents
- Require school inspectors to check on school accident prevention activities, including record keeping, safety precautions, accident prevention teaching, first-aid facilities, teaching and training
- Make an annual report on school accidents and present measures to reduce them
- Liaise with other Government departments where appropriate to set up measures to reduce school accidents e.g., Department of Transport on the 'Safe Way to School' programme

Local Education Authority can:

- Collect regular data on school accidents on standard forms
- Analyse data and provide feedback to school
- Require education advisors to check on the number of accidents in school; what is taught in accident prevention and what facilities are available for the teaching of first aid
- Set up arrangements for special payments to recognize the work of school first aiders
- Inspect playgrounds and gymnasiums from a safety point of view and remedy deficiencies

Teachers can:

- Be especially vigilant on playground duty at the start of a new term, consider the use of parents as extra help

- Appoint qualified first aiders and appointed persons as required under the Health and Safety at Work Act of 1974
- When refereeing strictly adhere to rules on the sportsfield and ban persistent offenders from playing
- Keep accurate records and regularly review incidents of accidents in schools
- Carry out a multidisciplinary review of school accidents once every term (include school Medical Officer or nurse, Health and Safety inspector and parent representative)

Following this review:

- Set up remedial measures for prevention wherever necessary and use a priority check list
- Carry out a planned programme of accident prevention and first aid in all classes (liaise with road safety, home safety and other advisers and with the Royal Society for the Prevention of Accidents (RoSPA) officers and District Health Authority Health Promotion departments)
- Make full use of advice in Department of Education and Science Safety Series numbers 1–6

School Medical Officers and Nurses can:

- Enquire of headteachers and class teachers about accident experience, teaching of accident prevention and first aid
- Offer help to schools where appropriate
- Check with local Accident and Emergency departments that regular information is made available to the Local Education Authority and individual schools
- Check with local Health Promotion/Education departments that adequate input is being made into accident prevention and first aid at schools
- Check accident records and first-aid box provisions and contents at school (statutory duty of DES and HSE staff)

Independent schools can:

- Keep standardized records (coordinated through the Independent Schools Association)
- Set up accident prevention schemes
- Teach first aid in school (Local Education Authorities and Health Authorities are sometimes willing to help independent schools in setting up safety and first-aid programmes. The Health and Safety Executive has a duty to provide this)

Parents can:

- Encourage schools to build and maintain safe playgrounds

- Offer to set up parents groups to help supervise playgrounds and sporting activities
- Encourage Parent–Teacher Associations to discuss school accidents and their prevention with staff

Children can:

- Observe rules in school e.g. no running in corridors
- Obey rules in sports activities
- Learn self-defence and refuse to participate in fighting and bullying
- Learn first aid and resuscitation

Legislation for accident prevention in school

Health and Safety (First Aid) Regulations 1981   Applied to educational establishments from July 1982 – these require the employer to ensure that adequate first aid cover for all employees exists while at work. Pupils are not covered here as they are not employees, but this cover has long been considered an essential provision under case law on people controlling educational establishments.

Health and Safety at Work etc. Act 1974   This covers both staff and pupils at school as it makes provision for employees and the health and safety of other people who may be affected by working activities, which, therefore, includes both pupils and other visitors into school.

Reporting of Injuries, Diseases and Dangerous Occurrences Regulations 1985   This places a legal requirement on authorities to maintain records of accidents to pupils and to report details of certain defined categories of serious accidents to the Health and Safety Executive.

Accidents in playgrounds

Given that childrens' playgrounds are designed for fun and enjoyment it is ironic that so many injuries occur within them. Some of the incidents that occur result from poor design and layout, whilst others occur because of the children's (sometimes aggressive) antics. In recent years more and more parents have concerned themselves with playground safety and exerted pressure on local authorities to improve the design and layout of playground equipment and surfaces. Nevertheless, each year one or two children are killed in playground accidents, 10 000–15 000 are admitted to hospital with injuries and 50 000–60 000 are taken to Accident and Emergency departments with injuries. Table 5.2 shows some details of playground accidents.

Who has playground accidents?

Children from all social classes use playgrounds and as with most other types of accident boys experience this type more than girls in the ratio 3:2. In Britain the 8–10 year olds are injured more often, but in Denmark (for example) younger children, 4–7 years old, are more often involved.

When do playground accidents occur?

A higher incidence of playground accidents occur in the summer months, associated with the increased usage of playgrounds at this time. They are more likely to occur when children are playing without supervision, but there are many occasions when accidents do happen in spite of the presence of an adult or older supervisory child.

Where do playground accidents occur?

The majority of playground accidents in Britain occur in public playgrounds – between 60–70 per cent. The remainder occur at schools (20–30 per cent); and

Table 5.2 Playground accidents

Accidents by age

Age	Number	Percentage
0–2 years old	30	6.9
3–4 years old	71	16.3
5–9 years old	160	36.7
10–14 years old	114	26.1
15–64 years old	61	14.0
Total	436	100.0

Accidents where equipment is involved

Article	Number	Percentage
Swing	84	34.7
Slide	55	22.7
Climbing-frame	54	22.3
Roundabout	27	11.2
See-saw	18	7.5
Swimming/paddling pool	2	0.8
Sandpit	2	0.8
Total	242	100.0

Source: Leisure accident surveillance system (LASS) for 6 months, Summer 1987.

at home (10 per cent). A very small proportion occur at the more specialized adventure playgrounds, which have been set up by local authorities, voluntary groups or private individuals in stately homes, safari parks or public houses. Any piece of playground equipment can be the cause of an accident, but the ones which appear most commonly in surveys are, in order of involvement:

- Swings
- Climbing frames
- Slides
- See-saws
- Roundabouts

Adventure playgrounds with their ropeways, high towers and slides are also involved from time to time. Rope swings and some of the more old-fashioned equipment, such as witches hats are also mentioned occasionally. Accidents can also occur in 'soft play' sites or in 'bouncing castles' particularly when children jump on top of one another, or fall off the edge onto harder ground.

How do playground accidents happen?

Playground accidents are most likely to happen when a child attempts to do something beyond his or her capabilities and either falls, panics or looses his or her nerve. Another reason for these accidents is when children of differing ages and abilities use the same piece of equipment. Older children are apt to jostle and shove the younger ones who will usually come off worst.

A large survey carried out in Lewisham, London in 1977 found playground accidents to be due to falls in 60 per cent of cases, and being hit by equipment in over 30 per cent. Several surveys have shown that as many as three–quarters of all injuries sustained here can be attributed to hard landing surfaces. The severity of an accident may be markedly increased (by a factor of 5–10) when the landing surface is hard. Where equipment is poorly designed or maintained then the potential for accidents also increases. Protruding pieces of metal and rusty patches will also contribute to the hazard.

Injuries sustained

Very often a child will only sustain simple cuts and grazes or perhaps a minor sprain. Sometimes, however, the outcome is more severe and will depend upon the equipment, the age and ability of the child and the type of accident. In younger children injuries more commonly involve the arm and head, whereas in older children legs are more often damaged.

The severity of injury is related to the type of apparatus, the height of the fall and the type of landing surface. The most severe injuries result from (in order of priority):

- Climbing frames
- Slides
- Swings
- See-saws

In the past witches hats and low-level roundabouts were also the source for many serious injuries but many of these have now been removed from playgrounds.

In general playground accidents result in slightly less severe injuries than most other types of accidents experienced by children. This should not lead to complacency, as some serious injuries still do occur.

Preventing playground accidents

Good progress has been made in recent years in reducing the number and severity of playground accidents. If this encouraging trend is to continue then we must look on childrens' playgrounds as important and relevant parts of the overall residential community, not incidental places set up in some unused corner.

Responsibility lies with those who site and design playgrounds, those who maintain and supervise them and lastly with the children and parents who use them.

Local Authorities – planning, amenities and recreation can:

- Site playgrounds close to housing to provide safe, local play areas for young children, which will reduce road traffic accident figures if children do not have to travel long or hazardous routes to playgrounds. In Sweden the law requires the provision of a municipal playground (with trained staff) to be placed within 300 m of any housing area that has more than 150 dwellings; smaller playgrounds must be provided for housing areas with more than 30 dwellings. In some cities in the United Kingdom there are bye–laws relating to the provision of playgrounds
- Erect equipment free of sharp angles or protrusions on which children can play without entangling limbs or heads, but which provides adventure opportunities
- Site play equipment in imaginative surroundings with exciting apparatus using interesting shape and colour; ensure that children will not come into line with any moving piece of apparatus, i.e. swings when they are moving around the play area
- Consider siting slides on mounds so that children do not fall from a height even from the top of the slide
- Set aside a fenced-in area for under-fives to provide a mini playground with appropriately sized equipment, keep older children from the area unless they are genuinely supervising younger children
- Provide safe surfaces, which includes anything other than concrete or tarmac. Thick rubber surfaces, tree bark and sand are all acceptable

alternatives that probably increase the safety provision. A shock absorbing surface should be placed under or around any apparatus from which a child is likely to jump or fall; this can reduce the severity of a fall by between five and ten times. Even with impact absorbing surfaces, however, falls from great heights would still be dangerous and so it is unwise to erect very high equipment. The British Standard has a minimum 'free fall' height of 2.5 m (see below)

Parents can:

- Supervise younger children at all times in the playground
- Teach children to use playgrounds safely by learning how to climb safely, not to run in the path of a swing, how to use other equipment correctly, not to push and harass other children particularly at the top of a slide ladder
- Put pressure on local authorities through parent groups to ensure safe provision in their local playgrounds
- In schools contribute to safety provision in playgrounds through the Parent–Teacher Association.

Children can:

- Behave sensibly in playgrounds with regard for other, particularly younger children

Although parents are the chief supervisors of their children in playgrounds, other countries make provision for additional official supervision. In Denmark, for example, in the summer months, supervisors are available in the larger parks. In Uppsala, Sweden, groups of parents have been trained in playground safety and therefore have been able to identify and have removed potentially unsuitable equipment and hazards. These groups have been involved in the planning of new housing estates and other provisions for childrens' safety.

The British Standards Institute – BS 5696 on childrens' playgrounds and equipment provides a useful reference point for the upgrading of playground equipment and provision, on minimizing hazards and providing design standards. In particular, it concludes that a free-fall height of play equipment should not exceed 2.5 m and embankment sides should not be more than 500 mm above the ground at any point. Further details are specified concerning swings and rotating equipment etc.

Fairgrounds

A special type of play area is the organized fairground or fun park, which, with its fast moving equipment and exciting atmosphere is potentially a recipe for disaster.

In recent years an increasing trend in fatalities and serious injuries at fairgrounds can be observed. Given that each year some 20 million people now visit fairgrounds this is perhaps not a surprising trend.

In 1972 a big dipper ride collapsed at Battersea Funfair killing five children and this raised public awareness to the potential problems. Soon afterwards the Home Office introduced a voluntary Code of Practice requiring an annual inspection of fairground equipment. A new Code of Practice was introduced by the Health and Safety Executive in 1984, which now requires an annual inspection by an independent competent person to be reported to the Health and Safety Executive.

The main causes of fairground accidents are:

- Use of old equipment
- Failure to regularly inspect and maintain equipment
- Fooling around by riders
- Poor supervision and attention to safety measures
- Increasing complexity of equipment requiring more sophisticated maintenance

To prevent fairground accidents it is imperative that as well as regular inspection (to the Health and Safety Executive's standards), all attendants must:

- Ensure safety belts and appliances are properly fastened
- Avoid fooling around by children
- Regularly maintain and replace any faulty or worn-out equipment

Accidents with fireworks

Fireworks are used throughout the world on celebratory occasions, civil and religious events. The Chinese New Year, certain Royal and historical occasions and in the United States the Fourth of July are all well-known occasions for the use of fireworks. In Britain once a year on November 5th around 100 million fireworks are used to celebrate Guy Fawkes night. Fortunately deaths from firework accidents are very rare, but each year between 30–40 children are admitted to hospital and 500–600 visit Accident and Emergency departments following injuries sustained. Incidents usually involve serious burns and eye injuries. In the 1960s when accident figures were very high a massive campaign took place to reduce accident figures and injury severity, which was very successful. By the early 1970s figures had dropped to below 1000 cases or one per 100 000 fireworks sold. This figure has now levelled out and since the early 1980s there has been a slow but steady rise again. Reasons for this include public complacency and irresponsible behaviour by youths. One encouraging sign is the fall in

Table 5.3   Types of fireworks involved in accidents

Bangers	914
Rockets	592
Roman candles etc.	498
Sparklers	315
Home-made/powder extracted	124
Unspecified	1072
All others	371
Total	3886

Fireworks involved in accidents in Britain 1981/1985 — RoSPA.

the proportion of children involved and another is that less banger and rocket injuries are reported.

Who has firework accidents?

The most susceptible group by far is 13–15-year-old boys but older teenagers and younger children are also at risk. For young children the greatest risk is of being hit by a firework let off by an older child.

How do firework accidents occur?

Firework accidents most often occur in family or private parties when inexperienced people are letting off fireworks. These accidents occur much less frequently in organized public displays. Firework accidents have been occurring to an increasing degree in recent years, in casual incidents, in the street, invariably involving teenage boys. A further worrying trend is the increased use of bangers by vandals and the irresponsible use of fireworks by young boys playing pranks with their friends.

Products involved

The products most frequently involved in firework accidents are shown in Table 5.3.

Injuries sustained

The most common injuries seen for firework accidents are:

- Penetration injuries at site of impact
- Burns – may be widespread if clothing catches fire
- Eye injuries (around 300 per annum of those for all ages)

Long–term scarring and loss of vision occurs in a small proportion of cases but they are sufficiently serious to be a cause for considerable concern. There may also be burns associated with the bonfires often lit at the same time.

Preventing firework injuries

Much of the steady fall in firework injuries during the 1960s and 1970s was due to a cooperative voluntary approach by the manufacturers coupled with certain legislative changes.

Manufacturers and traders:

- Reduced the number and explosive power of bangers
- Removed 'helicopter' 'flyabout' and 'Jumping Jack' fireworks from sale
- Presented and sold fireworks in boxes rather than as single items
- Restricted the sale of fireworks for a limited period around November 5th only

Legislators:

- Banned the sale of fireworks to children under 16 (maximum penalty for conviction is £200)
- Banned the letting-off of fireworks in the street (maximum penalty £200)
- Banned the manufacture of fireworks without a licence

In addition at both the national and the local level there has been wider publicity about the dangers of fireworks and much wider use of organized displays by local authorities and by various organizations.

The majority of firework accidents result from carelessness or 'fooling around' with fireworks. Strict observance of the Firework Code will keep injuries to a minimum. In the future, it may be necessary to further restrict the manufacture of certain types of fireworks, such as bangers and rockets.

Parents and organizers of displays can:

- Be alert to the dangers of fireworks and displays need to be kept under strict control. Casual use of fireworks should be vigorously discouraged

Local Authorities and Trading Standards Officers can:

- Keep up a continual vigilance during the period surrounding November 5th

One of the leading lobbyists for improvements in firework safety – the National Campaign for Fireworks Reform – has advocated much more stringent measures including the total abolition of bangers and banning of sales of fireworks to children under 18 years of age. The Campaign also advocates the organization of firework displays to be restricted to adults over

18 years of age who have had suitable training and are properly licensed by the local fire service.

There are some people who advocate the total abolition of fireworks, as in Australia, but with such a strong tradition in the country it is likely that people would start to import fireworks illegally from abroad, or make their own.

6

SPORTS AND LEISURE ACCIDENTS

Sports accidents

Sport is recognized as being of great benefit to growing children. It can provide opportunities to develop physical agility, strength and improve fitness as well as to forge team spirit and 'sportsmanship'. Indeed it is often said that today's school children do not get nearly enough sport and physical activity and that we should encourage further development of this within school and during leisure time.

There are always risks with physical activities, and accidents do happen in sport. This can be as a result of potentially dangerous activity, for example, ice hockey, physically aggressive contact sports, for example rugby, or careless mishaps when participants fail to obey rules or codes of practice. Whereas nobody would wish to discourage sport, or ban any form of it, there is increasing concern about the aggressiveness and urge to win at all costs displayed by some players, and often by parents of children taking part. In society today we are all urged to succeed and sometimes in sport this results in an unhealthy and unnecessary competitiveness, which increases the chance of injury.

The national prestige associated with success in sport at an international level has also unfortunately led to very intense and competitive training, often starting with young children. It is essential that a healthy balance is found where everybody can enjoy and benefit from their participation in a chosen sport and a few will excel. Some injuries are inevitable but when these become excessive in number or severity it is time to consider remedies.

In total, around five children are killed each year taking part in sporting activities (specialized activities such as horse riding and moto-cross are not included here – see pages 97–103). Between 7000–10 000 children are admitted to hospital each year and a total of 150 000 visit Accident and Emergency departments for treatment. As with most other forms of accident injury, boys outnumber girls (in a ratio of 2:1) and the number of accidents increases greatly with age. See Table 6.1.

Who has sports accidents?

As boys tend to play sport more often than girls, take part in more dangerous types of sports and play more aggressively than girls it is hardly surprising that they experience more injuries. The vast majority of incidents involve boys aged 10–14 years old. The one exception is horse riding (covered on pages 96–99) in which girls are more often injured than boys. Figures drop off as the boys approach mid- to late-teens when they leave school and very often discontinue their sporting activities.

No information is available on social class distribution of sporting accidents in children. Certain sports tend to be determined by class or finance, though there are many exceptions. In addition, regional variation in school sports occurs, for example rugby is played in most schools in Wales and the Borders of Scotland whereas in England it is more likely to be available only in fee-paying independent schools.

Boxing is often the prerogative of under-privileged inner city boys attracted to boys clubs, whereas mini-motorcycles attract a wide social range of boys, but more often those whose fathers have a mechanical bent or interest in motorcycles. Some sports require children to be mobile and able to travel to certain locations, but this is not a great deterrent today.

When do sporting accidents occur?

Accidents are most likely to happen at the start of a season when the participants are unfit and inexperienced. Towards the end of the season when competition may be more fierce and players tired, further accidents happen. Similar rules apply to the beginning and end of a particular game when accidents are more likely at the very beginning or towards the end.

Some sports are known to have a much higher risk of injury than others

Table 6.1   Leisure/sports injuries among children involving hospital treatment, estimates for the UK, 1988

Location	< 5 years	5–10 years	11–16 years	All < 17 years
Education areas	20 600	150 300	236 500	407 400
Transport areas	54 300	131 200	120 500	306 000
Recreational areas	28 000	74 600	69 900	172 400
Sports facilities	3 300	29 600	92 900	125 800
Public buildings	17 800	12 700	13 500	43 900
Other specified place	1 400	7 400	10 000	18 900
Place not specified	83 900	223 300	331 000	638 300
All places	209 300	629 000	874 400	1 712 700

Source: LASS 1989.

once the exposure has been taken into account.

A survey in Britain in the mid-1950s found soccer to have the highest incidence of injury when measured as a rate per 1000 hours of activity. Swimming was found to be the least injury-provoking. Not surprisingly most of the fast-moving, physical contact sports appeared on the list but non-contact sports were very low down.

In secondary independent schools (Public schools) where soccer is not usually played, rugby is by far the most injury-provoking game.

In the United States sports injuries are most likely to occur during American football, ice hockey and athletics. In Japan the most common sports injuries occur during skiing, baseball, karate and field athletics.

The extent of the sports injury depends on the type of sport undertaken, the activity level of the participant and factors such as the state of fitness and training of the player. In adults drug or alcohol levels will also have a bearing, but this is not relevant amongst children except if they move into the adult competitive world at a high level.

In children's sports the most important factor is to match children of the same size, ability and age. When these considerations are not taken it is inevitable that the smaller, younger or weaker child will sustain injury. Referees must also be sure not to turn a blind eye to acts of aggression or foul play, as this will often lead to injury.

Use of safety equipment is also vital where applicable. This applies mostly to water sports where buoyancy aids or life-saving equipment are paramount, or where headgear is necessary. In cricket, baseball and hockey protective clothing for batsmen, wicket keepers and goal keepers is essential for the protection of legs, hands and genitalia from the hard ball. One area of particular concern during the 1970s and 1980s was the increased number of spinal injuries in rugby, in particular to the lower cervical spine of a player in a ruck, during the collapse of a scrum or following a head-on tackle. More than three-quarters of these injuries result in some degree of permanent paralysis. Factors that exacerbate this are: lack of fitness, inexperience, foul play and mismatching of strength and skill.

Injuries sustained

Many sporting injuries are trivial and do not result in cessation of the sporting activity. Some injuries are the result of a sudden traumatic event, either accidental or deliberately inflicted by an opponent. Others may occur because of continual exertion or overuse of a particular part of the body, which is too much for the age and development of a young child. Some level of sprains and strains must be expected in some sports and most will have no long-term effect. One unusual effect of continuous vigorous athletic activity in girls may be the delay in the onset of puberty, for example in competitive gymnastics.

The outcome of the majority of sporting injuries in children will be a full recovery and return to sporting life. On occasions the injury may prevent the child returning to the same sport, or at least the same level of activity. Organizers and participants must always be aware of the possibility, albeit rare, of a fatality during a sporting activity. In children this may be due to a predisposing medical condition, such as structural abnormality of the heart, a sudden rupture of a blood vessel in the brain or a diabetic coma. Sudden death is more likely to occur in the young from being hit or kicked in the head causing brain haemorrhage or being hit in the chest causing sudden heart failure. Death may also occur suddenly from the complete severing of the spinal cord in the neck region following an awkward fall or having the head pulled forward forcefully as in rugby or American football.

Injuries to the epiphyses (growth plates) of bones are always a matter for concern for orthopaedic surgeons. Studies in the United States have shown that risk of injury to the epiphyseal area is quite low especially in pre-adolescents. Those most at risk are tall, lanky children or those who are overweight and muscularly weak. Soft tissue and skeletal changes may occur in young long-distance runners but it is thought that repeated impacts or traction of growth plates are not usually detrimental.

A development of arthritis in later life can follow damage during a young sporting career. A fracture injury to a joint or repeated vigorous unnatural movement – e.g., the hips in a hurdler – or poor technique can increase the likelihood of this effect.

Attention has recently been drawn to depressed fractures of the skull and other head injuries as a result of the child being hit by a golf club. In a report of eleven such accidents, none occurred while the child was under adult supervision, indicating that children must be warned about the potential dangers of playing with golf clubs.

Preventing sports accidents

It is unnecessary for participants in sports to be exposed to risk of injury and this can virtually be eliminated provided certain basic rules are obeyed.

Participants can:

- Make sure they are fit to play by taking part in pre-season training
- Maintain fitness levels as required for the sport and level
- Use graduated training – too much too soon will lead to strains and sprains
- Use protective gear when required – this must be of an approved standard, worn and maintained properly e.g.,

  headgear – cycling; riding; moto-cross; canoeing; boxing
  scrum caps – rugby
  gloves – cricket wicket keeper; baseball guard
  pads – cricket batsman; wicket keeper
  box – cricket; hockey goalkeeper

footwear – soccer; rugby; cricket; hockey; riding
buoyancy aids – yachting; canoeing
mouth guards – rugby scrum; boxing
goggles – swimming; squash; motocross
helmet and body protection – American football

Concern has been expressed that some protective equipment can cause rather than prevent injury such as helmets and face guards for American football. The face guards could be used for butting or face grabbing whilst the weight and design of the helmet permits excessive head extension, i.e. bending backwards that results in fractures of the neck vertebra. Newer rules now prohibit head butting and face grabbing and the new design of helmet restricts the possible range of backward movement.

Coaches and referees can:

- Ensure pre-match warm-up exercises are completed especially in hard physical games in cold weather
- Encourage equal and fair competition between children of same size, weight and ability
- Keep strict control of the game and penalize offenders by sending them off if necessary (counsel offender after the game)
- Check that playing conditions are suitable for the sport. The type of surface and weather conditions may markedly affect the potential for injury. Excessive heat or cold may also influence the effect on a competition for the development of hypothermia or exhaustion. Hard surfaces will increase fractures whilst newer synthetic surfaces (e.g., astro turf) may increase grazes, foot and joint injuries. They may also cause heat stroke during hot weather as they retain heat far more than conventional natural surfaces. This is particularly relevant when a lot of protective clothing is also worn, e.g., American football. The environment may also help reduce injuries, e.g. when padded rugby posts and flexible boundary markers are used
- Encourage gradual run down after activity
- Fence off field sports such as javelin, discus, shot and hammer to prevent these lethal weapons accidentally hitting another competitor
- Learn first-aid techniques and carry an adequate first-aid box

Parents can:

- Provide all necessary safety equipment, allow adequate training and preparation
- Discourage sports inappropriate for children i.e., boxing
- Avoid excessive obsessional encouragement of children's sporting activities, i.e. Little League syndrome in the United States
- Encourage good sportsmanship and fair play

- Provide adequate well-maintained equipment
- Curb their own aggressive instincts, which could encourage similar behaviour in children
- Take out insurance cover against your child sustaining injury while playing sport, to provide payment in the event of a serious disability. Some independent schools offer this provision as an option on school bills at a typical cost of between £20–25 per child per annum.

Ice sports

Fatalities amongst children in ice sports are very rare numbering only one or two per year. The number of injuries are unknown although local Accident and Emergency departments always report a spate of injuries following icy and snowy weather conditions. Many of these incidents simply involve falling over in the street or playground, but a significant proportion result from tobogganing and skiing.

It is only on very rare occasions in Britain that canals, ponds and lakes freeze enough to provide sufficiently thick ice for children to embark on skating or sliding. Great care must be taken, as the exact depth and strength of the ice cannot be depended on and the risk of falling in and drowning or of suffering hypothermia always exists.

A small number of injuries sustained at ice skating rinks are also seen at Accident and Emergency departments from time to time.

An increasingly popular sport for British children is skiing with a growing number of school parties venturing onto the slopes of Europe. This is a sport for the fit and trained participant and the most common group to experience injuries are adolescents in the 11–13-year-old age group, followed by those in the 14–16-year-old age group.

Injuries sustained

Accidents involving falls on ice include fractures of the radius or ulna; supracondylar fracture of the femur or of the tibia or fibula. Tobogganing and sledging accidents also result in fractures of the leg as well as head injury or facial lacerations and loss of teeth. The old-fashioned wooden sledge can inflict serious injury if it hits a smaller child, the newer plastic sledges may be more lightweight but they easily capsize and swing off course. Children often go down slopes on boards, plastic bags, tin trays and air bags amongst other things, and run the risk of hitting a tree en route.

In skiing accidents injuries may include sprains of the thumb; ligaments of the knee; fracture of the tibia. Of particular concern are the head and spinal injuries.

The inexperienced and less-skilled skiers are those most likely to be injured. In spite of the increasing popularity of this sport, surveys in Scandinavia and the United States have shown that there is an overall drop in the rates of accidents per day skied. This is associated with better teaching and improved boots and ski-boot bindings. There may, however, be a trend towards more serious injuries because of higher speeds and more intense competition.

Ice accidents often result from inexperience and lack of training. They may also occur from poor judgement of the hazards and by hitting unexpected or unforeseen obstacles including other participants. Carelessness and fooling around on the slopes is another factor. In more competitive events some participants may push themselves beyond their abilities and this can raise risk of injury.

Preventing accidents

Parents can:

- Provide appropriate safety equipment, i.e. boots and binders where appropriate
- Arrange lessons where appropriate
- Carefully supervise children on busy slopes
- Find quieter slopes for younger children

Children can:

- Wear warm clothing with thermal underwear, waterproof clothing, anoraks, kagools, gloves and headgear
- Avoid excessive fatigue
- Learn the necessary skills for the sport
- Move off slopes once the run has been completed
- Avoid skating on thin ice
- Wear a crash helmet (i.e., a cycle helmet) – compulsory for certain competitive events
- Avoid behaving recklessly on ski slopes or attempting manoeuvres beyond their abilities
- Beware of bad weather conditions and avalanches
- Obey the skiers code – avoid collision with other skiers

Drowning accidents

In injury terms drowning is often thought to be an all-or-nothing event. However, a small proportion of survivors do experience some permanent handicap.

Overall this is a steadily decreasing form of accidental death, but nevertheless around 60 children drown each year. Some 200 children are admitted to hospital following a near-drowning. There are no reliable figures for those that are seen in Accident and Emergency departments.

In the United States it is the third most common cause of death in the 1–4-year-old age group, and the second most common in the 5–14-year-old age group; in Australia it is the second most common cause of child death and the most likely location is the family swimming pool, followed by the family bath.

In Britain we have far less access to outdoor swimming facilities in comparison with the United States and Australia, and the seasonal exposure is concentrated into a much shorter period. In spite of this, drowning has until recently been the second most common cause of death in all children aged 1–14 years; it now ranks third behind road traffic accidents and burns.

Who drowns?

During the latter half of the 19th century 1000 children drowned regularly each year in England alone. These figures have fallen during the 20th century and by the 1960s there were 200 child deaths per year from drowning. This trend has continued and now approximately 70 children die in this way each year.

Boys outnumber girls in a ratio of about 3:1 in drownings, this differential is seen particularly in the 10–14-year-old age group, in which it is approximately 5:1. Overall 50 per cent of drownings occur with children under 5 years old, 25 per cent are 5–9 years old and 25 per cent aged 10–14 years old.

Although no detailed studies have been carried out to determine any socio-economic factors in childhood drownings, an OPCS study into parents' occupations has indicated that children in social class V are more at risk from drowning than those in social class I. This is attributed to their greater exposure to hazards such as inland waterways.

When do drownings happen?

More drownings occur in the summer months (between May and August), particularly in the school holiday months of July and August. This seasonal implication is mainly seen in children aged between 5 and 14 years old and is also more relevant amongst the male drownings.

Where do drownings occur?

Drownings can obviously occur where there is water of any kind. Young children can drown in a very small amount of water. Within the home the bath, Jacuzzi, bucket or bowl of water, paddling pool and ornamental garden pond can all be the site of a drowning, whereas beyond the home the public swimming baths, canals, rivers, lakes, industrial pits and pools or the sea are the sites of drowning. Airbeds, surf boards, inflatable rafts, boats, canoes, yachts and barges can all be involved in drowning accidents.

Most incidents of child drowning in the United Kingdom occur in inland waters. The commonest place is rivers and their tributaries, canals, followed by the bath, the sea, garden ponds, swimming pools, lakes and reservoirs.

The majority of cases of small babies drowning occur in the bath at home, often when the mother leaves the baby unattended while she answers the telephone, for example. Public swimming baths have a good safety record in terms of deaths: the presence of trained swimming pool attendants ensures that resuscitation is applied quickly so that many near-drownings occur in swimming pools rather than fatalities.

How do drownings occur?

Children playing near water accounts for nearly half of all childhood drownings in the United Kingdom. The younger the child, the greater the risk. Older children are more likely to be involved while actually swimming, paddling in the water or playing with rafts, inflatables or boats.

Nearly two thirds of the children under 16 years old who drowned in the United Kingdom in 1982 were not accompanied by adults; in the 0–4-year-old age group nearly three-quarters were unaccompanied in spite of the fact that none of them could swim.

Even in the 5–9-year-old age group only 11.5 per cent could swim, although the figure rose to 85 per cent in the 10–14-year-old age group. The main reasons for childhood drownings relate to the environment to which the child is exposed and the personal factors concerning the child and parents. Environmental factors obviously relate to which water locations the child is exposed to.

Personal factors for the child include:

- Inability to swim
- Disobedience
- Misuse of buoyancy aids or lifejackets
- Excessive risk taking (e.g. diving)
- Adventurousness
- Carelessness and inexperience
- Lack of awareness of hazards (may be impaired by depression or alcohol – unusual in children)
- One of a large family
- Tempted by objects in the water
- Injury (e.g. neck injury from diving) or sickness (e.g. epilepsy or diabetes) – rare

Children with epilepsy who swim are four times more likely to drown than normal children, but the absolute risk for this group still remains low.

Alcohol is a factor in as many as 20 per cent of all teenage and young adult drownings, and suicide is often significant in an even higher proportion of the older age group. Child abuse may also be a factor in some of the bath water drownings.

Personal factors for the parent or supervisor include:

- Lack of supervision due to being asleep; distracted; drunk; under stress
- Being older parents – less capable or confident
- Lack of or excessive discipline
- Unrealistic expectations of the child
- Child neglect
- Deliberate non-accidental injury

Two special cases that have gained publicity in recent years are:

- *Bath tub drowning* – this has been described in Australia, the United States and Britain. It occurs equally with boys and girls under 1 year of age. These tragedies can occur even in a very small amount of water. The following factors contribute to a high risk:
  - Highly mobile family
  - Lower socio-economic status
  - Younger siblings in larger family
  - Father in charge of child
  - Child being looked after by older sibling
  - Single parent family

  In the United Kingdom in 1982/3 three of the 76 recorded drowning fatalities were bath tub cases.

- *Whirlpool Spas* – this is a relatively recent hazard, the whirlpool or jacuzzi has a powerful suction outlet that can hold a child under water by the skin or hair. Fatalities have occurred in the United States due to this.

Other water-related injuries include:

- *Swimming pools* – head and spinal injuries due to hitting the bath side or bottom; leg injuries especially from slipping; chlorine poisoning
- *Yachting/Canoeing/Boating* – head injuries; fractures; lacerations; hypothermia after over-exposure to cold water
- *Home baths* – head injuries; lacerations

Injuries sustained

Drowning usually results in total recovery or death. For every recorded fatality there is another near-drowning incident. A recent study by Kemp and Sibert covering the United Kingdom found that around 6% of those who recovered from a near-drowning were left with a severe neurological handicap.

Severe hypothermia is one factor that may in fact enhance the chances of survival in drowning cases. Cases of immersion in icy water in Norway and Canada for 40 minutes with full recovery show that the severe cold can actually preserve the vital structures. A recent study published in the *British Medical Journal* also showed that some victims could be revived long after recovery from the water. The body is slowed down by hypothermia but with gradual warming and resuscitation recovery does sometimes occur. For this reason it is sensible to continue resuscitatory aid as long as several hours after a body has been recovered from the water.

The prognosis for victims rescued from fresh water is good; less good for those recovered from salt water. It is sensible to admit any child who has been immersed in water to hospital for a 48-hour observation period, unless recovery takes place very quickly and the child recovers totally in seconds. Observations should be made for these complications:

- *Neurological* – anoxic encephalopathy, e.g. mental impairment, spasticity, quadriplegia
- *Cardiac* – ventricular fibrillation sometimes complicated by alcohol or barbiturate intoxication and/or hypothermia
- *Respiratory* – aspiration pneumonia, barotrauma, mechanical lung damage, foreign body or chemical pneumonia
- *Secondary drowning* – usually 6–8 hours after near-drowning (but up to 48 hours) due to pulmonary oedema following inhalation of water – absorption into blood – dilution of blood – cardiac failure
- *Hypothermia*

Preventing drownings

In considering ways to prevent drownings both the environment to which the child is exposed and the personal factors concerning the child and his or her family need to be looked at.

Environmental factors

Natural – It is obviously impracticable to fence off all hazards, but this may be possible with a small local source, i.e. a local garden pond. Adult supervision is very important and this includes regular competent beach patrols at beach sites of known risk. Warning signs, although open to vandalism, and suitable life-saving equipment, i.e. life buoys, surf and boat rescue equipment should also be installed at high-risk sites.

Man-made – For all these, a case for fencing and supervision exists. Adequate fencing for a home in-ground pond or swimming pool should be at least 1.2 m high with self-latching and self-closing gates. Small ornamental garden ponds should be fenced or covered with wire netting if there is a toddler at home or if one is likely to visit (i.e. grandparents home). In some cases specific legislation for the provision of safety fences to fixed standards or for life-saving equipment may be necessary. Whenever children are taking part in water sports etc. the equipment should be appropriate for it – seaworthy boats etc. – and life jackets should always be worn.

Personal factors

Both the child and parents have responsibilities in preventing drownings.

The child can:
- Learn to swim
- Let parents know where he is going to swim
- Swim in company of other competent swimmers
- Obey instructions and never swim beyond permissible areas
- Avoid injury, i.e. head injury, by not diving into shallow water or where there may be hidden hazards such as rocks
- Avoid swimming whilst ill, e.g. severe epilepsy or diabetes
- Use buoyancy aids, life jackets, or wet suits where appropriate
- Learn first aid and resuscitation techniques
- Avoid swimming after a heavy meal or prolonged vigorous exercise
- Learn to handle boats and canoes and learn to deal with emergencies and changes in conditions
- Beware of swimming out of his depth to recover a ball etc. or of being blown out to sea on an inflatable raft or air bed
- Heed warnings on where or where not to swim and beware of undertow on surfboards, inflatable boats etc.

Parents should:
- Never leave a baby alone in the bath or even with another child in the bath
- Supervise when circumstances and conditions require
- Avoid distractions
- Learn first aid and resuscitation
- Ensure that the child is swimming in a safe place

Bites and stings

There has been increasing concern about the apparent increase in the number of dog bites. In particular media attention has focussed on severe bites to children by particular breeds of dog. Statistics show that, on occasion, a bite or sting may be fatal. Each year there are about 1000 admissions to hospital, and about 50 000 attendances at Accident and Emergency departments for this reason.

Who is involved?

Two age groups predominate among dog bites: toddlers aged 2–3 years old and boys in the 7–9-year-old age group. Overall boys predominate in the ratio of 3:2.

Where do the accidents happen?

A recent study showed that more bites occurred in the home or its immediate surrounds than outside the home.

Injuries sustained

Home accidents commonly involve the head and face, whereas accidents outside the home tend to involve the legs and buttocks.

The breeds of dogs involved is not known accurately enough to quote any figures scientifically. Media reports suggest that Pit Bull terriers and Rottweilers are dangerous because in some cases they are bred for fighting. Recent legislation relating to the registration and restraint of dogs, their muzzling and neutering, together with fines for their owners should ensure that serious dog bites become less frequent.

Dogs are of course not the only creatures that bite. Some pets such as gerbils, hamsters and cats also bite on occasions. The only wild snake in the United Kingdom that bites is the adder: the painful swelling of the limb that results and occasionally a degree of shock can be treated by anti-venom. Stings from bees and wasps can also produce allergic swelling, with pain and discomfort.

Preventing dog bites

Over and above the legislation recently introduced, children should be taught to behave correctly in the presence of animals, and vice versa. Some dogs may be jealous of a new baby or small child in the family and the dog and baby must be supervised by an adult at all times, or kept apart from each other. Older children must be taught not to tease dogs.

Horse riding

One or two children are killed each year following a horse riding accident in the United Kingdom. Between 2000 and 3000 are admitted to hospital and 12 000–15 000 seek help at Accident and Emergency departments. This is one of the rare examples of accident type in which girls, especially in the 10–14-year-old age group, outnumber boys.

Horse riding is a very popular activity – up to 2 million people ride each week – and whilst many may perceive it as the hobby of the rich, country girl, many children living in towns and of quite modest means also learn to ride. Risk potential for riding is quite high. The horse is a heavy, fast and sometimes unpredictable animal and any fall is potentially dangerous even with proper headgear. In riding the expectation of a serious accident is one per 350 hours of riding (compared with motorcycling – one every 7000 hours).

If a horse should stumble and the child rider should fall the distance travelled and the trajectory sustained can cause quite serious head injuries. These are often made worse by failure to use proper headgear – riding helmets have been much improved but still some riders fail to wear them or wear them undone. Other likely injuries arise from being bitten, kicked or trodden on by the horse in the stable; the horse falling onto the rider; legs being crushed; landing on the chest or abdomen in a fall.

Who has riding accidents?

In Britain and in other countries local surveys have shown that children under 15 years of age comprise around 60–70 per cent of all riding accidents. The majority involve girls aged between 10 and 14 years old, which outnumbers the involvement of boys by a ratio of 6:1. These accidents are more likely to happen to girls of professional parents.

When do riding accidents occur?

These accidents may occur at any time of the day, most commonly during the months of May to October, and especially during the school summer holiday months of July and August. If a local gymkhana or riding event takes place in the area they are also more likely to occur (although these are usually well supported by first aid and medical help).

A high-risk time of day is at dusk for child riders on the road, especially if neither the horse nor rider has any form of lighting and if reflective clothes are not worn.

Where do riding accidents occur?

The majority of riding accidents happen when children are out riding in fields or on bridleways or when they are practising jumps. Riding is particularly popular on the edge of large cities and towns. A small proportion of accidents happen when children are engaged in competition; even fewer whilst on the road either because of a solo fall or in collision with a motor vehicle.

How do riding accidents occur?

A riding accident may have one clear cause or be the result of a number of reasons. Some relevant factors are:

- *Inexperience* – rider and/or horse trying to do more than they are capable.
- *Lack of training* – Horse being startled – by the sudden appearance of anything unusual for example:
  - Presence of a motor vehicle
  - Child running into road
  - Children playing or shouting
  - Machinery starting up
  - Other animals
  - Tree branches waving in the wind.

Injuries sustained

In the majority of cases a child will be thrown clear of the horse landing either head or arms first. Sometimes the child will land on or be thrown into an obstacle such as a gate post or a tree and then more serious head, chest or abdominal injuries occur. Less frequently a horse will fall on top of the rider or the rider will be trapped underneath the horse and even less likely the child will be kicked, trodden on or bitten by the horse.

The typical injury requiring admission to hospital is a head injury which accounts for well over 60 per cent of all horse riding admissions to hospital.

In a survey of fatalities from horse riding accidents in Derbyshire covering all ages, it was found that of those who died from head injuries:

- One-third had no hat
- One-third had a hat but lost it in the fall
- One-third had an inadequate hat

The correct use of an adequate hat is therefore of paramount importance in the prevention of serious head injuries. Injuries requiring most prolonged admissions are fractures of the femur and internal injuries. The most common injury presenting at Accident and Emergency departments is a fracture, typically one sustained when landing on an outstretched arm, i.e. the Colles fracture to the radius or ulna, and less frequently fractures to the elbow, shoulder, clavicle or the fibula or tibia. Spinal injuries do occasionally occur in child riders but they are much less common than in adults.

The outcome of a fall from a horse is usually full recovery. Some riders with head injuries are severely concussed and a few develop post-traumatic epilepsy or other neurological defects. Some children with complicated fractures of the femur may experience problems of non-union.

For some, rehabilitation to full activity may take 18 months to 2 years and very occasionally may leave a child with a permanent limp or deformity. Head and spinal injuries may result in hemiplegia or paraplegia (paralysis). The outcome of these injuries relates to the nature and severity rather than the initial cause of the injury.

Preventing riding accidents

A reduction in horse-riding accidents will follow when parents, riders and instructors are all fully conversant with the hazards of this activity. Adequate training in handling the horse, a development of confidence, and the correct use of well-designed safety gear will do much to reduce both the accident numbers and the severity of the resulting injuries.

In particular:
Drivers can:

- Slow down to 15mph or slower on seeing a horse and rider on the road
- Avoid excessive noise, e.g. by braking or sounding a horn
- Give a wide berth between vehicle and horse
- Avoid cutting in
- Avoid any sudden movements, e.g. flashing lights, waving children

Parents and riders can:

- Ensure the child wears a properly fitted, secured helmet conforming to BS 6473 (see note below)
- Ensure the child learns to ride properly – ideally at a recognized riding school
- Ensure the child only attends competitions that are properly organized and supervised and are attended by fully trained first aiders

In addition Riders can:

- Join the British Horse Society (BHS)/Pony Club riding and road safety scheme (see page 187) and take the riding and road safety proficiency test
- Keep in single file on the left hand side of the road
- Keep the horse under tight control and look out for hazards
- Wear suitable clothing and riding boots
- Wear conspicuous clothing and reflectors
- Use a night light on the outside foot and stirrup

The Medical Equestrian Association takes a special interest in preventing accidents to horse riders and in providing medical care at competitive events.

Riding hat

The British Horse Society strongly recommend that a 'properly secured, well-fitting hard hat, acceptable BSI standards, should be worn by all riders under all conditions with particular emphasis on the young and the rider with limited experience'. Legislation now requires children up to the age of 14 to wear an approved riding hat when riding on the road.

For British riders the best form of protection is the hat to BSI Standard

6473 providing this is properly fitted and has its chinstrap securely fastened. These hats provide good protection for horse and pony riders in normal usage. For competitions the Jockey skull cap – to BS 4472 – may be obligatory. Cheaper imported hats are available on the market but these do not provide an adequate level of protection and may lead the rider into a false sense of security. Hats manufactured to BS 3686 may also not offer adequate protection.

Fitting a hat

When the retention system is fully adjusted and the chinstrap fully fastened it should not be possible to remove the hat. Any hat that has been involved in an impact should be replaced.

Motorcycle scrambling (moto-cross)

This sport involves riding specially-adapted motorcycles or mini-motorcycles over rough undulating ground. It may also include grass or dirt track riding. Deaths are rare but an estimated 1000–1500 children are admitted to hospital each year and 3500–5000 visit Accident and Emergency departments with injuries sustained while motor scrambling. The very young age – as young as 6 years old – that children start this sport is the biggest cause for concern.

Competition riding is generally very well organized and carefully controlled, there is usually first-aid cover and most large events have a doctor available. Having personnel competent in resuscitation is an important factor for the more serious accidents at these competitions.

Who has motorcycle scrambling accidents?

This is almost exclusively a boys sport. The official starting age is 6 years old; the majority of injuries occur to boys aged 10–14 years old.

How do motorcycle scrambling accidents occur?

Inexperience and over-enthusiasm are recognized causes for accidents, but because of the nature of the sport some tumbles are inevitable. The motorcycles are not ridden at high speed and the main hazards are the rider falling off, the bike falling on the rider or the rider being hit by the following motorcycle.

Local studies have shown that approximately half of all moto-cross accidents occur at organized events and the other half in casual riding. These are in addition to the small number of road accidents that children are involved in on motorcycles (see Chapter 3). Lack of experience and young age are the main risk factors.

Injuries sustained

Many of the injuries sustained are relatively minor but the potential exists for more serious injuries than in most other sports. The incidence of injury has been estimated at between 1 in 100, and 1 in 200 per race. The most typical injuries that occur in motorcycle scrambling are:

- Head and facial injuries
- Fractures of tibia or fibula; radius or ulna; femur
- Sprains and contusions of joints
- Internal chest or abdominal injuries
- Cuts, grazes and abrasions

The majority of minor injuries can be treated on the spot by the first aiders in attendance. More serious injuries, especially to the leg, may require a prolonged spell in hospital.

Apart from the very rare fatalities a small number of moto-cross accidents each year result in some form of permanent disability including brain damage, paralysis and loss of mobility.

Preventing motorcycle scrambling accidents

The rules of this sport allow children from 6 years old onwards to take part. Many paediatricians consider that children under the age of 12 years should not take part for two main reasons: younger children have not developed all the complex skills, physical strength and coordination required to be able to handle a scrambling bike efficiently and safely; any fracture in a young child around the growth plates (epiphyses) of bones can cause problems where growth is disrupted and deformity and loss of mobility can occur. In approved events an efficient organization and a well-designed course will go a long way towards preventing accidents. Keeping strict control of bike riders and spectators will minimize the number of accidents. Parental zeal can result in a scared child being encouraged to do things beyond his capabilities and parents should resist such pressure.

Riders and parents can:

- Make sure the child is fully fit and well trained for the event
- Ensure the bike is of a suitable design for the course, well maintained and of a suitable size for the child
- The child should wear safety gear at all times, including
  - Full face helmets
  - Goggles
  - Body and shoulder padding
  - Gloves
  - Boots

- Because of the involvement with agricultural dirt all motorcycle scrambling participants should ensure that tetanus immunization is fully up to date

Organizers and promoters can:

- Ensure full first-aid cover at all events
- Advise participants about safety clothing and equipment and make sure it is always worn
- Restrict the sport to children of over 12 years old
- Make sure all riders are fully trained and competent in the use of their machine
- Control parents by discouraging pressure for children to attain more than they are capable of

Motorcycle manufacturers can:

- Desist from promoting the sport as suitable for children of 5 or 6 years old and focus on necessity for protective and safety clothing and equipment.

Firearms and other weapons

Occasionally children are injured in accidents involving airguns, firearms or other weapons such as crossbows, blowpipes and knives. These incidents can be particularly devastating and each year approximately 5 children are killed, 200–500 are admitted to hospital and 1000–1500 attend Accident and Emergency departments because of injuries sustained. The number of incidents involving firearms will obviously depend on the attitude within any society to guns and firearms and on the strength of the law governing their use. The media too can influence an attitude, which could reinforce an idea of the normality of the use of guns.

In the United States guns are more available, more widely used and thus more accepted as a part of life. In the United Kingdom, with the exception of Northern Ireland, public opinion is against the availability of guns.

Unlike guns themselves other weapons such as crossbows, blowpipes and knives do not require licences. In addition, another hazard is the home-made weapons that youths are often inventing, for example blowdarts made from sharpened bicycle spokes, which are fired from converted bicycle pumps and can therefore cause considerable injuries.

Who is involved with firearms?

Accidents involving firearms almost invariably involve older boys injuring either themselves or their friends. Innocent children can also be involved.

When do firearms accidents happen?

These accidents can occur at any time of the year and at any time of day, but are far more likely in the summer months.

Where do firearms accidents happen?

Firearms accidents occur mainly during casual, sometimes furtive activities in home gardens, recreation areas or in woodland and wasteland. They typically occur when youths are shooting at caps or tin cans. Sometimes they occur during organized shoots. Even more rarely accidents occur when a younger child plays indoors with the firearms belonging to an older brother or parent.

How do firearms accidents happen?

Ways in which a child can be harmed in a firearms accidents include:

- Deliberate harm by another person (homicide)
- Deliberate harm, self-inflicted (suicide)
- Deliberate harm in warfare or terrorism. The child may be an innocent bystander (e.g. Northern Ireland) or a participant as in civil wars
- Accidental firing of guns or explosion of device. When playing with a device; when out shooting; when playing on waste land, quarries, mines or industrial premises

Children have little idea of the dangers of firearms and may not be fully conversant with safety measures and procedures. The attractions of airguns and other explosive devices are very considerable for young men. The main types of devices include:

- Airguns and/or air rifles
- Shotguns
- BB and pellet guns (United States)
- Pistols and/or revolvers
- Rifles
- Bombs
- Explosive devices (see Chapter 5 – fireworks)

Injuries sustained

The precise type of injury depends on the nature of the firearm or explosive, and where on the body contact is made. The bullets or pellets from single firearms may simply lodge in soft tissues, for example the buttock, alternatively they may penetrate a long way internally, for example the skull, chest or abdomen. The path of penetration may be diverted by hard bony structures and the final lodgement may be difficult to locate.

Bullets that explode internally on impact may cause devastating injuries to bone muscle and vital structures. Explosions may result in severe head, chest or abdominal injuries, loss of limbs, facial lacerations or loss of vision.

Injuries sustained range from fatal to relatively trivial. The most serious long-term disabilities include:

- Brain damage with intellectual impairment, stroke and epilepsy
- Spinal damage with paralysis
- Partial or complete loss of vision
- Loss of function of the arms or legs

Firearm injuries may be more serious than originally apparent. In all but the most trivial accident expert opinion must be sought at an early stage. The injury will often require expert surgical (or neurosurgical) treatment as some bullets and explosions may cause serious injuries at a distance from the entry point.

Preventing firearms accidents

Ultimately the only way to prevent these accidents is to ban all such weapons. Presently anybody over the age of 17 years of age can purchase an air rifle and obtain a licence for it without any training whatsoever. A total ban is unrealistic in modern society, the most acceptable alternative being to ensure that all people using firearms receive adequate training in their handling and use. An additional measure is to control very strictly the licensing and sale of all weapons. The use of any weapon should be prohibited by law until the applicant for a licence has demonstrated competence in its use.

In Sweden there is a total ban on the sale of offensive weapons. If this is not acceptable to our society then parents can go a long way in showing their disapproval by banning all toy guns etc. from the home as well as real firearms. This may at least help children develop a respect for guns as dangerous weapons.

If children must be in the vicinity of guns or must use them the following rules should be obeyed:

- Ensure secure and safe storage of weapons when not in use
- Prohibit indiscriminate use of weapons
- Keep children out of the line of fire
- Carry the weapon correctly and ensure safety catches are on

7

ACCIDENTS AT WORK, INCLUDING ON THE FARM; NATURAL AND MAN-MADE DISASTERS

Accidents at work

Society's attitude to children working has changed dramatically since the Victorian era; cotton mills and mines to the casual paper round or a stretch on the till in a hamburger cafe.

Yet in spite of the improved status of children in the world of work they are still exploited. Some children are put at considerable risk in certain occupations and children at work are overall more at risk than adults at work. The Low Pay Unit estimates that 30 per cent of working children experience an accident at work requiring medical attention each year.

Overall between 20 and 30 children are killed each year at work (including accidents on farms), an estimated 2000–5000 are admitted to hospital and as many as 5000 attend outpatients. Many of these are classified as road traffic accidents. As children are not classed as 'employees' by the Health and Safety at Work Act they do not have the same protection as adults if they are accidentally injured at work. Their parents may have no right to compensation for any injuries unless they can prove in court that the employer was negligent. If the child were employed illegally, however, the parent may be considered party to any negligence. Useful summaries of problems relating to children at work are contained in papers by the Children's Legal Centre, the Low Pay Unit and the Scottish Low Pay Unit.

Who has accidents at work?

Children of all social backgrounds in the 13–16-year-old age group take on part-time work in shops or cafes and take on paper rounds. Some take on a casual job to finance a hobby or for recreational purposes, some to support smoking, drinking or paying for drugs. Others need to work to supplement the family income. Much of the employment is illegal (see page 109).

No official figures are available but an estimated 35–40 per cent of children aged 11–15 have part-time jobs. Such activity is more likely in rural areas than towns. Both boys and girls are involved in accidents at work but boys may be involved in more physical jobs and therefore they have more accidents.

When do work accidents happen?

These can occur at any season and any time depending on the nature of the work. The most common is a road traffic accident involving a newspaper delivery boy. This may occur before school in the morning or, more likely, in the afternoon or early evening especially in the dusk of winter months.

Where do work accidents happen?

The major risk areas are:

- Farms (see separate section on pages 109–112)
- Paper rounds (risk as a cyclist or pedestrian see Chapter 3)
- Shops (problems relating to lifting heavy stock or boxes)
- Leisure activities including pleasure boats, fairgrounds, circuses and the theatre; there may be accidents because of the nature of the equipment or because of the breakdown of the equipment
- Sport (horse riding stable boys and girls e.g., with falls and animal bites)
- Child care or baby sitting
- Gardening
- Furniture removal
- Garage work
- Construction work
- Painting and decorating
- Catering in hotels, restaurants and pubs
- Cleaning and domestic work
- Sewing
- Hairdressing

How do accidents at work happen?

Work accidents are most likely to happen to children because of:

- Lack of training
- Inexperience and unsuitability in relation to the child's development
- Carelessness and irresponsibility; long working hours and fatigue

Children at work require more attention, supervision and guidance than adults, yet they often do not get this from their superiors.

Injuries sustained

The majority of these accidents will be minor, recovery will be rapid and the child will be able to return to his casual job. Accidents as pedestrians or cyclists in the course of work are more likely to be serious and may result in death or permanent disability.

The Low Pay Unit Survey of London and Bedfordshire children in 1982–83 found that nearly one-third (30 per cent) of children working had experienced an accident in their current job (during a 1-year study). Nearly 3 per cent of all the children needed to see a doctor as a result of the accident. Similar figures were found in a Birmingham study in 1990.

The most common injuries were:

- Cuts – especially on glass
- Fractures, sprains, lacerations from falling and slipping
- Muscle injuries from lifting heavy weights
- Animal bites

One benefit of a minor accident at work for a child is to raise awareness of the hazards of the workplace. In the event of a more serious accident the child may be unable to carry on his or her preferred job.

In order to keep attendance at hospitals to a minimum it is imperative that a proper first-aid kit is available and that care can be provided when and where necessary.

The Health and Safety at Work Act 1981 requires employers who have more than 50 staff to have written instructions on safety procedures, to appoint a first aider and safety representative and to provide first aid equipment and facilities at work. Employers with less than 50 staff must still provide a first-aid box and appoint a safety representative.

Reducing children's accidents at work

Regulations to protect children at work are vague and, therefore, unscrupulous behaviour on the part of employers is a potential problem.

Children at work are not only at risk with respect to their health and safety but also their education, if too much time is spent on a job or if the hours make the child too tired for school work.

Remedies include improvements to the working environment and appropriate education of the worker in the task. Legislation also needs to be tightened up. The Employment of Children Act 1973 has been passed by Parliament but never put into force. The active implementation of this Act would make a major contribution towards reducing childhood accidents at work. In the meantime the main thrust of protection for children comes under the Health and Safety at Work Act. In principle the Act limits the numbers of hours children (aged 13–16) work, where they may work and what they may do.

- It is illegal to employ children under the age of 13.
- *Hours* – Only between 7am and 7pm and for 2 hours on a school day or Sunday.
- *Place of Work* – Children may not work in or on: factories; warehouses; construction sites; commercial kitchens; street markets; commercial transport.
- *Limitations* – Children may not operate circular saws; clean machinery; lift heavy objects; handle poisonous substances.

Farm accidents

Agriculture has changed dramatically over the past 50 years from a highly labour intensive occupation to a mechanized, technological industry. Hazards have changed accordingly and now represent a threat to any adult or child working or living on a farm. On average around 10 children are killed each year in farming accidents, between 1000 and 1500 children are admitted to hospital and as many as 5000 attend outpatients for treatment. Table 7.1 gives some details.

Hazards on a farm range from heavy and complicated machinery to highly toxic chemicals. They include the use of large storage barns and silos as well as ponds and slurry pits. In addition, farm animals, which are normally docile may also become dangerous if they are protecting their young and are threatened by people.

Who has farm accidents?

Fatalities from farm accidents can occur at any age but again they are a more frequent occurrence with boys. The types of accidents vary according to age; toddlers are most likely to be involved in drownings, falls from tractors and

Table 7.1 Children killed on farms in Great Britain, 1981–1984, by activity

Activity	Deaths
Playing	17
Working with/helping/watching adult at work	12
Passengers on machinery	5
Horse riding/other recreational activity	4
Total deaths 1981–1984 (4 years)	38

Source: HSE.

being run over by vehicles; school age children are victims of a wide variety of accidents; older children are most likely to be involved in incidents with machinery and tractors.

School children who live in towns and who are visiting a farm either as an individual or on a school trip may not be aware of potential dangers and are therefore at extra risk.

In recent years nearly 60 per cent of all farm accidents involving children have involved those who live there, whose parents are farm workers or those whose close relatives run a farm.

Approximately one-third of the incidents involving 10–15 year olds have happened while the child was actively working on the farm. An encouraging trend is the overall fall in the number of farming accidents involving children in recent years, which follows a long period when there was no sign of any decline.

When do farming accidents occur?

Farm accidents are most likely to occur during the summer months. Not only is farming activity greatest at this time but more visitors are likely to be around at this time. These accidents may occur at any time of day but are most likely in the later afternoon.

Where do farming accidents occur?

Accidents can obviously happen anywhere on a farm but the most hazardous locations or incidents are: falls from tractors or trailers; crushing by falling objects; drownings; getting caught in machinery; being run over; burns and scalds; strangulation; electrocution.

The main reasons for child fatalities are: self-propelled machinery; liquids (drownings); falls; falling and swinging objects; fire and hot fluids; static machinery; electrical appliances; animals.

The most dangerous hazard is being in the vicinity of tractors and associated machinery, and for young children, in the vicinity of slurry pits, cesspools, ponds and reservoirs. Another hazard for older children is drowning (or suffocation) in grain silos especially during loading or filling. Children are also at high risk when climbing on roofs of buildings or elsewhere on farms. Poisoning, thankfully, is a rarity in spite of the potential danger; the last recorded child fatality due to poisoning on a farm in Britain was in 1973.

How do farm accidents occur?

Typically accidents happen on farms where children are not supervised – even if this is only for a short time. Often incidents will occur when children stray into work areas where they shouldn't be. Often the parents will be fully aware of potential hazards but the children are ignorant, sometimes an operator of a machine may be unaware of the child's presence and thus of the dangers.

At other times a particular hazard may have been left exposed or in the wrong place, threatening the safety of children.

A relatively frequent cause of accidents is when the farmer's children or relatives are allowed to ride on the tractor. The child falls off the tractor, for example over the wheel guard and is run over by the tractor wheel or, often, by the trailer. Another common accident is when young children play in barns and are injured or even suffocated when a bale of hay or straw falls on them. Farm yards themselves may be full of dangerous or heavy equipment, and there may be stairs to lofts without banister railings, and ladders that young children may be tempted to climb.

Injuries sustained

In farm accidents the child usually survives with a nasty scare but serious injuries are always a possibility. Typical injuries sustained are:

- Fractures of limbs, especially legs
- Head injuries from falls
- Crushing or tearing injuries to limbs, chest and abdomen
- Penetrating injuries and lacerations from animals and equipment
- Burns, e.g., from barn fires
- Poisoning from toxic chemicals or plants
- Drownings in ponds, cesspits and water tanks
- Firearm wounds
- Asphyxiation or suffocation in grain

The risk of tetanus following any skin break in farming accidents is an added problem. Routine immunization can eliminate this potential risk, particularly for those living or working near or on the land.

Head injuries and penetrating injuries to the abdomen and chest are likely to constitute the 10 per cent of injuries that are long-lasting or will cause a permanent disability.

Preventing farm accidents

Education

Responsibility for farm safety almost always rests with the farmer. In addition to taking responsibility for himself, his wife and children he must also ensure that his staff and any visitors are also protected.

Although children cannot be supervised every minute of the day it is vital that an adequate watch is kept whenever they are near buildings or equipment that could represent a hazard. They must also be supervised whenever they are around sources of water or fluids or when they are with animals. Farmers must ensure that children are only doing tasks within their capability.

Responsibility also rests with HM Agricultural Inspectors of the Health and Safety Executive (HSE) who arrange safety exhibitions at agricultural shows and give talks to interested parties.

Environment

Attention to certain details of the farm environment could also help reduce incidents. These include:

- Keep children away from work areas
- Set up a children's play area away from farm activities
- Build safety features into farm equipment
- Fence off static equipment, wells, cesspools, slurry pits and grain silos
- Store all chemicals safely and securely in containers with correct labels, away from children
- Secure gates and ladders
- Keep guns locked away from children
- Take care in handling animals (particularly those with young)

Enforcement/legislation

Overall advice on this problem is contained in the Health and Safety Commissions' Preventing Accidents to Children in Agriculture: Approved Code of Practice and Guidance Notes. The HSE's Agricultural Inspectors are empowered to visit farms (zoos, safari parks, stud farms, racehorse stables and fish farms) to carry out inspections, advise farmers and enforce legislation if necessary. Other aspects are covered by safety legislation, for example the fitting of a suitable safety cab to tractors and the safe storage, appropriate marking and correct usage of toxic chemicals.

When children are working on farms they are covered by local authority bye-laws. These should in the future by replaced by the Employment of Children's Act 1973, which, although published, does not show any signs of becoming adopted in its present format. The Health and Safety at Work etc. Act 1974 is a much more effective piece of legislation and it requires that:

- Young people under 13 cannot drive or ride a tractor or other farm vehicle; and there are regulations relating to children riding in trailers
- Young people under 16 years of age cannot operate a circular saw; remove a guard from any machine
- Young people under 18 years of age cannot lift or carry loads likely to cause injury; feed produce into a thresher; operate a circular saw except under supervision; work with an agricultural or a smoke generator

All fatal or serious accidents on farms must be reported to HM Agricultural Safety Inspectorate under the RIDDOR regulations.

Natural and man-made disasters

Whereas some disasters (natural, weather-related) are predictable to some degree, others are clearly not (environmental, travel). In cases of natural disasters it is not possible to prevent the event but with accurate forecasting it may be possible to make contingency plans. Modern technology enables scientists to predict the onset of earthquakes, volcanic eruptions, cyclones and flooding. People can be evacuated, buildings boarded up and emergency services mobilized. Often, however it is not possible for adequate arrangements to be made, or the extent of the crisis may not be recognized in time, for example, the Bangladesh floods of May 1991, and this in turn may make the scale of the disaster massive.

Man-made disasters should be more controllable, but in the case of environmental accidents (Chernobyl), or sea, air, road or rail crashes, large numbers of people can be suddenly affected by a large-scale accident. If we include deliberate disasters such as warfare or terrorism here the incidence rises further.

Warfare

Throughout history the loss of life through warfare has been enormous. Up until the beginning of this century warfare tended to be concentrated in battles at set places and times that would result in injuries to the combatants; bystanders tended to avoid injury. Modern developments have changed the face of war and now with the advent of powerful explosives, fire and lethal arms innocent adults and children are frequently caught in crossfire.

The ultimate devastation can be seen with the explosion of the atom bombs in Nagasaki and Hiroshima in 1945, and modern warfare has claimed many lives since. The recent wars in Africa, Central America, Vietnam, Iraq and Yugoslavia have shown again how innocent children can be caught up in conflict.

Dealing with disasters

The medical role in dealing with the aftermath of a disaster is clear. Firstly there is the immediate resuscitation and care of the seriously injured, the treatment and rehabilitation of the sick and injured as well as public health matters of restoring water supply, sewage disposal and drainage, provision of food, clothing and shelter and psychological care of people shattered by the disaster. On-going health care, immunization and prophylaxis programmes may also be required.

All health authorities and public agencies responsible for health care facilities must plan with each other to respond to disasters when they occur. This includes local and regional planning for relatively small disasters such as air or rail crashes or motorway pile-ups. It also includes national, regional and local planning for the potentially larger disaster of conventional warfare or the ultimate disaster of nuclear war.

Children in the age group 5–9 years, for example, may be left to fend for themselves in the immediate disaster as parents care for younger siblings. Although they may have been deemed old enough to cope they will not be equipped to do so and thus may be injured proportionally more than would be expected. In a disaster such as the Bradford football ground fire in 1985 the child fatalities were predominantly in 10–14 year old age range for boys, 15–19 year old age group for girls. Here, these were the age groups most likely to be attending the match unaccompanied. There were also quite a number of adolescents involved in the Hillsborough football ground disaster in 1988.

Experience in Britain following disasters has shown counselling help for the survivors is needed after the disaster. Feelings of guilt and shock require a sympathetic hearing, skilled counselling and prolonged support for many months afterwards. The local authority is often the appropriate link to provide the coordination. Provisions should be written into regional and local emergency plans. Provision of support may be provided immediately by police, ambulance, fire, rescue and voluntary agency staff. Later the medical and nursing staff at Accident and Emergency departments may provide support followed by long-term care from social workers, the churches, voluntary agencies and general practitioners, practice nurses and health visitors. Sometimes special groups such as the Bradford and Hillsborough Support Groups are set up to provide special help on a more permanent basis.

Provision following a disaster

- An emergency telephone number widely and continuously publicised
- An automatic friendly helpline
- Drop-in centres
- Financial and legal support
- Over-all coordination by one agency, usually the appropriate city, county or district council
- Full support from other agencies such as health authorities, general practitioners, social services, voluntary services, churches and religious groups
- Visits to site, hospitals, relatives by public figures including civic dignitaries, politicians and royalty – although these should not be excessive and should be treated sensitively
- Setting up a Public Enquiry plus any relevant internal enquiry
- Sensitive media treatment and full cooperation by key people including chief executives and directors of agencies involved

8

NON-ACCIDENTAL INJURIES

Assault, homicide and abuse

Fatalities amongst children due to assault or homicide number between 40 and 50 each year. An estimated 2000–3000 children each year are admitted to hospital suffering from injuries due to assault or abuse. The actual number is unknown, because most will be reported as home injuries or sport and leisure accidents.

Babies and toddlers are the victims of most of the fatalities and serious injuries inflicted by parents; both sexes are equally involved. Serious injuries incurred by children assaulting other children are more frequently seen amongst older boys.

The term 'child abuse' includes 'non-accidental injury' as well as other commonly used terms such as 'baby battering' and all of these refer to persistent and repeated abuse, often of a physical nature, of a defenceless baby or child. Sudden infant death syndrome, cot deaths, may occasionally result from a form of child abuse but this is very rare.

Most incidents of this type occur because of parental problems, a problem child or a family crisis. Again, figures are not clear on the precise incidence of child abuse as a number of child abuse fatalities are probably ascribed to other causes. A reasonable estimate is around 100 deaths a year (one a fortnight) in Britain. This figure is much lower than in the United States, for example, where in a population five times the size of Britain's, there is a death due to child abuse every day. In addition in Britain 1500 children are seriously non-accidentally injured each year, with 400 suffering brain damage. Moderate injuries are inflicted on a further 5000 children and as many as 60 000 are be considered to be seriously neglected.

Not all fatalities are the result of child abuse; some may be the result of a suicide pact or of multiple killing of members of a family. The problem of infanticide is also not covered by these figures.

Contrary to popular media opinion the number and rate of deaths due to homicide and purposely inflicted injury on children under 5 years of age is in fact decreasing and has done so progressively throughout the 20th century.

The National Society for the Prevention of Cruelty to Children (NSPCC) received 20 384 reports of a serious nature involving 38 034 children in 1991. The NSPCC Child Protection Helpline answers around 120 000 calls per annum, most of these directly from children.

Local studies confirm that a typical health district of 250 000 people, around 25–30 children will be taken to their local Accident and Emergency or Paediatric departments annually with suspected non-accidental injury.

Child abuse may take one or more of these forms:

- Physical trauma
- Burns and scalds
- Sexual abuse
- Malnutrition
- Poisoning
- Drowning
- Failure to carry out prescribed treatment
- Severe and subtle forms of psychological mistreatment and mismanagement
- Neglect of basic needs

Background factors in child abuse

Parental factors:

- Marital disharmony
- Unemployed father
- Low income and poor money management
- Single parent family
- Young mother (under 20 years of age) – three times more likely to lead to abuse of the baby compared with mothers over 20 years of age
- Parental illness, especially mental illness or attempted suicide
- When one parent is a step-parent (especially stepfather)
- Low intelligence
- Isolation from family and friends (25 per cent of abused children in this category) especially in high-rise city flats and new urban housing estates or very isolated rural areas
- Parents who were themselves battered or emotionally deprived as children (the vicious circle of deprivation)
- Unwanted or difficult pregnancy

Child factors:

- Inadequate bonding between mother and child from birth

- Pre-existing handicap in child e.g., cerebral palsy
- Difficult or miserable child
- Prolonged separation of child from mother from birth or at any other time (perhaps due to illness)

A particular problem for the single mother is when the father returns temporarily, either causing havoc in the family or is an alcoholic, abusive or aggressive.

Recognizing child abuse

Recognizing and confirming child abuse is not always straight-forward or easy. The general practitioner, health visitor or Accident and Emergency staff may maintain an 'index of suspicion' with any child injury, and certain indications increase the likelihood of child abuse.

Warning signs of physical child abuse

- Repeated injuries and attendance at Accident and Emergency Departments
- Delay in taking the child for treatment
- Inconsistent or unlikely explanation for cause of injury
- Multiple injuries other than those caused by the trauma
- Injuries of unknown cause
- Injuries of a bizarre or unusual nature (whole body x-rays will often show fractures in varying stages of healing, or signs of old fractures especially of skull, ribs, arms and thighs)
- Characteristic head injuries and skull fractures. The skull sutures may be widely separated, often in the parietal area
- Subconjunctival haemorrhage
- Multiple bruising and scarring on the body
- Bilateral black eyes
- Subdural haematoma
- Apparent acute illness, or more often repeated minor illnesses, which may be the result of poisoning

Sometimes no single obvious sign exists but the staff may be suspicious that something is wrong. The child may be constantly miserable, failing to thrive or showing obvious signs of lack of care. The parents themselves may show unusual behaviour or reaction to the injured child. In turn the baby or child may show obvious fear or suspicion of one of the parents (so-called frozen watchfulness). Great caution is required because the degree of danger to the child is not necessarily directly related to the severity of the injury.

Psychological or sexual abuse may be more difficult to detect although gross negligence and malnutrition should be obvious. Children exposed to psychological abuse often show bizarre or withdrawn behaviour. Those that have been sexually abused may be unduly precocious or sexually knowledgeable for their age and social experience.

In addition to doctors and nurses in hospital clinics or general practice, other people may be the first to recognize signs of child abuse, for example, social workers, teachers, probation officers and education welfare officers. The method of management of child abuse has been changed by the introduction of the Children Act in 1991: this is discussed below.

The injured children never recover from the psychological and physical damage of long-term child abuse. In many cases the child is maimed for life, whereas others find it difficult to form lasting and strong personal relationships as adults. In adolescence the abused child will be more prone to attempted suicide, self mutilation, anorexia nervosa, solvent abuse and truancy from school. As these children become parents the cycle of deprivation and abuse is likely to continue.

Sexual abuse

This is identified as: the involvement of dependent, developmentally immature children and adolescents in sexual activities they do not fully comprehend, to which they are unable to give informed consent or that violates the social taboos of family roles.

This form of abuse may occur in as many as 1 in 10 children. Incest (within the family) usually, though not always, involves father and daughter or step-daughter. The adult is likely to tell the child to keep the practice a secret and thus this abuse often does not come to light for a long time. The child may also be unwilling to confide in other people for fear of breaking up the family. Often only if the child's genitals are injured, a sexual disease is contracted or if the child is a girl and she becomes pregnant, is the abuse discovered.

Sexual assault outside the family is also common, and may be the result of a chance encounter or if children are recruited into 'child sex rings'; adult males entice young children into secret 'rings' and they indulge in a wide range of sexual activities. Obviously, the children are likely to experience behavioural problems.

If any suspicion of sexual abuse or assault exists the child should be examined by an experienced doctor, preferably a female paediatrician, police surgeon or gynaecologist. Many children recover from these ordeals without any long-lasting effects but their treatment requires careful and skilled handling. Others are destined to repeat the activities in adulthood or take up prostitution.

Parents and teachers may help to prevent sexual abuse by talking freely about the problem in appropriate classes, or by advising girls in particular of the dangers of this form of attack. They can also encourage children to tell their parents or friends frankly about any worries they have.

Remedies for child abuse

There are no easy remedies for child abuse as it is often the result of unemployment, poor living conditions, low income and other social factors.The family need support in an atmosphere of trust rather than recrimination.

In child abuse cases the simplest and safest measure (in terms of injury limitation) might appear to be to remove the child from his or her home. However, the solution is not that easy and may result in further emotional deprivation for the child and perhaps risk the child assuming that he or she is guilty of the offence rather than the perpetrator. If it is possible to provide support and protection within the family then every effort should be made to do this.

Early intervention is also of prime importance, and there are some indications that although there may be a rise in the number of children injured the severity of injury is falling. The most important consideration is that the child receives continuous, dependable loving care. When this seems unlikely the separation of the child from the family on a permanent or temporary basis might have to be considered.

The management of child abuse

Although the legal, social and health aspects of the management of child abuse need not be discussed here, a summary of the Children Act 1989, which came into force in 1991, is justified because it introduced so many important changes.

This Act has been regarded as the most comprehensive and far-reaching reform of child care to have ever come before parliament. It stems from a 1985 government review of child care law but also from a series of enquiries into specific cases and in particular into the Cleveland crisis.

The philosophy underlying the Act is that the state should not interfere with family life unless this is necessary for the child's welfare. Parents should continue to be responsible for their children, with local authorities providing support to help to keep families together, and they will no longer lose parental rights when their child goes into care. The views of the children themselves must always be taken into consideration, and all medical and psychiatric examinations and assessments in relation to care proceedings can only be carried out with the consent of the child, if he or she has sufficient understanding to make an informed decision. An additional principle is that a delay in the institution of matters concerning the welfare of the child will be of prejudice to the child.

An Area Child Protection Committee (ACPC) in each area will be brought together under the aegis of the Social Services department and chaired by a senior member of that Department. Membership is multidisciplinary –

Social Services department, the Police service, medical practitioners (both hospital and general practitioners), community health workers (especially health visitors), teachers and voluntary agencies should all be members. Information about a child and his or her family must be shared with the various agencies, and the welfare of the child is of paramount importance in considering the question of confidentiality.

Another important new change is the establishment of family proceedings courts. These are at the level of magistrates courts and the magistrates are selected from a specially trained panel. The aim is to create a less adversarial procedure and to ensure that the court minimizes delays by controlling the timetable.

An Emergency Protection Order can be issued by a court enabling a social worker to remove a child for up to 8 days, with a possible extension for a further 7 days. The parents can challenge this order in the court after 72 hours. The Police have authority to remove a child for up to 72 hours if the risk to the child seems extreme. The parents have to be allowed reasonable contact with the children under the emergency procedure order.

Should the social workers suspect that a child is being abused – and this term covers the four categories of abuse: neglect, physical injury, sexual abuse and emotional abuse – another new order, the Child Assessment Order, can be made should the parents refuse access.

Some changes have also been made on the grounds of making a Care Order; that is, the child suffering likelihood of harm in the future has been added to the reasons for taking a child into care. Local authorities can no longer take a child into care without court proceedings, and wardship has been abolished.

This new Children Act has been well received, though financing its provisions will be a major problem. For example, local authorities, in safe-guarding the welfare of children in need, must provide day-care for the under-fives, and after-school care for older children.

Reducing child abuse

Children can:

- Seek advice from friends, teachers or other suitable adults
- Call Childline 0800 1111 for advice
- Call NSPCC Child Protection Helpline 0800 800 500

Parents can:

- Abstain from all violence against children
- Adopt a loving, caring attitude to children rather than a punitive one

Social Services/ social workers can:

- Train all staff in understanding child abuse and required procedures

- Set up Area Child Protection Committees
- Keep 'at risk' registers (Child Protection Register); counsel parents
- Give practical help and support
- Liaise with voluntary organizations to set up self-help groups
- As a last resort take children into care or hospital following an Emergency Protection Order (allowing the child to be detained for 8 days) agreed by Case Conference and Magistrates court

Education Authorities can:

- Plan programmes of education in parent craft and child care to be followed up when relevant by health authorities in antenatal and child health care clinics
- Encourage parents to take responsibility in preparing their own children for parenthood
- Include sex education for older children in the curriculum

Doctors and Nurses in Accident and Emergency departments can:

- Take a careful history for every child seen at hospital following an accident. If there is any suspicion of non-accidental injury find out more and if necessary admit the child into hospital
- Look for warning signs (see page 117) in injured child or parents

Nursing staff can:

- Set up and maintain liaison between Accident and Emergency departments and community nursing services.

General practitioners and health visitors can:

- Recognize factors likely to precipitate child abuse
- Facilitate contact with appropriate agencies
- Counsel and advise parents
- Set up mother and baby groups to help support mother in baby-care skills
- Arrange for attendance at pre-school play groups
- Carry out regular developmental checks and proceed to more detailed assessments of children suspected of being abused

Voluntary agencies can:

- Set up Child Protection Teams (NSPCC has set up 60 such units)
- Encourage parents and neighbours to seek early advice
- Set up drop-in centres for young mothers
- Encourage mothers to use play groups, day centres and baby-sitting circles

Police can:

- Appoint a special police liaison officer with training in and responsibility for child abuse

Everyone concerned can:

- Alert the Social Services if child abuse is suspected

Suicide

This is a rare but tragic form of accident in children. The total deaths by suicide in children in England and Wales in any one year ranges between one and seven, all in the 10–15-year-old age group. This is in marked contrast to suicide in adults, which accounts for as many as 20 per cent of all accidental deaths. During the twentieth century suicide rates for all males have been falling and for females rising, although there have been no marked changes for childhood incidence.

In the United States there has been a marked increase in suicide during the decade 1970–80. In the 15–19-year-old age group the total figure doubled from 1968–76, and for the 10–14-year-old age group there was a 36 per cent increase in the same period. The rates are greater in the United States than in Britain, which has one of the lowest suicide rates in Europe.

The only group that has shown an increase in death rates because of suicide in Britain during the 1970s is young adults in the 15–24-year-old age range and slightly more so for women than for men. In view of the increasing incidence in the United States and social pressures on children in this country the potential remains for an increase in suicide in older children in Britain. If a known history of mental illness, social problems or suicidal tendencies exist in a child, expert advice should be sought.

Who commits suicide?

Girls make more suicide attempts than do boys, although boys are twice as successful in their attempts. Overall successful suicide rates are much lower for girls but self-destructive action (parasuicide) occurs three times more often in girls than in boys. Around 10 per cent of boys who attempt suicide kill themselves, and in 40 per cent of cases they will have made previous attempts. Most children who attempt suicide are from disturbed backgrounds, have a long history of mental illness, are depressed, have personality disorders or have close experience of suicidal behaviour in others.

These children have access to effective means and have opportunities to use them. They have a degree of conceptual maturity that enables them to plan ahead. Parasuicide, in contrast, is an impulsive act in someone less likely to be depressed, but these children are likely to come from a broken home, be argumentative and resentful towards parents.

Background factors found in children with psychiatric disorders other than attempted suicide include:

- Antisocial behaviour
- Social isolation
- School problems
- Mental illness (including alcoholism) in the family
- Physical illness in the family
- Broken homes
- Rejection by family or friends
- Failure in mother/child bonding

Background factors in suicidal children include:

- Violence in the family (two-thirds of children attempting suicide have experienced some violence)
- Marital disintegration (half of children attempting suicide have parents who are divorced or separated)
- Recent bereavement in the family
- Low income (one-third of the children have families on social security benefits)
- Children of above average academic ability (but underachieving)
- Male sex (for completed suicide)
- Other members of the family have attempted suicide
- Physical ill health in the child

How are suicides committed?

The suicide, or attempt, may be masked as another form of accident: road traffic, drowning, poisoning or burning. The most common methods are:

- Taking medicaments, poisons
- Hanging
- By firearm
- Drowning
- Gas
- Cutting and piercing
- Jumping from a height

The majority of overdoses in teenage girls in Britain are an emotional response to a particular problem rather than a genuine attempt at self-destruction. Tragedies occur when the attempt is made with drugs such as paracetamol as the toxic threshold of this drug may be as low as 30 tablets, compared with aspirin for which, with similar doses, there is a much better chance of recovery.

Reducing suicides

Certain factors have helped reduce the overall incidence of successful suicide in recent years. These include:

- Availability of counselling from organizations such as the Samaritans, RELATE marriage guidance, and CRUSE for bereavement counselling
- Replacement of prescribed barbiturates with less lethal benzodiazapines
- Improved diagnosis to aid treatment facilities in hospitals plus follow-up of all attempted suicides
- Better treatment of psychiatric illness
- Decrease in availability of lethal coal gas

These factors have not been so significant in lowering the number of teenage attempts and clearly there is a requirement for special attention for the needs of young adults. When children seek help or attempt a suicide they should be taken seriously and supported by professionals. Particular care needs to be taken during times of family crisis and stress.

9

WHAT CAN WE DO TO PREVENT CHILDREN'S ACCIDENTS?

If an accident is defined as 'something that occurs that is unforeseen', the implication might be that it is unpreventable. This is clearly not the case. Accident prevention is an area with plenty of scope for education and improvement of the environment and products. In addition, regulations and legislation can also be introduced.

In order to address the problem of accident prevention we need to:

- Analyse the problem
- Determine preventable factors
- Specify and plan intervention
- Allocate responsibility
- Implement a programme
- Evaluate effectiveness
- Revise the intervention programme

Because of the 'chance' implication of the word 'accident' William Haddon, the former president of the Insurance Institute for Highway Safety in the United States substituted the term 'injury control' rather than 'accident prevention'. In this book we retain the term 'accident prevention' with 'accident' being used by the World Health Organization meaning as 'a sequence of events that lead to injury', and 'injury' as used in the Oxford English Dictionary sense of 'hurt or loss caused to or sustained by a person or thing'.

Another reason for retaining the word 'accident' is that it is a generally-used word by the population as a whole. 'Accident prevention' has an understood meaning whereas 'injury control' does not. This is important because one of the essential features of accident prevention programmes is that they are almost invariably multidisciplinary.

The substitution of the term 'injury control' might well mislead people into thinking that the main object of the exercise is to improve the first aid and subsequent management of the injured child. This is not without importance, but our main aim must remain primary prevention.

In analysing accidents, information is available on three main aspects:

- The *person* or persons involved, i.e. the **host**, (e.g. sex, age, stage of development, physical, mental and emotional health, social background)
- The *agent* that causes the accident or disease (e.g., the glass on which the child cuts himself, the poison he drinks)
- The *environmental circumstances* with which the agent and the host come into contact with one another (e.g., failure to provide a protective barrier, i.e., a fireguard, pedestrian crossing)

Haddon produced **ten basic strategies** to counter damage because of accidents. They are summarized, with modifications directly relevant to children, using as an example injury caused by fire, flames or hot fluids:–

1 Prevent the **creation of the hazard** in the first place
   For example: careful disposal of smoking materials to prevent fires
2 Reduce the **amount of hazard** brought into being
   For example: install a sprinkler system to douse the fire
3 Prevent the **release of the hazard** that already exists
   For example: fitting fire-proof doors, containing a fire in one room
4 **Modify the rate or spatial distribution of release of the hazard** from its source
   For example: fire-fighting activities
5 **Separate** in time or space **the hazard** and that which is to be protected
   For example: fitting smoke alarms in houses to ensure the early evacuation of people at risk
6 **Separate the hazard** and that which is to be protected by interposition of a **material barrier**
   For example: fireguards
7 **Modify relevant basic qualities of the hazard**
   For example: using non-flammable materials
8 Make what is to be protected **more resistant to damage** from the hazard
   For example: making fire-resistant furniture, or clothing
9 Begin to **counter the damage already done** by the environmental hazard
   For example: immediate first aid with cold water following a burn or scald
10 **Stabilize, repair and rehabilitate** the object of the damage
   For example: post-traumatic cosmetic surgery

These 'ten strategies' are not necessarily designed as a basis for accident prevention programmes, as Haddon himself admits. The analysis merely provides an aid to the understanding, setting up, and coordination of actual and possible control programmes and teaching. Our own approach to accident or injury prevention takes this into account, and supplements these ideas with the necessary activities of measurement, planning, intervention and assessment.

The whole process can be seen as a continual cycle of:

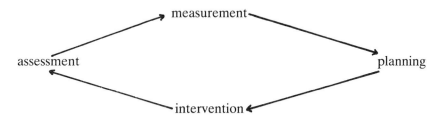

In this chapter we describe how the prevention of accidents to children depends on:

Education

Teaching the children themselves, their parents, teachers, health professionals with whom they come into contact and people who have the responsibility of designing the environment in which our children are brought up both inside and outside the home.

Changing the environment

Ensuring that our homes and the world at large are as safe as reasonably possible, bearing in mind the necessity for children to learn for themselves and to lead interesting and natural lives.

Improving product safety

Encouraging manufacturers to improve and modify their products to be child-compatible and safe.

Making and enforcing legislation

Requiring local and national Government to make and enforce laws which support prevention programmes.

Education

At school we accept that children will learn certain basics of language and mathematics. There are a number of other subjects which are now included in the 'core curriculum' in the United Kingdom. When we come to 'fringe subjects' and the 'hidden curriculum' there is less widespread agreement and even some dissension.

Children need to learn about the hazards of their environment and how to cope with them just as they should learn English and mathematics. It is not unreasonable to expect children to learn specific skills like crossing the road or riding a bicycle. However, this is not the position at present. We often expect children to acquire these skills almost by magic or expect them to learn the particular skill without any background knowledge of human attitudes and behaviour.

There is much more to education for accident prevention than simply teaching children. We need to teach parents about the hazards their children are likely to experience, and how to avoid putting their children at excessive risk. We need to educate professional people who come into contact with children in their work, and who may be able to influence children's behaviour towards avoiding accidents. We need to educate designers, manufacturers and salesmen that the products they are handling may be unsafe for children and therefore require modification.

Importantly, we have to educate politicians, local authority officers and architects who have the responsibility for shaping and designing the environment both within and outside the home, that children have special needs which should be considered at all times, with safety being an important aspect. The decisions they take may act directly or indirectly towards making an accident or conversely may assist towards reducing accidents.

In educating for safety we are looking to improve or enhance the classic triad of: knowledge – attitudes – behaviour.

It may be possible to increase **knowledge** so that a parent or child has a very clear understanding of the hazard. This will depend on previous education and, in the case of the child, on age and sex. There are a large number of hazards that we cannot expect a baby or toddler to understand; even an older child cannot fully appreciate all the hazards of crossing the road, for example.

When we come to changing **attitudes** the task becomes much more difficult. Some children and even some adults will decry the use of safety equipment like lifejackets, car safety seats or cycle helmets because use of these items creates a cissy image. This is particularly true in the attitudes of parents towards some aspects of home safety, car safety and sporting activities.

Finally a number of **behavioural** factors may start to come into play. A boy may well wish to display his 'macho image' by doing stunts on his BMX bike and the teenage girl may wish to rush the fences in her local gymkhana. A defiant child may simply go off to the playground in spite of remonstrations from parents. Indeed, teenage tantrums may often result in some mishap, as a result of loss of control.

The role of parents

Parents have a particularly important responsibility for providing a reasonably safe environment for their children to live in. Equally important is setting a good example, for instance, in their behaviour in crossing the road and in their use of household equipment.

Parents may say that education in safety matters is the responsibility of teachers, road safety officers and anyone other than themselves. Yet we **can** protect our children and teach them about the hazards of fire, hot water, sharp knives, glass and medicines and so avoid serious accidents.

In particular parents can teach children about:

- The use of child restraints in cars
- How to ride a bicycle and use a helmet
- The danger of hot water
- Safe use of medicines
- How to swim
- The potential dangers of animals and insects
- The dangers of climbing

The role of teachers

Teachers have a vital educational role in accident prevention first and foremost by recognizing its importance as part of a planned programme of education for health. The teacher may then build on this with specific accident prevention activities in, for example, laboratory safety; cycle proficiency; safety in sports and recreation; safety in the playground.

The role of health professionals

Health professionals may have an influence on parents and children that they themselves often seriously under-rate. Doctors or nurses may often feel that it is inappropriate to start talking about prevention when they are treating the child for an injury. But this is largely a matter of opportunity and correct approach.

Some health professionals have unique opportunities for one-to-one personal contacts with parents and children. General practitioners, community health doctors and health visitors may often be able to impart an accident prevention message. On a wider scale school doctors and nurses may be able to markedly influence a number of activities in schools that will contribute towards reducing accidents.

The particular areas where health staff may be able to influence accident prevention include:

- *Paediatricians and accident and emergency specialists* can set up **Child Safety Centres** at main hospitals and paediatric units to educate parents. These can also be used as a resource centre to educate professional colleagues, teachers and other influential members of the public. A number of childrens units in Australia have these centres even with bizarre displays of snakes and poisonous spiders to attract interest.
- *Paediatricians* may advise on special problems relating to accident prevention in handicapped children.
- *Midwives* may counsel parents of newborn babies especially on the use of infant car safety seats.
- *Health visitors* may advise mothers of babies and toddlers during routine visits on all aspects of home safety and on the use of infant safety seats. The health visitor may find it useful to use a 'Check List' or a child development learning pack to help her advise on each item.

The Cumberledge report on community nursing recognized that community nurses were well qualified to put across health education messages in lessons that people could readily understand and in a way that would encourage people to follow the advice they are given.

The health visitor usually has a good one-to-one personal relationship with the mother and is familiar with all the problems experienced by her family. She has credibility and respect with most parents. In the course of several visits she may be able to select suitable targets for attention and advise on specific safety matters. The health visitor has local knowledge and information and is specifically trained in communication skills. She is able to see how the child is developing and so relate accident prevention advice to the particular stage of development of the child. She should also have ready access to the facilities of the District Health Authority Health Promotion/Education Unit. Health visitors can probably do more than any other professional in the early stages to reduce the high toll of accidents to toddlers and young children.

A particular point of contact between the health visitor and the mother in relation to accidents and their prevention is when the health visitor makes a home visit to a child following attendance at an Accident and Emergency department for an injury. The aim of this follow-up visit is to confirm that the child is now recovered and to ensure that the home contains no further hazards likely to cause accidents in the future. However, health visitors can find these visits difficult as some mothers may feel that they are being accused of abuse or of deliberately hurting their child. A recent study of the 'Role of the Health Visitor in Accident Prevention' highlighted this problem and, as a result, a training pack for health visitors to help them in such home visits has been commissioned by the Child Accident Prevention Trust from the Community Education Development Centre.

Health professionals could also work to improve education amongst parents of children in ethnic minority groups, in particular. These groups of people could benefit greatly from improved, carefully prepared education programmes (in appropriate languages) especially concerning the safe carriage of children in cars, home improvements and for care with fire, for example.

Such programmes could be carried out after careful discussion with ethnic minority leaders, the Community Relations Council and link workers or interpreters where these are employed by the Local Health Authority.

There is a reasonable case here for positive discrimination in order to give extra attention where a problem has been identified. Overall, a raising of racial awareness in health authority staff and others by using local Industry Language Units or similar organizations will also help professional staff to be more effective in their educational roles with ethnic minority groups.

Preventing accidents for children in ethnic minorities is much the same as for other socially disadvantaged groups. Social and environmental improvements, better incomes and full employment will all help reduce accident numbers.

General practitioners (GPs) may cover a wide range of accident prevention activities in an opportunistic way during consultations or visits. The GP Contract introduced in 1990 offers considerable opportunities for GPs to become more active in health education.

The role of architects, town planners, engineers and designers

We see a pressing need for most of the professional groups involved with designing and planning to fully understand the implications of all the activities they undertake. They need to encourage the development of more user-friendly design.

Amongst the many activities that need to be covered by this group include:

- Design and layout of housing estates, schools and playgrounds
- Design of buildings, especially homes
- Siting of glass doors and windows
- Fitting of equipment like window latches, electricity sockets
- Development of the 'Kidsafe House' concept now widely practiced in Australia

The role of politicians

Politicians at national and local level have an important educational role because they are constantly in the public eye, and are often quoted in the media. They, therefore, have a considerable educational potential by passing on specific knowledge about accident prevention, by being actively involved in safety issues and by influencing colleagues to pass laws to improve safety.

They may also be able to mobilize resources specifically into the accident prevention field.

The role of manufacturers and producers

Manufacturers and producers may not be able to influence the public directly but they can, by setting high standards and good examples in the products they make, exert a considerable influence on public behaviour. They do also have ready access to the advertizing medium and so may take the opportunity to educate their clients in safety matters. Perhaps the most notable examples are the Volvo and Saab motor companies, who have used safety as a selling feature. Other manufacturers have also begun to realize that people do want to have some idea of their prospects of survival in the event of an accident. Safety is now becoming a saleable entity.

The role of traders and distributors

Tradesmen and distributors have a golden opportunity to pass on valuable information to clients and customers. Every trader and distributor should be fully conversant with the safety aspects of the product they are handling, with its correct use and the ways with which it may be misused. They should be prepared to pass on this knowledge when required.

Tradesmen may also help to raise awareness and knowledge amongst parents by making available brochures and catalogues that explain the purpose of their products. Sadly, many high street stores have neither brochures nor any staff trained in the safety aspects of the products they sell. They might actually increase sales by paying attention to this public need.

Specialist safety centres, like the well-established 'AKTA' ('Living Safety') in Sweden, have a great deal to offer in the form of skilled advice and technical help.

The role of sports coaches, trainers and referees

All of these have an important educational role in teaching children the rules of games and the reasons for these; methods of training to raise fitness and specific skills for playing the game safely and fairly. They also have a most important influence in imparting a sporting attitude to the game and in curbing undue aggression or unfair competition, for example, between individuals of different sizes and skills.

The role of recreational activity supervisors

These people who include youth club leaders, voluntary organization leaders (Scouts, Cubs, Brownies, etc.) as well as playground supervisors and recreation and leisure activity managers, all have a responsibility similar to teachers and coaches to equip their charges with an understanding of the hazards of the activities they are undertaking and to increase knowledge and use of the safety precautions required.

All these people also have a most important role in teaching basic first aid and ensuring that there is always someone around who is well versed in the skills of resuscitation.

The media

The important role of the media in education is discussed in Chapter 10.

Does education work?

It has been fashionable for many years to say that safety education does not work. To illustrate the benefits or otherwise of education in accident prevention we have looked at some specific safety initiatives, and examined the results of these.

Use of in-car safety devices by pre school children in Newcastle, Australia

Children aged 3–5 years of age showed a 25 per cent increase in restraint usage following a 2-week educational programme at their pre-schools. There was no change in usage by children in a control group who were not exposed to the educational programme nor in a group whose parents had been exposed to coercion by threatening them with law enforcement (Bowman JA, *et al.*, 1986).

Hazard reduction workshops for mothers in newly developing suburbs in Brisbane, Australia

A group of 22 mothers who participated in a series of workshops on 'Hazard Reduction' and 'Simple First Aid' were followed up for a period of 12 months. When compared with a control group of 22 mothers not exposed to any intervention the families of the trained group experienced only half the number of accidents as the untrained groups. (Taylor C, 1982)

However, not all campaigns are positive in their results. For example:

High school education of teenage drivers in the United States

When the routine teaching of driving skills was removed from a group of high schools in the American Mid-west the death and injury rate because of car occupant road traffic accidents fell. The withdrawal of teaching meant not only less teenagers on the road at a younger age but also resulted in those who did go on the road taking greater care than those who had previously received formal training. (Robertson S, 1980)

Motorcycle training in the United Kingdom (Raymond S, Tatum S, 1977)

An extensive study of motorcycle training of teenagers was carried out in the north and south east of England during 1972. Results showed that the riding performance of the trained sample was significantly inferior to that of a control group. The trained group also had a slightly increased accident rate. Training did effect a positive change in performance in some areas being most effective in the youngest riders. The trained group was thought to have a more positive attitude to safety but less confidence in their riding ability. Training merely gave them a false sense of security.

All this does not mean that education has no place. If people do not know that a certain substance is harmful, that a certain action is hazardous, or a particular environmental feature is dangerous, then they will never take appropriate action. Equally they will not be prepared to spend time or money on installing safety devices or in altering the environment. They will not be prepared to accept advice or direction, including legislation, on a problem if they do not see the reason for it. Education is crucial for creating a climate of opinion in which safety features in the product or the environment, or a particular safety action, becomes acceptable and is therefore used. A good example is the seat belt laws in the United Kingdom which have been accepted so readily by a very large proportion of drivers and front passengers. An expensive programme like the 'Clunk-Click' television advertising did not bring about the desired voluntary increase in wearing seat belts but did at least alert people to the problem. If the legislation had been introduced in an atmosphere of ignorance it would have been far less acceptable.

The inter-relationship of education programmes with other means of education is illustrated by an assessment of the BBC television series on children's accident prevention 'Play it Safe' which was carried out in Newcastle-upon-Tyne by Colver. After the series, 9 per cent of mothers from a socially-deprived area of the city took some action to improve their child's safety, but after a visit from their health visitor who gave advice such as where to obtain safety devices etc., the proportion of mothers who actively did something of their own accord rose to 60 per cent.

Investment in accident prevention

In hard financial terms the costs of childhood accidents are considerable. Some of these costs are borne by society as a whole, others by parents, and, in the longer term, some by the child himself. Investment into general accident prevention measures has already produced dividends, and further investment in the right areas may be expected to produce still further dividends in the future.

Some insurance companies and private enterprises are now finding investment in accident prevention is worthwhile. Others find sponsorship improves the company image.

In addition to general investment a case for quite specific intervention exits, in for example, safety glass, window locks, playground equipment or use of car safety seats. In these cases relatively small investments may be expected to produce quite good dividends in preventing childhood accidents.

One measure, for example, that would probably produce considerable financial dividends is the wider use of cycle crash helmets. Cyclists in the high-risk 10–14-year-old age group are at least as likely to be killed or seriously injured per kilometre travelled as the average two-wheeled motor vehicle rider. It has been estimated that the chances of death from head injuries whilst cycling would be reduced by a factor of nearly 20 if a good hard skull helmet was worn.

In a study carried out by the Transport and Road Research Laboratory it was estimated that the cost savings of wider usage of crash helmets would only be very marginal. A more recent study from Southampton University has concluded that even if only one in eight cyclists wore a helmet there could be a saving of £3.5 million annually on costs of loss of output and ambulance and medical treatment costs for cycle accidents. The study additionally found that half of all children would be prepared to use a crash hat and that the majority of parents, when presented with the facts about head injuries to cyclists, appreciated the need to provide their children with helmets.

The specific value of education in accident prevention is often difficult to prove. We cannot really be satisfied, however, until we have given education every chance to prove itself. Improvements in teaching, targetting specific topics and use of modern teaching aids must all help to raise awareness and change behaviour.

Changing the environment

Environmental and engineering measures are important components of the accident and injury prevention process.

Engineering measures concern the design, construction, manufacture and maintenance of equipment that may be used specifically by children or with which they will come into contact.

The environment operates at three levels:

- *The overall macro-environment* – including the planning of transport systems and their inter-relationship, the urban and rural environment and the natural environment.
- *The local environment* – houses, schools and public buildings.

- *The micro-environment* – at the level of design of products that people use in their daily lives. This relates to product safety and to the agent more than to the environment.

The overall environment

The transport system

An important aspect of planning relates to transport policy as a whole. At present this encourages the motor car and lorries above public transport by rail or bus. Even in towns it favours the motorist over the quite legitimate cyclists and more numerous pedestrians. The continuous increase in the volume of goods vehicles of ever increasing size and weight clearly contributes to the traffic problems compared with the benefits of rail or water transport for much of these goods.

Walking and the use of cycles for short journeys should be encouraged by providing cycleways and pleasant walkways (as has been done in most northern European countries). This would make a great deal of difference to the city environment by the reduction of noise, fumes and congestion. It would of course separate almost completely the conflict between the motorized road user and the energy saving more vulnerable cyclist and pedestrian.

The importance of appropriate town planning, such as the establishment of pedestrian and cycle routes on the Dutch 'Woonerf' system as a means of reducing child pedestrians fatalities has been stressed by the Organization for Economic Cooperation and Development (OECD) in its report on traffic safety and children.

Currently pedal cycling is unsafe in relation to the number of miles travelled. It could be made much safer if government policy were to change. Many factors enter into the politics of transport policy, but probably the most important factor of all is the immense political pressure wielded by the motor vehicle industry together with the heavy goods vehicle lobby and the motoring organizations. The promotion of cars with wasteful acceleration and totally unnecessary and illegal maximum speeds is an example of the low status afforded to safety. Similar considerations apply to motor cycles: Japanese manufacturers not only encourage the sale of bikes of an engine capacity that is forbidden in their own country, but also have promoted in the past the sale of mini motorcycles for use by children as young as 4 or 5 years of age.

The urban environment

The majority of people in Britain spend the majority of their time in an urban environment.

Large-scale planning involves consideration of the community and the interaction of its various components, for example the siting of schools, playing fields and play areas, the separation of motor vehicles from pedestrians, and the provision of cycle tracks. Such environmental changes may be large-scale and expensive if applied to existing locations, but are less expensive when new houses and areas are being built. Many new towns have been well designed from the point of view of traffic segregation, access to amenities and protection from a dangerous environment. Older towns and cities have left us with a legacy of many hazards.

Some other aspects of urban design have been less satisfactory. High-rise flats and their stark concrete surroundings have proved almost universally unpopular. Life in them has many difficulties and dangers that were not recognized when they were first built.

A number of studies have shown that mothers fear for the safety of their children in tower blocks. Such environmental limitations show society's apparent disregard for children's health and safety.

In Scandinavian and northern European countries, society is much more sensitive to children's needs. High-rise flats in these countries have easier access to play areas and parks. They are built in a more friendly style with a more imaginative layout. Other nationalities, like the French, the Italians the Chinese and the Indians have a more closely knit, family-centred approach to the care of children. Much of their urban environment allows easy and free interaction between people.

An example of the failure to consider children's needs in the urban environment is that during the planning of the new Newcastle metro railway, there was no intention by the planners to put a barrier at a level crossing in a housing estate. It was said that, 'Children who could not understand the meaning of a red flashing light should not be out on the road alone anyway'. But the reality is that they do go out alone and, therefore, do become exposed to such hazards.

A more direct example of the inter-relationship between safety and town planning is the study by Barbara Preston of all child pedestrian accidents occurring in one year in Manchester and Salford. These were correlated with:

- The category of the road
- What the child was doing at the time (going to school, playing, etc.)
- Certain social indices relating to the families, their houses and the environment

The highest accident and injury rates by far were found in the wards with the worst social indices. This affected boys aged 5–7 years old particularly who were playing in the streets because they had nowhere else to play. Lack of play space was the main difference between the high- and low-accident areas. It follows that the provision of sufficient alternative play areas would be a very effective way of reducing accidents to young boys, in the worst accident areas.

Confirmation of the effectiveness of this type of approach has been made in Scandinavian studies.

A more recent study (Sharples PM, *et al.* 1990) has looked at the causes of fatal childhood accidents involving head injuries in the North between 1979 and 1986. Of the 255 children who were killed, 136 (53 per cent) were playing at the time of the accident; 61 per cent of the accidents occurred within 1–2 km of the child's own home and 63 per cent occurred between 3pm and 9pm. There was a significant relationship with social deprivation, there being a 15-fold decrease in mortality between the local authority wards that ranked highest in the overall deprivation index and those that ranked lowest. The study commented that,

> *'Two hundred and fourteen (84 per cent) children during 8 years were fatally injured as pedestrians, cyclists or while playing and this emphasizes the importance of extending preventive measures much further. There is an urgent need to provide safe and stimulating play areas close to home in overcrowded and deprived areas and to implement town planning measures to make the urban environment safer for child pedestrians and cyclists.'*

The rural environment

The rural environment for all its beauty and tranquillity has many hazards. We must recognize that the shortest excursion away from the protection of a town will bring with it many risky adventures. Woodland and streams have many traps for the unwary.

The potential for injury from the many different farming activities should not be underestimated. They range from heavy machinery, to grain silos, to slurry pits and all the toxic effects of poisonous chemicals, fertilizers and insecticides. Even the farm animals are not without their dangers.

These are covered in more detail in a separate section on farming accidents in Chapter 7.

The natural environment

There is not a great deal we can do to change the overall natural environment. However, the effects of polluting gases on the ozone layer and the subsequent global warming, does affect the climatic pattern and natural disasters such as cyclones, storms and flooding. So man can, after all have quite a profound effect on the natural environment.

We can also have a more immediate effect on controlling the natural environment locally, for example by building sea defences, drainage systems and flood barriers. Even these efforts sometimes pale into insignificance when natural forces take over and cause devastating storms and floods that kill and injure many people.

We cannot control earthquakes, hurricanes and cyclones but by better forecasting we can at least take precautions to reduce their worst effects.

The local environment

There are numerous environmental features of homes which have a high potential for accidents. If these unsafe features are eliminated or modified there is great scope for accident reduction.

The Child Accident Prevention Trust has produced *Guidelines on Child Safety in Housing* a design manual for architects, house builders and housing managers. This gives information on the numbers of accidents associated with specific features of the home, how these accidents might be reduced by changes in design, and the cost of implementing these measures.

The Consumers Association has also published papers on home safety that include comments on the use of products as well as design features.

Although children spend the majority of their time indoors in their own homes, they do go into buildings, in particular into schools. Surprisingly, however, a senior architect in the Department of Education and Science once commented that he did not believe that a single accident had occurred in a post-war school in England and Wales as a result of bad architecture or bad design. In fact many examples of accidents involving glass doors in particular and many other unsafe features exist.

The general principles of accident-avoidance by good design are the same for all buildings.

The Royal Institute of British Architects (RIBA) and the National House Builders Federation (NHBF) have recognized these needs by issuing guidelines to members and by including features on safety in their journals. A number of house builders try to build safety features such as smoke detectors and circuit breakers into their houses. Swedish kit house builders in particular incorporate these features right through from the design stage for both energy conservation and safety to be taken into account. In Australia an imaginative cooperation between the Master Builders Association and the Child Accident Prevention Foundation of Australia has produced a 'Kidsafe Homes Kit'. This details a range of features that, installed from the beginning, will mean that a new home is as safe as possible for children.

Making and enforcing legislation

There are occasions when education is not enough – legislation is required to dictate and enforce safety provisions, particularly in the case of children.

New laws have to be made to keep pace with modern life and existing ones must be updated or amended. The procedure for making law is long and tedious.

If the government in power decides to present a bill it has a good chance of success. If it is presented as a Private Members Bill it still has a good chance if sufficient members support it. Otherwise a bill may never get through the various stages of parliamentary procedure and will not become an Act of Parliament.

Recent acts that affect the safety of children include the Children Act 1989, The Consumer Protection Act 1987 and the Building Act 1984. These were all presented by the government. Others that have become law through the persistence of individual members include the Private Members Bill tabled by Stephen Day MP on the wearing of seat belts by children in motor vehicles.

Other ways of getting laws enacted or of drawing attention to a particular safety problem include a **parliamentary written question**, which any member of the public may ask their MP to table. If expert advice is needed then the question may be raised through an MP by a specialist organization like the Parliamentary Advisory Council on Transport Safety or the Child Accident Prevention Trust (see Annex).

A formal debate may be held on a government Green Paper (for discussion) or White Paper (with firm proposals). After this the government may, if it wishes, come forward with definite proposals for a bill or for **regulations** to be put forward to amend an existing Act of Parliament. The use of regulations is a much easier process because it does not need the lengthy process of three readings, committee and report stages. Some Acts of Parliament are sufficiently 'all embracing' to allow legislation to be added relatively easily.

An **Early Day Motion** may be put forward at certain times during the parliamentary session. This can allow an important issue to be debated and for formal motions to be passed. When it is appropriate this procedure can also lead on to the framing of a Bill.

During **Prime Minister's Question Time** set questions are raised by the opposition, usually on topical items covering key issues of the day. This can be a time for issues of public safety to be raised.

Two other devices for raising awareness in parliament are **Private Members Bills** and **Emergency Debates**. The **Private Members Bills** are very much the 'luck of the draw', and all members have the opportunity to present a Bill if their name is drawn from an open ballot. Many private Members Bills are never supported but occasionally (as in Stephen Day's Bill) they may go all the way through and become law.

An **Emergency Debate** is usually only called (by any member) and accepted by the speaker following some national crisis. Any disaster like the Zeebrugge ferry or Hillsborough soccer disasters (see Chapter 7) will prompt an emergency debate when many of the safety issues will be given a good airing. The **Public Enquiry** that usually follows will invariably end up with a series of recommendations which the government will often take up and require to be implemented.

Local authorities may also pass **Local Bye-laws** by a far less complex process. Procedures vary around the country but they often result from one councillor raising an issue (e.g., dogs fouling pavements) and having it agreed by a majority of the council. Not all local bye-laws work in the best interests of child safety. The most notorious example must surely be the prohibition of cyclists from many footpaths and passageways in residential areas. If we wish to encourage children to cycle safely away from traffic then surely every effort should be made to encourage them to use these off-road routes. (We are aware of the need also to protect the vulnerable pedestrian from the cyclists).

Professionals and members of the public should be aware of the possibilities for local action through the council. Local agitation can get school pedestrian crossings accepted and playground standards improved. Given the will the possibilities for local action are very considerable.

We present here some examples of legislation that are directly or indirectly relevant to the safety of children. Some of the reasons behind the laws and their actual or potential effects in reducing accidents are explained below. Others are covered by the different chapters relating to specific accidents. The list is by no means exhaustive and it is always changing. It does reflect the current state of the art.

For many of these acts and regulations slightly different rules apply in Northern Ireland, Scotland and Wales. Precise details may be obtained from national British Standards or local Trading Standards offices (see telephone directory). They may also be obtained from the Northern Ireland office in Belfast, the Scottish office in Edinburgh or the Welsh office in Cardiff. In the Channel Islands and the Isle of Man most British laws apply but some may be completely different.

Legislation relevant to children's safety

General legislation

Various children's acts (see Appendix) cover the rights of children in society and seek to protect them. Recent additions cover the requirements of all professional groups working with children to take into account the wishes and feelings of the child. Other consumer and general safety acts require that goods should be safe and fit for use, and this obviously concerns children as much as adults. Environmental acts ensure that air pollution and waste disposal are properly restricted to ensure safety, and also require dogs to be controlled and this should reduce the risk to children from dog attacks.

Home safety

Fire hazards are a main cause of home accidents and various acts seek to restrict the hazards to children by holding adults responsible for the safety of children around household heaters and fires. Regulations concerning the flamability of furniture and furnishings should reduce the chances of toxic fumes harming children in the event of domestic fires.

Poisonings are another potential source of harm at home and regulations require that aspirin and paracetomol be purchased in child-resistent containers. Pharmacists, by professional agreement, now dispense all drugs in child-resistant containers or in strip or blister packets, unless the recipient requests otherwise. The sale of other poisonous substances is restricted and clothing that comes into contact with the skin must not contain a specific chemical which is deemed potentially harmful to children.

Household equipment can be dangerous to children and one specific act covers the size of gaps permitted in the manufacture of children's bunk beds.

Toy safety

Products designed specifically for use by children – toys – must conform to the Toy Regulations. It is an offence to supply toys that do not conform to these standards. Children are protected by the fact that toys must not cause harm or injury if used in a reasonable manner bearing in mind the normal behaviour of children. Some items may have a notice saying they are unsuitable for children under 3 years of age, particularly if they contain small parts. Certain chemicals must not be used, parts such as eyes (of dolls or soft toys) must be firmly attached and voltage used in toys is restricted.

Benzene is not allowed in concentration in any item intended as a toy. Items that could be mistaken for food and could confuse children are disallowed and firearms or fireworks may not be sold to children.

Building safety

Many safety features required in new buildings protect children. These include provision of handrails, limiting the gaps between bannisters to 10 cm on stairs, restriction of spread of fire within buildings and attachment points for fireguards in fireplace surrounds. All plugs and sockets must conform to safety standards and must meet British Standards Institute (BSI) standards.

Safety of products used by children

Items used by children such as carry cots, prams, pushchairs and clothing such as hooded garments are covered by regulations.

Safety at school

Various regulations and acts cover the safety of children at school, in addition by tradition and common law practice schools stand *in loco parentis* and are expected to take reasonable care on behalf of their children such as a parent might take. Children in primary schools particularly must be supervised, and under Local Management of Schools (LMS) each school will be responsible for the health and safety of its pupils.

With LMS parents and governors will have more say about what is taught in schools and this could have particular relevance for the amount of 'safety' included in the curriculum.

Schools must provide a certain proportion of first aiders on their staff and injuries must be notified.

Playground safety

Childrens safety in playgrounds is covered by a separate set of regulations and new playground equipment must be as safe as is reasonably possible. Further regulations are expected soon.

Safety at work and in agriculture

Children (under 16 years of age) are not allowed to work in mines or other industrial settings, they must not carry heavy loads, work circular saws or handle poisonous substances. Children under 13 years of age may not drive tractors or other agricultural machinery, and are not allowed to work in paid employment.

Children on the road

In cars children (and adults – July 1991) must use the seat belt provided or an approved safety seat when travelling in cars, where one is fitted. In practice this means that children must always be restrained when travelling in the front seats of motor vehicles. When seat belts are fitted in the rear they too must be used, or a childs safety seat, baby seat or booster seat or harness combination may be used. The only time children are not required to be restrained in cars in when all the seat belts are being used or where they are not fitted.

Miscellaneous acts

Other acts protecting children, not catered for under the above categories, include those concerning children in public houses and bars. Here children under 5 years of age may not be given alcohol (except on medicinal grounds); children under 14 years of age are not allowed in bars except in separate rooms provided by a public house; children aged 14 years of age and over are allowed in a bar but may not consume alcohol; children over 16 years of age may buy beer, port, cider or sherry to drink with a meal.

Children under 16 years of age may not buy cigarettes and it is an offence to sell to under-16s.

Enforcing legislation

Many of these regulations will protect children by their very existence, particularly in the case of regulations concerning the manufacture of goods. Others, however, are more difficult to enforce.

Rules concerning use of safety devices, particularly seat belts, are clearly difficult to monitor and enforce. In theory car drivers are responsible for children under 14 years of age and must ensure that they wear seat belts or approved devices when travelling. In practice many adults either do not want to or do not bother to use their own seat belts particularly in the rear seats and for these people it will always be difficult to convince them of the requirement for children to abide by this law. Since 1989, however, the police are entitled to enforce the law and insist that front seat occupants and both adults and children in the rear of cars wear seat belts where available. This should encourage some parents to conform. However, this depends on a police officer having both the opportunity and occasion to stop a vehicle with an unrestrained child and to enforce the law. This will always be difficult to assess unless the child is standing up or climbing around the car.

Overall these regulations are more likely to be enforced by consumer pressure (in the case of product safety) and accepted practice (children in cars) than by the 'arm of the law'.

Improving product safety

Accidents and injuries to children can be caused by many harmful and dangerous products ranging from soft toys to equipment used by babies and children. The most significant way to reduce the danger of such products is to ensure that all playthings and equipment used by children are 'child safe' In this section we are specifically concerned with the things with which children come into contact, i.e. consumer products.

Toys

Toys that appear endearing and attractive to children, notably teddy bears and soft toys, can contain many hidden dangers. Historically, there have been problems with eyes on metal posts and buttons and removable parts being swallowed or inhaled by young children. The safety and testing of toys has improved considerably, and now the new Toy Safety Regulations have been introduced that will help parents in their choice.

Home fittings and equipment

Around the home much of the equipment and many fittings may not be safe for children. One solution for parents is to examine each room of the home in turn and to 'child-proof' it.

Overall, parents should bear in mind that the first thing babies do to explore the world around them is to put anything and everything in their mouths. Parents should therefore try to ensure that things the baby might reach are clean and safe, and that the baby's toys can withstand his chewing, sucking, pulling and pushing without coming to pieces!

Products made specifically for use by children are the primary cause of only a relatively small proportion of accidents. Nursery furniture, toys and play equipment of all sorts may be involved in quite a number of children's accidents, but they will not necessarily be the crucial factor in the production of the accident or injury. There is nevertheless a genuine and justifiable concern that children's products should be designed and manufactured in such a way that they are safe. This is necessary even when used in the way that they are intended to be used, as well as in 'foreseeable misuse'. It is often difficult to ensure that children will use a toy merely in the way an adult thinks it should be used!

Safety is defined by the British Standards Institution (BSI) as 'freedom from unacceptable risks of personal harm' and 'foreseeable misuse' by children is defined by the International Standards Organization (ISO) as 'the use of a product in ways not intended by the designer, manufacturers, etc., but predictable when related to the activities of children at various stages of their development.'

Many people think that children's products are safe purely because they are sold for children. This is a false assumption. A survey carried out by the Consumer's Association (publishers of *WHICH* magazine) in the United Kingdom in 1983 showed that over 75 per cent of parents thought that cots and high chairs must comply with safety regulations. This is not so. Nearly all (98 per cent) thought that manufacturers should make sure that the products they make are safe. In fact for the vast majority of products they are under no legal compulsion to do so but increasingly nursery products are covered by BSI (see below).

In terms of product safety there are three levels at which a product may comply, these are:

1) Compulsory safety standards enforced by legislation and regulations
2) Voluntary standards which are not enforceable
3) No safety standards required

Children's products covered by regulations or standards in the United Kingdom include:

- Two-wheeled pedal cycles to BS 6102 Parts 1 and 2
- Baby car seats (use up to 10 kg) to BS AU 202a
- Carrycot restraints for cars to BS AU 186a
- Child car seats (use up to 18 kg) to BS AU 202 and 3254
- Child car booster seats (for use with rear seat belt or harness up to 36 kg) to BS AU 185
- Safety film for glass to BS 6206C
- Stair and door gates to BS 4125
- Pushchairs and buggies to BS 4792, and to Pushchairs (safety) Regulations (1985)
- Carrycots to BS 3881, and Stands for Carrycots (safety) Regulations (1966)
- Prams to BS 4139 and to Perambulator and Pushchair (safety) Regulations (1978)
- Harness (reins) to BS 6684
- Highchairs to BS 5799
- Cots to BS 1753
- Cot mattresses to BS 1877
- Toys to BS 5665 and Toy (Safety) Regulations (1989)
- Nightdresses to Nightdresses (Safety) Regulations 1967 (SI 1967/839) or to BS 5722
- Playpens to BS 4863
- Baby nests to BS 6595
- Dummies to Babies Dummies (Safety) Regulations 1978 and to BS 5239
- Bottle heaters to BS 3456
- Cycle helmets to BS 6863
- Coiled kettle flexes to BS 6500
- Smoke detectors to BS 5446
- Child-resistant Packaging (Safety) Regulations 1986
- Floor-standing fireguards to BS 6539
- Wall-mounted fireguards to BS 6778
- Spark-guards to BS 3248

Other regulations are referred to on pages 153–4

When a manufacturer puts a BSI kitemark on a product this guarantees certain minimum standards. It means that the BSI has carried out independent testing of samples of the product against the appropriate British standard. The presence of the symbol (the kitemark) and an appropriate BSI number confirms that the standard has been met in every respect.

It also means that the manufacturers may be visited at any time by BSI staff to ensure that products are consistently up to the required standard. This monitoring includes the right of BSI to take away random samples of the product for independent testing at any time.

It is possible for a manufacturer to claim that he complies with an appropriate British Standard. He may also use words to this effect on his product. It is only *bona fide* kitemark licensees who are able to provide BSI assurance that the claims are valid. Such an approach may often lead consumers to think that a product is made to BSI standards when this is not so. Both consumers and shop assistants can help here by learning more about the safety aspects of products and looking specifically to see whether products do comply with standards.

The safest piece of equipment available will only be effective if used correctly. For young children the use of safety harnesses in prams, pushchairs and highchairs cannot be stressed strongly enough. The best tested car seat will only be effective if the straps are tight and the buckle fastened when in use. Standards can only influence design and manufacture; use is up to the parent.

Particular care should be taken when families are away from home and using out-dated equipment (perhaps borrowed from relatives) that may not conform to current safety standards. The width of bars on cots, the 'tipability' of pushchairs and the stability of highchairs should always be checked. Similarly when holidaying at home or abroad parents should check that standards are satisfactory. Even within parts of Europe, manufacturers may not be as attentive to safety as the standards that may be expected in the United Kingdom.

Responsibility for product safety

Recent legislation in the European Community and in the United Kingdom has put an increasing onus on manufacturers and traders to ensure that their products are safe. In 1982 a government White Paper was issued that emphasized the importance of standards in the whole field. Later a memorandum was signed by the government and the BSI, in which the government agreed to support the standard system and to use existing standards in such matters as purchasing and to refer to standards in regulations. Finally a 'General Safety Duty' was introduced that stated all consumer goods must meet sound modern standards of safety. Goods are covered by regulations of the 'deemed-to-satisfy' (i.e., that the goods meet an equivalent standard) type.

In addition, specific standards will be approved and specified to either British or foreign standards. The question of the standard of reasonable safety will take into account a number of factors. These include the degree of risk posed by the product, the availability of proven technology to prevent the hazard, the cost of safety, the question of labelling, warning and instructions generally, and the level of safety applied by published standards.

The role of manufacturers and retailers

British manufacturers and retailers are rightly concerned with the safety of their products. This is not only from a purely technical and ethical point of view but also because any adverse publicity associated with reports of the manufacture or sale of unsafe products is clearly damaging to their image and sales figures. 'Rogue' manufacturers and retailers are unusual and the majority of goods that are unsafe have been imported from abroad. Many of the loopholes that allowed the importation of such goods are closed now that the 'General Safety Duty' of the Consumer Protection Act is in force.

The safety of children's toys has been of particular concern to the public because of the association between accidents and faults in design or manufacture. The new Toy Safety Regulations should ensure satisfactory standards, and lower accident potential.

Standards, although of great importance, are not the only way of ensuring safe products. New products are constantly being developed, manufactured and sold. Standards cannot always deal with some specific aspects even though there are general standards, for example on electrical safety. It is, therefore, important that safety should be built-in at the design stage.

Labelling and warning notices

Requirements relating to the labelling of various products exist in the United Kingdom as well as in most other countries. They can be divided into two main categories:

- Labels relating to the use of the product, such as the age-group for which it is intended or other limitations relating to its use. This applies particularly to products intended for the use of or by children, such as toys, nursery furniture, prams etc.
- Labelling of products that may be used by children but in which the adults may have a special responsibility to ensure the child's safety such as with drugs and household chemicals

Labelling is in the main directed at adults who can read and understand the significance of the label. It is important that parents and other adults should be informed that a certain substance they are bringing into the home is hazardous, particularly where poisonous and toxic substances are concerned. In spite of all this attention, the value of labelling as an effective means of accident prevention has been questioned.

Some labels are designed to be a hazard warning to both children and adults. A study in New Zealand showed that there was no difference in the incidence of poisoning in houses in which a special symbol 'Mr Yuk' was used to prevent children being poisoned, compared to a well-matched control group. However, in Canada a similar symbol is thought to have helped reduce the incidence of poisoning. The campaign was accompanied by an extensive educational campaign over some years. It was, therefore, difficult to disentangle the effect of the educational efforts from the effect of the symbol. Bland messages such as 'keep all medicines out of the reach of children' have had no apparent effect on the incidence of child poisoning in the United Kingdom.

The design and printing of labels is also important. The size and position of the warning can be such that it is almost totally inconspicuous and therefore useless. Some warnings may be present for legal rather than for practical purposes. The statement 'this toy is not suitable for children under the age of 3 years' may satisfy a legal requirement in relationship to its size, but such a notice is of no value in houses in which there is more than one small child and in which toys are likely to be all stored together.

Warning labels should never be relied upon to warn consumers of hazards (which should themselves have been remedied).

Safety packaging

The method of packaging certain products can be important in prevention of children's accidents. The use of child-resistant containers or a non-re-usable unit dose packaging for pharmaceutical preparations is one of the best examples. Another is 'tamper evident' packaging that prevents the contents being obtained at all until the seal is broken. This has become of greater importance in the United States because of the illegal insertion of toxic or poisonous materials into goods on sale in stores. The seal prevents the removal and replacement of an ordinary top.

Organizations involved in product safety

In recent years there has been a very considerable increase in all aspects of product safety. A number of organizations have been active in this field at international and national levels. Considerable progress has been made in reducing the hazards resulting from products or from faults in products.

For anyone working in the safety field it is often useful to know who is involved and what they are doing. We include below some of the organizations involved in general safety or more specifically in child safety.

International organizations

The Treaty of Rome that established the European Economic Community (EEC) has as one of its prime objectives the removal of barriers to international trade. One such barrier is differing standards. Harmonization within the community is achieved through the **Committee European de Normalisation** (CEN). The equivalent in the field of electrical safety is CENELEC.

These bodies produce their own standards. When they are covered by an EEC Directive they become legally binding on the member states. There are a few exceptions to this general rule. If a state thinks the Directive will be detrimental to the health or safety of its citizens, it may not immediately have to introduce the regulations. Because some standards in some countries will be lower than in others, the CEN standards and EEC regulations can sometimes be significantly lower and different from those in Britain.

A product that would pass the lower standard of Country A can be deemed to satisfy the higher standard of Country B for the purposes of regulations. This is one of the drawbacks of the 'deemed to satisfy' procedure. As a general rule EEC regulations are limited to general safety requirements such as undesirable levels of heavy metals in paints, rather than to specific ones. In spite of this a 'Directive on Toys' has been published and others may well follow.

In view of the obvious difficulty in getting concensus among the various nations the time taken to produce a CEN or CENELEC standard is even longer than that required to produce a national one.

The Commission of the European Community took an important initiative in setting up a 'Child Safety Campaign' during 1987–88. The objective of the campaign was to achieve a significant reduction of all severe children's accidents in and around the home in EEC countries by the year 1995. An important part of this campaign included specific safety requirements for certain children's products.

Coordination and cooperation at an international level between standards-making bodies is achieved by the **International Standards Organization** (ISO) and the **International Electrical Commission** (IEC). These are not official United Nations agencies, but they are organizations of which 80 different countries, including the United Kingdom, are members. ISO and IEC standards are binding on member states and the problems of obtaining concensus are formidable. In the field of child safety ISO is currently producing a standard for child-resistant containers to prevent poisoning.

The International Standards Organization also has a Council Committee on Consumer Policy (COPOLCO). Recently this council recommended to the main ISO council that a background document on 'Child Hazards in Relationship to Standards' be drawn up for the guidance of member states when drafting standards. This recommendation was accepted by ISO and an *ad hoc* working group has been established to draw up the guidelines.

Consumer organizations within Europe place the question of safety high on the list of priorities relating to consumer products. The United Kingdom has its own consumer representatives in the European Community Group initiated and supported financially by the Department of Trade and Industry. The European Commission itself has a Consumer's Consultative Committee. Outside the Commission the umbrella organization of consumer groups within

Europe is the **Bureau European de Union des Consommateurs** (BEUC) with offices in Brussels.

There is, in addition, an international voluntary body; the **European Consumer Product Safety Association** (ECOSA). This is a relatively new organization based in the Netherlands and associated with the Consumer Safety Institute. It produces a regular newsletter that has much useful information on international activities in product safety.

On a worldwide scale agencies involved in product safety include the **World Health Organization** (WHO) through its Accident Prevention Programme administered from the headquarters office in Geneva and its European office in Copenhagen. The **Organization of Economic Cooperation and Development** (OECD) has shown a direct concern for the problem. In 1983, its Committee on Consumer Policy produced a very valuable report on measures to protect children. It has analysed the current state of affairs in the 25 member states, looking at the different types of hazards and the measures taken to prevent them.

Whilst all of these international organizations may appear to be complex and bureaucratic they do serve very useful purposes. Standardization of products allows much easier exchange and adaptability. Comparisons between countries may stimulate action when one country is found to have higher product-related accidents compared with others.

British organizations involved in product safety

The British Standards Institute (BSI) plays a vital part in ensuring product safety. This is an independent body financed by industry and the Government. The broad aims of standardization are summarized by the BSI as including 'protection of consumer goods and services' and 'promotion of quality of life, safety, health and the protection of the environment'.

The standards-making aspect of the BSI's work is performed by a series of technical committees. Manufacturers are strongly represented on these committees. Quality control is carried out by inspectors employed directly by the BSI.

Consumer interests are represented where possible and necessary on some technical committees. Such interests are mainly the concern of voluntary bodies. As the time and expense involved can be quite considerable there can sometimes be problems in ensuring an adequate balance of consumer representation. This has led to the criticism that the 'lowest common denominator' is accepted rather than the highest possible safety standard. It also means that it may take many years before a concensus is reached on a particular standard.

At a higher level within the BSI, consumer interests are represented by the Consumer Policy Committee (CPC) whose chairperson is on the main BSI Board. The Child Accident Prevention Trust and the Royal Society for the Prevention of Accidents are both represented on the CPC. At a lower level there are four coordination committees looking at specific aspects of standards being drawn up, with safety experts attending to give advice in appropriate areas. The coordination committees report back to the CPC.

There are still some standards that specifically exclude young children from their provisions, for example in some electrical safety standards. As part of existing tests, an adult-sized mechanical 'test finger' is used. The BSI is currently developing a standard child test finger that can then be used in test procedures. This will be used, for example, to test the mesh sizes of fireguards. Another anomaly is that some kitchen electrical equipment is specifically not tested for safety against children who are the very people most at risk.

There is an increasing recognition of the special problems of children. A previous statement to the effect that the standard excludes young children and the elderly is to be replaced by the following:

> '*So far as is practicable, this standard deals with the common hazards presented by appliances that are encountered by all persons in and around the home. However, except in so far as this standard deals with electric toys, it does not in general take into account the use of appliances by young children or infirm persons without supervision: for such use additional requirements may be necessary.*'

The Association for Consumer Research (Consumers Association [CA]) answered the rise of 'consumerism' as a voice in society which has developed in the United Kingdom since the late 1940s. The part played by the CA has been paramount in this movement. Its national organization undertakes the testing of goods and services from a professional and technical point of view. It also assesses the relative merit of products in their every day use by questionnaires to its members. The results of the tests and questionnaires are published in *WHICH?* and other specialist magazines.

In 1985 the Child Accident Prevention Trust was awarded a half-share of the CA's Jubilee Research Award, which was used to draw up a guide to child safety equipment. In this guide the different types of safety equipment, for example fireguards, stair gates, child car restrains are listed, together with their availability and current price. Additional finance from the Department of Trade and Industry and others have allowed a wide distribution through health promotion/education officers and health visitors free of charge to mothers of young children.

Other consumer organizations in the United Kingdom include the Institute of Consumer Affairs, the National Consumer Council and the National Federation of Consumer Groups. The roles of RoSPA and the CAPT are discussed in Chapter 10.

The **Institute for Consumer Ergonomics** in Loughborough and a number of other postgraduate institutions like the **Cranfield Institute of Technology** have taken a special interest in product safety. By carrying out specific research projects these establishments provide detailed analysis and comment on numerous aspects of product safety. Their expert reports may then be used for changing standards or improving the design of products.

Government organizations like the **Transport Research Laboratory** (TRL) at Crowthorne in Berkshire and the **Building Research Establishment** (BRE) and the **Fire Research Station** (FRS) similarly carry out and coordinate research of a more specialized nature.

The implementation of recommendations and advice made by the academic and government institutions may contribute significantly to improvement in product safety and the prevention of accidents.

Summary of legislation and regulations on safety for children

General legislation
The United Nations Convention on the Rights of the Child
The Children Act 1989
The Children and Young Persons Act 1969
Consumer Protection Act 1987
The Environmental Protection Act 1990
Children and Young Persons (Amendment) Act 1986
Child Care Act 1980

Home safety

Fire safety:
The Children and Young Persons Act 1969
The Community Homes Regulations 1972
The Nightwear (Safety) Regulations 1985 and Nightwear (Safety) Amendment Regulations 1987
The Furniture and Furnishings (Fire)(Safety) Regulations 1988 and the Furniture and Furnishings (Fire)(Safety) Amendment Regulations 1989
Heating Appliances (Fireguards) Regulation 1973

Poisons:
Child Resistant Packaging (Safety) Regulations 1986 and the Medicine (Child Safety) Regulations 1975
The Poisons Act 1972
The Dangerous Substances and Preparations (Safety) Regulations 1980 and Amendment Regulations 1985

Household equipment:
The Bunk Beds (Entrapment Hazards)(Safety) Regulations 1987

Toy Safety:

The Toy (Safety) Regulations 1989
The Toy (Safety) Regulations 1974
The Benzene in Toys (Safety) Regulations 1987
The Food Imitations (Safety) Regulations 1989
The Novelties (Safety) Regulations 1980 and Amendment Regulations 1985
Firearms Act 1968
Explosives Acts 1875–1976

Building safety

The Building Act 1984
The Plugs and Sockets (Safety) Regulations 1987

Safety of products used by children

The Stands for Carry Cots (Safety) Regulation 1966
The Childrens Clothing (Hood Cords) Regulations 1976
The Perambulator and Pushchair (Safety) Regulation 1978
The Pushchairs (Safety) Regulations 1985
Trade Description Act 1968

Safety at school

Education (School Premises) Regulations 1981
Health and Safety at Work Act 1974
Education Reform Act 1988
Health and Safety (First Aid) Regulations 1981 and approved codes of practice

Playground safety

The Occupiers Liability Act 1957 revised 1986
The Uniform Contract Terms Act 1977
Health and Safety at Work Act 1974
Consumer Safety Act 1978
Consumer Protection Act 1987

Safety at work and in agriculture

The Factories Act 1961
The Offices, Shops and Railway Premises Act 1963
The Agriculture Act 1965
The Children and Young Persons Act 1963
Reporting of Injuries, Diseases and Dangerous Occurrences Regulations 1985

Health and Safety at Work etc. Act 1974
Health and Safety (First Aid) Regulations 1981

Children on the road

Motor Vehicles (Wearing of Seat Belts by Children in Rear Seats) Regulations 1989.
Horses (Young Persons) Protective Headgear Act 1990

Miscellaneous acts

The Licensing Act 1964
The Children and Young Persons Act 1933 section 7, section 12
The All-Terrain Motor Vehicle (Safety) Regulations 1989
The Nurseries and Childminders Act 1948
Dangerous Dogs Act 1991

10

WHO IS RESPONSIBLE?

Whenever one tries to decide who was responsible for an accident we are always likely to blame the stupidity of the child or the carelessness of the parents. As children get older, of course, they assume more responsibility for their own actions and safety. Nevertheless, parents and guardians must be responsible for their children's actions at all stages of their development.

However, it has been emphasized strongly, wherever possible, that parents and children should take responsibility for their own behaviour. In this chapter we look more at the official agencies and other bodies which do, or should, take responsibilities for child safety.

Safety Organizations

Organizations which have a responsibility for accident prevention may be divided into three categories:

- Statutory organizations (national and local government)
- Voluntary organizations
- International organizations

National government

The World Health Organization has recommended that one body responsible for accident prevention should be established at national level. Many northern European countries have such a structure. In the United Kingdom the responsibility is shared between many government departments.

The Department of Health is responsible for the management and treatment of injuries (see below), **The Department of Transport** for road safety, **The Home Office** for fire safety, **The Department of the Environment** for environmental safety and **The Department of Trade and Industry** for product safety. Finally **The Department of Education** is responsible for the national curriculum, which includes health education.

In spite of this fragmentation, things may well change. The Department of Health (DoH) in a White Paper 'The Health of the Nation' has outlined a strategy for continuing improvement in the general health of the population which includes five key areas. One of these is accident prevention. Targets have been set in this to reduce the death rate for accidents among children under fifteen by 33% by the year 2005. A Paper on the role of the National Health Service (NHS) on road accident prevention in childhood, produced by the Child Accident Prevention Trust on behalf of the Health Education Authority at the request of the DoH has also suggested that the lead should be taken by the DoH.

A very important function relating to accident prevention which the DoH should, and could, be concerned with is data collection. Satisfactory data on accidents is absolutely essential before really effective preventive programmes can be established. The Home Accident Surveillance System (HASS) collects data at certain NHS Accident and Emergency departments, but is supported by the Department of Trade and Industry, which has extended this into a Leisure Accident Surveillance System (LASS). These two systems have been of immense value to people concerned with accident prevention.

The DoH has not been able to establish any uniform data collection system through the country. A computerized Accident and Emergency system (CAER) has not proved to be very satisfactory, and hospitals are tending to go their own way with Accident and Emergency records. A possible data collection system for children's accidents is the CHIRPP system (The Children's Hospitals Injury Reporting and Prevention Programme), which is in use throughout children's hospitals in Canada and Australia. Perhaps this could be introduced into Paediatric Accident and Emergency departments in the United Kingdom.

There is no doubt that we need to see much greater use both nationally and locally of accident information to highlight particular accident problems.

The Department of Health is primarily responsible (over and above these two functions of preventive strategies and data collection) for the provision of hospital care and emergency ambulance services through the regional and district health authorities. It is also responsible for the provision of general medical services through general practitioners (GPs) who are under contract to the local Family Health Services Authorities (formerly the Family Practitioner Committee). Accident prevention measures and support may be provided by

- Accident and Emergency departments in hospitals with their back-up facilities
- Hospital inpatient facilities for the treatment of injuries sustained
- Diagnostic and treatment services by GPs. Some GPs and their staff also carry out education in accident prevention in the community (a recent paper by Sibert has looked in detail at the doctor's role in the prevention of accidents to children)

- Ambulance service
- Rehabilitation services
- The collection of hospital outpatient and inpatient data on accidents and injuries (very few health authorities carry out systematic analysis of the data collected)
- Domiciliary nursing services particularly by health visitors with their special concern for young children
- Health education officers who may include accident prevention in their role
- Allowances, pensions and other financial support to injured and disabled people
- The Medicines Division, Medicines Inspectorate and the Committee on the Safety of Medicines, the Department of Health has an overall responsibility for the safety of drugs. Primary, secondary and tertiary prevention measures are all covered in this list, though primary prevention is seldom given the emphasis that it deserves.

The Home Office has the responsibility for fire safety in England and Wales and for the operational efficiency of the fire brigade. Research into fire safety is carried out in cooperation with the Home Office Scientific Research and Developmental branch and the Department of the Environment Fire Research Station. The Home Office also has the responsibility for the problem of drowning. Even so, it is the Royal Life Saving Society (see page 188) and the Royal Society for the Prevention of Accidents that collect statistics on drownings. The maintenance of law and order through the police force is also the responsibility of the Home Office.

The Department of the Environment has the responsibility for the Building Regulations through the Building Regulations Division. These cover England and Wales, except inner London where local regulations apply. The department also has the responsibility for open spaces and recreation areas including parks and playgrounds. Numerous regulations relate to the environment. These are administered and enforced by the local authorities.

The Department of Transport is responsible for major communication networks and through local authorities, for the building and maintenance of the road systems. It provides a policy framework and finance for the Transport Research Laboratory (TRL). It also makes a grant to the road safety division of RoSPA, which is responsible for road safety education through road safety officers employed by the local authorities.

The Department of Trade and Industry (DTI) runs the Consumer Safety Unit that is responsible for collecting information on home accidents through the Home Accident Surveillance System and the Leisure Accident Surveillance System. It also looks at specific products and problems brought to its notice by Trading Standards Officers, voluntary organizations and others. The DTI draws up regulations under the Consumer Protection Act 1987 and regulations, prohibition notices and orders under the Consumer Safety Act 1978.

The Department of Employment and The Health and Safety Commission are responsible to the Secretary of State for Employment and operate the Health and Safety Executive. This supervises the administration of the Health and Safety at Work Act 1974, which is mainly concerned with factory safety but it is also relevant for children when they are at school, because the working conditions of teachers and other staff at school are covered by the Act.

The Department of Education is responsible for general educational policy and finance, although most of the education policies rest with local education authorities and with school governors and headteachers. Safety within schools, including during sports lessons, rests with the school authorities and with the Health and Safety Executive (as detailed above).

The Ministry of Agriculture and Fisheries has responsibility for the political and fiscal control of farming and the use of farmland. The Ministry used to have an Agricultural Safety Inspectorate but this was incorporated into the Health and Safety Executive in 1974. The Health and Safety Commission noted in it's 'Plan of Work 1983–84' the high rate of agricultural accidents and included among its priorities a reduction in the number of accidents to children on farms.

The Ministry of National Heritage has taken over the management of the Sports Council, this in turn supervises the National Childrens Play and Recreation Unit.

The Scottish Office, Welsh Office and Northern Ireland Offices each have responsibility within their own regional localities. Scotland has the greatest degree of devolvement mainly through the Secretary of State for Scotland and the Scottish Home and Health Department.

The Central Office of Information (COI) is the government agency that provides and disseminates a wide range of materials via the media on behalf of government departments. This includes film and television clips on road safety or home safety matters.

The Office of Population, Censuses and Surveys (OPCS) is a branch of the Government Statistical Service and is responsible for the production of the Registrar General's annual reports on death and health matters. It also produces the 'Monitor' series that includes the quarterly publications on births and deaths and deaths by accident as well as certain pamphlets on specific subjects such as on fatal accidents occurring during sporting and leisure activities.

The National Radiological Protection Board was established by the Radiological Protection Act 1970 and is responsible for carrying out research and development. It provides information, advice and services to those involved in all aspects of radiation. In 1983, the board produced a document on 'the criteria of acceptability relating to the approval of consumer goods containing radioactive substances'.

Local government

Local Authorities enforce legislation through County, City, Borough or District Councils. Education, Social Services and Environmental Health are all organized locally. The abolition of the Metropolitan County Councils means that responsibility for accident prevention has fallen back onto small locally based authorities.

Education Services operate under the policy direction of the Local Authority Education Committee. The headteacher of a school, together with the school governors carry the responsibility for the curriculum and now, under Local Management of Schools (LMS), for the budget of the school. Previously this allowed schools to provide a widely varying degree of accident prevention and safety education etc.. Now, under the national curriculum the requirements are more stringently laid out.

Social Services Departments come under the policy direction of the local Social Services Committee through the Director of Social Services. The departments have a duty to look after the health and safety of children in their care. They are also concerned with the problems of child abuse (non-accidental injury). In addition, social work departments provide financial, material and personal support for children who are handicapped or disabled following an injury. Such overall support to a family may be vitally important in contributing to preventing further accidents.

Environmental Health Departments function through Environmental Health Officers (EHOs) and have a wide range of responsibilities and duties. The standards of hygiene in restaurants, cafes, shops and hospital kitchens as well as rubbish disposal and pollution are all covered by EHOs. Some departments employ a Home or Home and Water Safety Officer – although in spite of numerous recommendations this is still not a statutory post. If no Home Safety Officer is employed, the Environmental Health Officers may undertake these duties especially in relation to the education and training of others (including school children) in home safety.

County Engineers and Surveyor's Departments employ a Road Safety Officer (RSO) (with few exceptions). This is a statutory post, and if there is no separate RSO the County Surveyor will be designated RSO. Training Courses for RSOs are offered by the Royal Society for the Prevention of Accident's (RoSPA) Road Safety Division. Much of the RSOs time is spent in training school children in pedestrian safety and organizing cycling proficiency testing.

Consumer Services are operated by local authorities through Trading Standards Officers, who are responsible for enforcing the Consumer Safety and Consumer Protection Act.They are also the first point of contact for members of the public with complaints or concern over the quality and safety of goods that they have bought or have seen for sale.

Public utility companies are not geographically co-terminous with local authorities and cover wider regional areas. Water, gas and electrical companies are all directly responsible for the safety of their products.

Police Authorities also cover a wide area. The role of the police is to enforce the law as a whole, including Road Traffic Acts. As well as enforcing the law the police also have responsibility for education either through direct talks with school children or through the admonition of young children who unwittingly or knowingly infringe minor traffic laws or other laws. The importance of the police function with respect to safety cannot be overemphasized.

Fire Authorities are committees of elected representatives whose purpose is to provide fire-fighting organizations and services for their particular areas. Fire brigades operate with the local government fire authorities and include fire prevention advice amongst their responsibilities. Increasingly fire prevention officers are seen to have a role in giving talks in schools and in providing free advice to members of the public on request.

Independent and voluntary organizations in the United Kingdom

Among the many 'quasi-autonomous non-governmental organizations' (QUANGOS) the following are of particular relevance to safety:-

The Health Education Authority (HEA) is financed by the Department of Health and has health promotion, disease, accident and illness prevention as its main role. In the past, accident prevention has not been a main activity – probably because of RoSPA's role in this field – but with financial support from the Department of Health and advice from the Child Accident Prevention Trust (CAPT) the HEA produced the booklet *'Play it Safe'* to coincide with the first BBC TV series in 1982. It is equally involved in the second series and its associated Child Accident Prevention campaign, and has also commissioned the report on the role of the health service on the prevention of children's road accidents.

The Transport Research Laboratory (TRL) is funded by the Department of Transport and is the largest road research organization in Europe. Vehicle and road-user safety is high on the priority list and research on, for example, vehicle design, car passenger restraint systems, pedestrian and cycle safety is continually underway. The TRL also brings expertise to groups such as RoSPA and CAPT. Research findings are applied in countries around the world, as well as in Britain.

The Schools Council is financed jointly by the Department of Education and by local authorities. Its purpose is to undertake research and developmental work in the curriculum, teaching methods and examinations in schools. Some of the school council courses relate to home safety. There are specific collaborative projects with the HEA that include more about accident prevention.

Voluntary organizations

(Further details are given in the product safety section of Chapter 5)

The distinction between independent and voluntary organizations relates merely to the proportion of financial resources received from governmental funds.

The Royal Society for the Prevention of Accidents (RoSPA) is a charity and the longest established and largest accident prevention organization in the United Kingdom. It plays an important role in advising government departments and other organizations about accident prevention. Much of RoSPA's work is in the educational field in the forms of journals, papers, posters, films and other resource materials as well as administering the National Cycling Proficiency Scheme and the Tufty Club for child pedestrian safety. The national headquarters is in Birmingham but much of the work is carried out through a network of regional divisions where staff work with local education authorities and local council safety committees. The major divisions of RoSPA cover agriculture, home, leisure, occupational, road and water safety education.

Child Accident Prevention Trust (CAPT) was formed in 1979 and as it suggests covers the special case of children. CAPT is a scientific advisory body that researches into accident prevention and accordingly advises agencies in this field. It also publicises accident prevention measures and when necessary lobbies parliament. A similar organization is the Child Accident Prevention Foundation of Australia, the main driving force behind accident prevention in that country. The multidisciplinary nature of CAPT is shown by the wide variety of individuals and organizations concerned in some way with childhood accident prevention.

As well as the Department of Health, which provides the Trust with its core funding, the other governmental departments mentioned above are all represented together with other organizations with an interest in child care.

The Medical Commission on Accident Prevention (MCAP) was started by an initiative by the Royal College of Surgeons. It maintains a leading scientific and advocacy role but its work on childhood accidents is now carried out by CAPT.

The British Safety Council is mainly concerned with occupational safety and does not deal specifically with children's matters.

The British Medical Association does not directly undertake specific activities in the field of accident prevention. Nevertheless, it is represented at a number of other organizations. It also engages in medico–political activity, for example in the support of seat belt legislation or activities relating to drinking and driving or matters concerning speed limits.

The Parliamentary Advisory Council for Transport Safety (PACTS) is a group of Members of Parliament (MPs) interested in transport safety, together with representatives from many different safety organizations. Vehicle manufacturers and traders, motoring organizations and special interest and pressure groups are all well represented. PACTS deals with air and railway transport as well as road transport and also carries out research into transport accident problems making representations and recommendations when appropriate. Some of these matters may be taken up in Parliament by the MPs on the Council.

The British Standards Institution and the Consumer's Association are both covered in Chapter 9 under product safety and standards.

The Royal Life Saving Society has the prime purpose of preventing death by drowning. It collects data on drowning from information provided by the police and from this and other services produces an annual report 'Drownings in the British Isles'. It is also involved in all aspects of water safety and life saving and can provide training in resuscitation.

The National Association for Safety in the Home (NASH) is a recently formed body concerned mainly with fire safety.

Other professional bodies with an interest in children's safety include the **British Paediatric Association** (BPA) and the **British Association of Paediatric Surgeons** (BAPS), which have a joint accident committee. This is mainly concerned with the services for injured children rather than with accident prevention. Both it and the **British Paediatric Accident and Emergency Medicine group**, which has been recently formed, have a close association with the CAPT. Other interested bodies include: **The British Association of Accident and Emergency Medicine (formerly the Casualty Surgeons Association), Health Visitors Association, Royal Society of Health, Institute of Environmental Health Officers** and the **Trading Standards Officers Association** all of which are involved in preventing children's accidents.

Local activities include a number of multidisciplinary groups concerned with accident prevention. Within the overall health field several Regional Health Authorities (RHAs) as well as the Scottish and Welsh Health Departments have set up Health Promotion Planning Groups that in many cases include accident prevention. The West Midlands and Northern RHA have prepared action plans on the prevention of accidents in childhood.

A survey in 1984 showed that potential for the formation of local groups still exists provided they can be serviced by a central source. The importance of local groups should not be underestimated. The Swedish State Commission for Investigation of Childhood Accidents is very strongly in favour of local initiatives. Voluntary groups of parents and other interested parties can often identify local needs for environmental improvement that can be very effective. One suggestion in the report is that each area should have its own Childhood Accident Prevention Officer. Such an approach has unfortunately not yet been accepted in the United Kingdom.

Local groups formed under the aegis of the 'Play it Safe' campaigns are discussed below.

International organizations

Many of the international organizations concerned with safety have been mentioned in the previous chapter under product safety. A summary of the most important groups and their activities is given here.

The World Health Organization (WHO) has its headquarters in Geneva, with regional offices around the world. Members are not necessarily members of the United Nations. WHO has both a global and a European programme. The European initiative has been looking into the backgrounds of accidents and has established a database that can collect data internationally.

The Organization for Economic Cooperation and Development (OECD) has considered safety in a number of publications including one entitled *'Product Safety: measures to protect children'*(1984) and *'Traffic Safety of Children: road research programme'* (1982).

The International Standards Organization (ISO) and other organizations concerned with standards and their harmonization between different countries are referred to in detail in Chapter 5.

The European Community (EC) functions through the Commission itself, which has many different Directorates. The Commission is advised by the European Parliament, which passes laws affecting member states, and also by the important Economic and Social Committee that advises the EC about the feasibility and appropriateness of measures being considered.

Media influences

Advertising

In today's society undoubtedly advertising commands a strong control and influence over us all. Advertisements extol specific life styles in an attempt to sell a product, for example in car advertising the image is repeatedly pushed that speed is power and that is what we should all be aiming for. Few manufacturers agree that safety sells with the exception of a few, notably Saab and Volvo whose 'safety cage' is well known and respected.

Volvo sells its cars on the basis that they are a safe family car. Advertising is based on impact absorbent bumpers and child safety locks and they even give away child seats. Previous advertising lines such as, 'Always keep your valuables in a safe place' show that a market for such advertising strategies exits. A standard feature of 940 and 960 model saloons is now an integral child safety seat converted from the central rear armrest – and Volvo advertise this as a strong selling point. However, most manufacturers prefer to sell for speed or style rather than safety.

Advertisements are bound by the rules of the **Advertising Standards Association** (ASA) and all advertisements must be 'legal, decent, honest and truthful'. Guidelines for car advertising stress that 'it is not acceptable to emphasize speed in car advertisements' yet many do seem to imply this. Complaints made to the ASA may be rejected on the grounds that other selling features were more prominently pushed in the advertisement and hence many manufacturers still rely on selling speed.

The only measure the public can take is to write to the ASA every time it considers advertising fails to comply with the 'Code of Advertising Practice'.

Copies of any letters can also be sent to the chief executive or sales director of the relevant car manufacturer. They should point out that excessive speed can kill innocent people and ask that they encourage safer driving practices rather than reckless abandon and disregard for other road users.

The Department of Transport undertakes its own advertising on television and radio, in magazines and newspapers and on posters to highlight specific safety campaigns that are underway. Recent campaigns have included 'Belt up in the Back', and 'Drinking and Driving Wrecks Lives'. Another recent series of advertisements was designed to appeal to young people to inform them that the wearing of cycling helmets is both necessary and fashionable. The Autumn 1991 campaigns specifically aimed at making drivers aware that they could reduce the number and severity of accidents to children by reducing their speed.

Television

Safety and accident prevention usually comes to the attention of the general public as a result of specific campaigns or when legislation is being discussed (e.g., seat belts). It may depend on seasonal elements (e.g., drink driving at Christmas time). For the rest of the time safety does not come to the fore in most people's minds. There are some television programmes that have taken safety issues on board, these include:

Play it Safe (BBC) have been the most important television programmes on child accident prevention. This was initially a series of ten 10-minute programmes presented by Jimmy Saville, each programme commentating on one specific type of accident or injury. A booklet of the same name proved to be one of the most popular and successful pieces of literature published by the Health Education Authority. CAPT held the secretariat of a group that encouraged the formation of multidisciplinary local groups, but regrettably very few of these lasted any length of time.

In 1991 the BBC remade the series with a half-hour documentary and eight 10-minute programmes presented by Anneka Rice. It is hoped that the local groups to be formed on this occasion will be more effective and long-lasting, as a 2-year campaign has been mounted, supported by a multidisciplinary group (Action for Child Safety) under the wing of CAPT. A previous study of Approaches to Local Child Accident Prevention (ALCAP) together with a campaign pack and other support literature will help in the formation of the local groups and with ideas as to the approaches they might adopt.

That's Life (BBC) with Esther Rantzen has taken on issues concerning riding hats, playground safety, bicycle helmets, car safety seats and toy safety.

Watchdog (BBC) with Lynn Faulds Wood broaches issues such as home products, kitchen fittings, prams, playpens, toy safety, bicycle helmets, car safety seats and first-aid matters.

Top Gear (BBC) with William Woolard and Chris Goffey discussing aspects of car safety and road safety in general.

Current safety campaigns and measures

Britain has the best overall road safety record in the European Community in terms of road deaths per capita and per mile travelled. It has a better record for car users than for cyclists and pedestrians. However, the three main causes of death on the road have been identified as:

- Drink driving (a key factor in one-third of road deaths)
- Dangerous drivers (including excessive speeding)
- Dangerous motorcyclists

Overall, human error is responsible as the prime factor in 70 per cent of road deaths and a factor in 95 per cent.

The Government made a thorough review of road safety policy in 1987. A plan of action to reduce road casualties by a third by the year 2000 was the result of this survey into what would be realistic and practicable.

The review recognized that a number of measures contributed to the reductions made in casualty figures over the past 15–20 years. These included:

- Changes in personal behaviour and methods of travel
- Improvements in road design and structure
- Pedestrianization of town centres
- Improvements in road lighting
- Numerous low-cost engineering schemes
- Changes in traffic law
- Changes in education and driver and rider training

The Government decided to focus on three main areas:

- Raising public awareness that everyone has a responsibility for road safety
- Targeting the most vulnerable road users, i.e., children, the elderly, pedestrians, cyclists and motor cyclists
- Using proven cost-effective methods that can cut casualties by calculable amounts, especially in vehicle construction and road engineering

In these priorities the Government decided to pay attention to four sectors:

- The road
- The vehicle
- The driver
- The vulnerable road user

In a £12 billion road-building programme over the next 10 years the overall cost benefit analysis is expected to include savings on fatalities (at nearly £700 000/person) and injuries.

National and local governments may make moves to improve road safety. These ideas are often outlined in current government White Papers or framed in certain Acts or Regulations. Overall, a package of educational measures to increase knowledge and change attitudes and behaviour plus legislative changes, plus engineering measures all help to reduce accidents.

Specific improvements

There are even more areas that may not be immediately obvious, but where one or other agency may have some responsibilities. **British Summer Time**, for example, was discussed in a Government Green Paper that asked for views on changing summer time. Options were:

- Leave it as it is
- Alter the start and end dates to coincide with the majority of European countries
- Change to single summer time (Greenwich Mean Time + 1 hour) in the winter and double summer time (Greenwich Mean Time + 2 hours) in the summer

Reasons for extending summer time are based mainly on providing longer daylight hours in the evening for work and leisure. As far as safety is concerned this would also give more daylight hours in the evenings for children to get home safely.

It is estimated by the Transport and Road Research Laboratory that a change in British summer time would result in a net saving of 220–250 lives, 800–900 serious injuries and 1200 slight injuries each year in the United Kingdom. The reduction in evening-time accidents would be slightly offset by a possible increase in morning accidents. Overall, because more accidents happen on the way home in the evenings than on the way to school or work in the mornings the net result would be a reduction.

Overall 80 per cent of those responding to the Green Paper were in favour of changes to British summer time but the Government has not yet made any decision on any of the three options. The main objections to change come from people in Scotland where the changes would have a less beneficial effect.

Black spots In addition to large-scale schemes, the Government is keen to encourage low-cost remedial engineering measures at problem sites. Working closely with local authorities the Government aims to increase these cost effective schemes on local roads with the introduction of simple changes. Most highway authorities carry out Accident Investigation and Prevention (AIP) schemes that pick out accident 'black spots' where there are a high number of fatal or injury-producing accidents. These sites may be remedied by re-aligning or widening roads, building roundabouts or setting up other traffic control measures. Sometimes the simple introduction of new road signs or road markings, installation of traffic lights or changes in junction priorities are sufficient to notably improve accident figures

Traffic calming measures include the use of severe speed restrictions, for example, below 20mph and physical barriers and road humps (sleeping policemen). These will all aid to providing 'living streets' where pedestrians have rights as well as motorists. Proposals in this area have recently been put forward in a Department of Transport Paper *'Children and Roads: a safer way'*. The Traffic Calming Act 1992 will enable most of the measures to be introduced.

Speed Control is a concern of the Transport and Road Research Laboratory that monitors motorway speeds. Automatic counters have been installed at 25 motorway sites. These can measure vehicle speed and analyse types of vehicle, in order to monitor trends. On motorways many drivers exceed the 70mph limit (many cruise at average speeds closer to 80mph). The safety implications of this depend very much on road conditions. Fog, heavy rain, ice and volume of traffic can all exacerbate dangerous conditions and often call for speed limits well below the usual legal level.

A strong motorway lobby has been pressing for motorway speed limits to be raised to 80mph. The counter to this is that as an average speed limit on motorways is already some 10mph above the limit this would merely mean the average cruising speed rising to 90mph. The corresponding kinetic energy of impacts will therefore be that much greater in the event of the inevitable concertina collisions.

European initiatives include the European Community project 'Drive', which aims to create an integrated Pan-European road transport environment. Using electronic systems traffic will be better controlled and drivers will be better informed.

With the introduction of free trade in Europe efforts will centre towards harmonizing a single set of safety requirements for Europe.

The European Commission aims to standardize driving conditions by introducing:

- Uniform speed limits
- Licensing of minibus drivers
- Minimum tyre tread depth
- Setting a legal limit for drink/driving of 50 mg alcohol/100 ml blood
- Fitting and use of rear seat belts (front seat belts are already universally used)

Whilst supporting the aims of the Commission the British Government does not consider that detailed implementation of road safety law is within the

Commission's jurisdiction. However, Britain already complies with, or will soon do so, all the measures being suggested. It has one of the best records in the EC for doing this.

11

THE NEED FOR EVALUATION

Are our prevention activities really working?

In nearly all activities nowadays we need to evaluate performance and measure outcome, and nowhere more so than in childhood accident prevention. These accidents cost millions of pounds, and bring great hardship and suffering to parents and children. If we can show that there has been a real reduction in the numbers of accidents and in costs we have partially justified any investment. If we can show that the savings made are greater than the cost of the intervention measures then the activities are perfectly justified.

Of course it is seldom so simple. A change in accident rates or numbers may have already occurred when the intervention measures were introduced, perhaps due to other unrelated activities or many combined factors. This is why it is seldom possible to say that the introduction of a specific measure really has made a proven quantifiable difference. No wonder it is so easy for the critics to say 'let's spend all our money on treatment that we know works' – even if it doesn't! We must make the effort to evaluate our work even if at the end we can only say 'something must have happened because our numbers, rates and costs are falling'. Better still, of course, if we can point to a specific problem, introduce measures at a set time and measure a reduction in injuries thereafter. The introduction of compulsory usage of front seat belts in cars in the United Kingdom in February 1983 is one such example. This chapter outlines some of the areas in which evaluation may be made and describes some of the ways in which it may be achieved.

Costing an accident

The hard economic facts of running organizations, carrying out safety measures or educating others in safety matters do not allow for open-ended investment into safety. It is, therefore, essential to build in a cost benefit analysis into any safety programme.

In costing an accident there are many factors to consider: the initial cost of treatment for the injured person, the follow-up treatment, the care and any rehabilitation that may be necessary. In a fatal accident it may be possible to put a figure on the loss of life, as the Department of Transport can do for road traffic accidents, but this takes little account of the real loss to the person's family. Where a permanent disability results there may be regular long-term costs for on-going treatment. For these serious accidents there are costs for: the family travelling to visit the injured child; time off work for the parents; loss of schooling and reduction in employment potential for the future.

Many of these aspects are difficult if not impossible to cost, and the overall effect is therefore of much greater cost than that initially estimated. An examination of the overall costs of children's accidents by the treasurer of CAPT, John Whalley, should prove useful as a baseline for future evaluation of childhood accident prevention work.

Costs of road traffic accidents

The Department of Transport makes an annual estimate of the costs of road traffic accidents. In 1990 the estimated costs of road traffic accidents were:

	Per accident	Per casualty
Fatal accident	£742 840	£664 935
Serious injury accident	£25 930	£20 160
Slight injury accident	£2 440	£410

The total costs of road traffic accidents in the UK was estimated to be £6770 million for all accidents and £5330 million for injuries.

These figures for casualties apply to all ages and allow for 'lost output', ambulance costs, costs of treatment, damage to vehicles and property, police and insurance costs, and a notional cost of pain, grief and suffering. The costs of childhood road traffic accidents cannot be calculated in the same way as those for adults because they are not yet in employment. Nevertheless, using similar criteria the costs are very considerable.

Costs to a health region in the United Kingdom

A detailed study of the costs of childhood accidents in the West Midlands (comprising ten per cent of the population of the United Kingdom) in 1984, found that the total cost of these accidents to the National Health Service was approximately £10 million for just 1 year.

The study did not take account of the costs of ambulance services and long-term rehabilitation. It found the average cost of each accident to be just over £50 with road traffic accidents being twice as costly as any other form of accident. The average cost for a permanent disability was £8000.

Overall the study underestimated the true costs. It did not take full account of the long-term adverse effects of accidents and the lifetime of support and care required for some severely disabled people.

Cost effectiveness

A cost-effective programme is one in which the savings are greater than the cost of the intervention. Such an ideal is seldom achieved in practice because it is not usually possible to say that it was solely one programme that produced the beneficial results. Only by introducing alternative schemes or by having a control area with no alteration could one say that one scheme was better or worse than another.

The analysis becomes more complicated when consideration is given as to who is the beneficiary. The agency that puts the money into the programme will not necessarily be the one to gain the benefit. Small-cost engineering schemes, for example, to improve the road environment may be carried out by the local authority. The beneficiaries will be:

- The general public who pay taxes
- Some individuals who now avoid an accident at a particular black spot
- The police
- Ambulance services
- The hospitals
- Social services

None of these, except the general public will have put anything into the measures from which they benefit, but the investment will still have been worthwhile for the whole community.

Loss of life years

There are a number of ways in which to measure loss of life years. One is to count loss of **productive life years**, these being the years in which an average person may be expected to work, for example from 15 to 65 years of age. Another is to count the years lost up to the normal life expectancy, which varies from country to country. A simpler and more standard way to measure years of life lost is to take a cut-off point of 65 years of age for both males and females. The number of **life years lost** from 0–65, may be counted up for a given condition such as road traffic accidents or cancer or heart disease. It may then be aggregated as a total or as a rate per 10 000 people at risk. By using this formula the importance of a condition while taking relatively small amounts of life early on will become apparent in comparison with another condition which takes many lives but only in later life. The rate may be applied to all diseases, a particular disease, a whole country or region or a health district or a local authority area. When comparisons are made between total and rates of life years lost, accidents follow closely behind cancer and heart disease in total years lost. An improvement in the years of life lost rate over a period of time would be some indication of an improvement in loss of life, especially young life, during that period. It would need to be consistent and statistically significant to be confident that we were seeing a true fall in loss of life years.

In addition to measurement of numbers of deaths and death rates due to various conditions there is the use of Standardized Mortality Ratios (SMR). Years of life lost are regularly being used by public health physicians as one of the ways of measuring outcome. The Chief Medical Officer in his annual report on the state of health of the nation and the directors of public health in their annual reports are now beginning to include these measures for comparisons of health status. The public health common data set produced by the University of Surrey is a standard reference source for this data. It shows, for example, that the highest SMRs for road traffic accidents in England and Wales are in a band stretching across from the West Midlands to East Anglia. The highest rates for years of life lost due to road traffic accidents are to be found in the socially-deprived parts of the northern industrial cities. The first is due to higher losses among teenagers and young people on roads with fast-moving traffic. The latter is because of young child pedestrians and cyclists being knocked down in inner cities.

It cannot be allowed to pass without notice that conditions like cancer and heart disease, which are common in later life, attract far greater investment into methods for treatment and prevention than accidents that mainly affect the young. Yet the potential for a cost benefit gain must be far greater for accident prevention than for any other condition.

Education programmes

Sometimes educational programmes are shown to be ineffective, or at best only marginally effective, and thought to be unworthy of investment. In some cases a strict evaluation will show that specific target groups exist for whom well-researched and quite specific intervention programmes may work. Even here there may be problems because the group most in need is the very one with the least background knowledge, the most permissive attitudes and the greatest unwillingness to change its behaviour.

Criticism has been made in the past that educational programmes cannot prove their effectiveness. Some examples of specific programmes are given in Chapter 9.

It is true, however, that over the years, parents and children around the world have become much more aware of the hazards of their every day environment. In most developed countries, where the standards of education are relatively high and all parents and children are exposed to some understanding of accident prevention, accident rates are falling. There are some notable exceptions in some countries, such as pedestrian and cycling accidents, in which this may not be so. There are also always epidemics of accidents because of the introduction of some new craze or product. Part of the credit for this steady reduction in accidents must go to the dedicated parents and teachers in homes, clinics and schools who have endeavoured over the years to relay the important accident prevention messages. Part must also go to changes in the environment and to changes introduced by legislation and regulations and improvements in product safety.

Redesigning and modifying educational programmes

After evaluation of the effectiveness of prevention programmes it will be necessary to modify and re-adjust the educational message to further improve the programme. The problem itself may also change – new hazards may emerge, new attitudes arise and new approaches develop. These changes may all lead to a need to modify the accident prevention programme.

In addition, once an evaluation has been made it is most important to discard measures that have been proved to be of little or no benefit. It is also necessary to modify other measures in order to make them more effective. However, great care is needed before totally discarding a measure. It may not have resulted in a decrease in accidents or rates but it could well have been responsible for halting an increase. This in itself is a benefit.

Changes in knowledge, attitudes and behaviour

An ideal safety educational programme is one in which everyone knows all the risks, has developed the 'right' attitude towards these risks and behaves in a way that minimizes these risks. No such programme exists but we can go a long way towards it. Life-style questionnaires have now been developed that accurately measure the knowledge of children and mothers relating to safety. Survey techniques that are well within the range of modern psychology can test children's attitudes and aptitudes. Much more difficult is the ability to measure changes directly resulting from the educational process. It is relatively easy to say that children do know more about the hazards, are exposed to less hazards and do take less risks but much more difficult to say whether they learned this from their peers, at school or through the educational process.

The final stage of the whole accident prevention process is evaluation. This is best done by measuring the number, severity and outcome of the accidents in question. Measurements can also be made of the level of interest and knowledge shown in the problem before and after any educational campaigns are carried out. Indirect measurements such as the numbers of a particular type of safety device (e.g., fireguards, car safety seats) sold may also be used as an index.

The cost effectiveness and cost benefit of interventions should be assessed as far as possible. The need to measure the severity, size and outcome of accidents and injuries brings into focus the need to collect data and to disseminate the information accurately and efficiently.

12

WHERE DO WE GO FROM HERE?

A summary of ideas and recommendations for future action.

During this century remarkable progress has been made in reducing many types of children's accidents. In contrast there has been only moderate progress in a number of other areas where improvement might have been expected. In this chapter we pull together our ideas on future developments.

In Britain we have seen a reduction in:

- Poisonings – through the use of child-resistant containers
- Burns – some types in particular following the introduction of inflammable night clothing
- Pedestrian accidents – although there is still a long way to go
- Drownings

In the case of poisonings and burns it was possible to reduce injuries through the introduction of one specific measure, backed up by legislation. In the cases of pedestrian accidents and drownings many factors relating to the environment and human behaviour made it possible to reduce accidents effectively.

The challenges during the remaining years of this century and the early years of the next will be:

- To define precisely why certain accidents persist
- To determine the cause of the accidents
- To find measures of prevention or reduction of their severity

A programme of action

There are a number of key general areas in which improvements can and should be made. These include:

- Data collection and analysis

- Setting of realistic targets and programmes
- Interdisciplinary cooperation and liaison
- Evaluation of the effectiveness of these activities

In addition, there are a large number of specific activities within the various preventive programmes that have considerable potential for achieving improvements in the future. These may be broadly grouped into:

- Education
- Environment
- Legislation (including product safety)

Education

There has been a great deal of activity in the field of education in recent years and this has clearly been very necessary. It is vital to continue this work, yet much of the evaluation that has been carried out has not been able to prove consistent and persistent changes in attitudes and behaviour because of education. We would welcome some further evidence of the effectiveness of education to give greater credibility to the many programmes that are being carried out by dedicated workers around the country.

Teaching the teachers and community leaders

Future educational efforts should be directed towards professionals as well as the children themselves and their parents.

There is a need for architects, builders, town planners and designers as well as teachers, health professionals and social workers to take a greater interest in and responsibility for child safety. Members of Parliament, local councillors, Members of District Health Authorities and the National Health Service Trusts, school governors and Parent Teacher Associations (PTAs) should also become more involved.

If we were to see a firm commitment from these policy and decision makers, we could confidently predict further reductions in accidents of many types.

Active participation by health staff

Medical staff and nursing staff, especially those involved in caring for children, in trauma and community nursing, are taking an increasingly active role in educating parents and their professional colleagues. They will need to play a much greater part in the future in local and national political arenas, lobbying and pressing for reforms and improvements where these are necessary.

Choosing the best methods

Choosing the technique most effectively suited to presenting information is always difficult. It is vital to get it right. In the field of safety education and accident prevention there is still room for improvement. There is a need for a systematic study of methods used and a need for a complete review in order to change attitudes, improve knowledge and change behaviour. Many people still do not see accidents as a problem or of any relevance to them. Work undertaken for the Child Accident Prevention Trust and the Health Education Authority by Pam Laidman showed that mothers develop psychological defence mechanisms against accepting accidents as a problem. They also have a reluctance to act on professional advice.

Still further improvements are needed in presenting material to both parents and children. A wider use of the techniques used by advertisers and on television by presenters is needed to get the attention of parents and children.

Training

The effectiveness of training for specific tasks needs to be more clearly demonstrated. In the past critical evaluation of some cycle and motorcycle training schemes has produced equivocal results. Some studies have even suggested that training results in increased confidence (but not necessarily competence). This results in increased activity and consequently in increased accident figures. Yet, a thorough grounding in the basic techniques in, for example, riding a bicycle or a horse, is necessary before facing the complex hazards of the road environment. Efforts made at training are to be applauded, but we must examine how they can be more reliably directed towards ensuring the aquisition of genuine survival skills.

In future years it may even be necessary to restrict children of certain ages from access to the road on bicycles, for example. Children need to reach a certain level of maturity before they can even begin to cope with the complex environment of a road. In some northern European countries children cannot go on the road at all, even accompanied, until the age of 7 or 8 years of age, and unaccompanied until the age of 12 years.

Schools programmes

Every school must adopt a **Planned Programme of Education for Health** that includes life and survival skills. Every school leaver should be versed and practised in all the basics of first aid, including resuscitation (as in Norway and Russia). They should also be able to swim and rescue others in the water and be aware of the hazards of the environment including the home and the road. They should know what precautions or remedies to take to survive these hazards. In due course we will also have educated the next generation of parents.

Dangerous sports

The increase in some sporting and recreational accidents should be viewed with some concern. We would not wish to overprotect young people or to ban sports. Yet sports where aggression is deliberate and encouraged would not seem to be appropriate for children in whom the potential for injury is unnecessarily high. Boxing must be included in this category because even for young amateurs the aim is to inflict injury directly on ones opponent. Rugby football could also fall into this category unless it is controlled and refereed properly and effectively. It is certainly one of the most violent forms of contact sport and great care needs to be taken to control unnecessary aggression and violence. Clearly international players need to set young viewers a good example!

Other dangerous leisure activities include horse riding and mini-motorcycling. In both of these the aim must be to avoid children participating at ages when they have neither the skill nor the coordination to participate safely, and to use safety equipment (particularly protective head gear) when appropriate.

Canoeing, hang-gliding and mountaineering all involve children taking part in activities for which they may not be properly trained or sufficiently experienced to do so safely. Care must be taken to see that adequate supervision and support is available.

Trainers, coaches, teachers and parents have considerable responsibility for teaching children to play the games fairly and safely, to control aggression and to take reasonable precautions to avoid injury to themselves and other players.

The environment

Within the scope of the natural and man-made environment there are many areas for improvement. We would not wish to make significant alterations to our natural environment but certain hazards that have been shown, by local studies, to be harmful to children can be removed or fenced off. It is with the man-made environment, however, that the greatest potential for improvement exists.

Towns and residential areas

In the wider urban scene we need to re-think the whole urban environment. Major urban planning has in the past been dominated by transport needs and those of the motor car, in particular. We now need to develop much more 'user friendly' environments where a more satisfactory balance can be achieved between the needs of the motor car and its driver and the needs of others in the environment.

The Dutch 'Woonerf' – or 'living street', where people and traffic can mix without a serious threat from the traffic in visually attractive surroundings is certainly a step in the right direction.

Another recent development has been the World Health Organization's Healthy Cities project in which individual cities invite a multidisciplinary group to improve the overall health of its citizens and of the environment in which they live; this naturally includes accident prevention. Some cities have included the reduction of children's accidents as a major component in their programme.

Within residential areas the special needs of children need to be considered to a much greater extent. Outside the home the need for attractive and stimulating play areas are required, which are appropriate in character to the developmental level of the children using them. These should be as far away as possible from major traffic risks. There should also be pedestrian or cyclist-only areas.

The home

Within the home, children's needs also tend to be overlooked by those responsible for designing the environment in which they live. Architects and home builders must be encouraged to remember that children will live in the houses and they should ensure that kitchens, for example, are ergonomically designed to suit the needs of the adult using them and the safety requirements of children in the home. Potentially dangerous stairs, balconies, windows, glass doors and other home hazards should not be incorporated into homes designed for families with young children.

Cars

Further improvements needs to be made in interior design and layout of equipment, seating arrangements and the provision of safety restraints and devices; the exterior of new cars still needs to be more pedestrian-friendly and the shell of the car should be stronger to give better protection to the occupants. Serious consideration must be given to stricter controls on speed limits of cars, motorcycles and lorries. If drivers cannot keep within the law willingly then mechanical means may be necessary, perhaps in the form of governors on all vehicles likely to be driven at excessive speeds.

A further extension of the seat-belt law is needed to ensure ultimately that all passengers and drivers are strapped into all vehicles for all journeys. Available child safety devices have improved vastly in recent years both in terms of the types of restraint available and in the ease of use. These must now be available to all parents at a reasonable cost, with complete ease of use and fitting, to suit the ages or weights of all babies and young children in order to encourage maximum use of them. Finally, consideration should be given to the wider use of airbags, which are particularly effective in preventing facial and head injuries caused by hitting the steering wheel.

Legislation

Product safety

We would like to see greater recognition by designers, manufacturers, importers and retailers of the importance of the safety aspects of all products. It is better to include safety considerations at the design stage than to have to add them as as afterthought. Products designed especially for children, nursery furniture, toys etc., should have safety as a major feature, but other products with which children come into contact should also be considered for safety at an early stage. Safety standards, British, European and others, have important roles to play. In addition, we welcome the new legislation in the form of a General Safety Duty that puts an onus on all manufacturers to show that their products are safe. In spite of this progress we still consider it necessary to maintain continued vigilance over all new products. New and sometimes gimmicky toys are constantly coming onto the market, presenting new hazards. These are mainly imported and are usually very quickly identified as dangerous by parents or Trading Standards Officers. They do occasionally slip through the net and tragedies can happen. Sometimes goods are illegally imported or are sold illicitly especially on street stalls or Sunday market-type outlets. With the new proposed legislation liaison between Customs Officials and Trading Standards Officers should improve and make it easier for Trading Standards Officers to take preventive action with dangerous products.

Much has been done to improve product safety, for example safer designs of kettles and irons, and yet these new designs are still not widely used.

Playgrounds

New playgrounds should all be built with careful consideration in relation to housing and other amenities. Safe-play equipment should be routinely used with a maximum free-fall height of 2.5 m. Safe, soft landing surfaces should be used under all equipment. Overall the layout of playgrounds should take account of the natural movement of children within them.

On housing estates mini-playgrounds should be strategically placed amongst homes where parents can easily watch their children. Larger playgrounds should be placed within safe, easy access of all large housing developments so that children do not have to cross busy roads to use them.

Schemes currently underway in Newcastle-upon-Tyne and parts of London following the example of Scandinavian countries have much to commend them. These factors can all contribute to making the urban environment a pleasant and safe place for all to live in.

Housing

Modern house designs have improved in recent years but there is still a lot to be done. Every home should have smoke detectors; safety glass fitted in all doors and patio windows; stairs should be covered in and not open-plan; fitted lockable medicine cabinets should be available; window locks should be fitted; and oven guards provided.

Some of the less serious but still important modifications include:

- Bannisters with vertical railings and a miniature grippable handrail for children
- Balconies with vertical railings and lockable access doors
- Circuit breakers on electrical fittings
- Residual current devices in power point circuits

Other desirable features are listed in the Child Accident Prevention Trust Guidelines on Child Safety and Housing (see Bibliography). Further safety devices are also listed in the Consumers Guide to Child Safety Equipment. Even taking into account all the possible improvements, young children will still fall from bunk-beds and down stairs. Hopefully their falls will not be so frequent or so severe if the recommended improvements are all implemented. Building regulations that relate to these safety features also need to be more clearly defined and enforced.

In the gardens of private homes we would like to see toddler-proof street gates and adequately fenced ponds and swimming pools. In countries such as the United States and Australia the warmer weather conditions mean that swimming pools are used at home and drowning is more common. Simple precautions such as adequate fencing may save toddlers' lives.

Toys and safety equipment

Children's toys and safety equipment need regular updating. New safety equipment in particular such as car safety seats and crash helmets always require careful development. The ultimate in car safety or in bicycle design has still not been reached in the United Kingdom. There is still great scope for improvement of cycle crash helmets and in riding hats. There is also work to be done in making cyclists and motorcyclists more conspicuous on the roads either by building in lighting systems to vehicles, by attaching bright objects to the vehicles or by improving rider conspicuity. These are all relatively simple life-saving measures.

Role of designers

Designers, manufacturers and traders need to become more aware of the potential hazards of their products. The potential for law suits or litigation under product liability is a deterrent but it does not entirely remove the prospects for further dangerous products to get onto the market.

Even items that are inherently sound may be misused or used other than for the purpose or age group intended, and this could render them dangerous. Here the onus is on the user not the trader but those selling or demonstrating their products are still responsible for making sure that the purchaser understands fully how to use the item.

A special case for children is for equipment such as cots and car seats that need to be designed exclusively for children of a particular age and stage of development. There is a need for anthropometric studies to find out more about sizes of, for example, children's fingers, heads and gullets. Ergonomic studies could then use this information to work out the best designs to suit children and their parents, bearing safety in mind.

Road safety

Many aspects of road-safety legislation have an effect on childhood road traffic accidents. In addition to the seat-belt legislation directed towards reducing injury severity, there are many laws that directly relate to the reduction of accidents.

Some of these laws are not fully effective because they are abused or not fully enforced. We would like to see a number of improvements that we consider could make a major contribution to reducing accidents. Some require national parliamentary changes but others are best dealt with at local bye-law level. The laws that would be particularly useful by being more rigorously enforced include drink driving, speed limits and dangerous driving. Laws that might be changed to good effect include extension of speed limits in built-up areas and reduction of speeds in exclusively residential areas and near to schools. Tougher learner requirements for young drivers and riders would not only protect them from serious injury but would also protect large numbers of child pedestrians and cyclists too. Finally serious consideration should be given to the compulsory wearing of cycle helmets as in parts of Australia.

Setting targets

Targets need to be set for improvements, not purely for their own sake but in order to set realistic goals and to measure achievement. If nothing is being achieved the measure may need to be dropped or modified. The fact that there is no further reduction is not in itself a measure of failure. It may be necessary to keep up the pressure (as in immunization programmes) in order to maintain the *status quo*.

More important, is the selection of target groups. Children in tenement housing, for example, are much more at risk from fires and falls from windows than most other children. Toddlers living on busy residential roads are at high risk of being hit by cars. The remedies for these groups rest not purely in accident prevention but also in social and environmental reforms, full employment, living wages, education and many other factors for which political and social action is required.

There are numerous other examples of groups who have specific problems for whom specific programmes should be directed, for example, home accidents for babies and toddlers, and sports and leisure safety for teenagers.

Initiatives for the 1990s

In its Alma Ata declaration in 1977, the World Health Organization (WHO) put forward the goal of 'Health for All by the year 2000', and in 1985 the European Office published its 'Targets for Health for All'. Target 11 is

'By the year 2000, deaths from accidents in the (European) region should be reduced by at least 25 per cent through an intensified effort to reduce traffic, home and occupational accidents.'

This has been a valuable stimulus to the various countries' accidents prevention programmes.

The United Kingdom government now has an ideal opportunity to influence accident prevention activities under the terms of the White Paper published in July 1992. In it the government has made a commitment to achieving better health for everyone in England (separate plans have been made in Northern Ireland, Scotland and Wales). The government outlines ways of improving health and sets out specific targets for health gain in five Key Areas. These are:

- Coronary heart diseases/stroke
- Cancers
- Mental illness
- Accident prevention
- HIV/AIDS/sexual health

This is the first time that any health gain targets have been set in England and the first time that accidents have been given such a high priority by the government.

The specific targets that have been set for children's accident reduction by the year 2005 are:

Reductions in death rates for:

- Children aged under 15 years by at least 33 per cent   } from the base
- Young people aged 15–24 by at least 25 per cent   } rates for 1990

We have been impressed by the progress in recent years but still feel there is so much to be done. We look forward to the much wider application of methods already proven and to other methods still only experimental but which promise much for the future. We do not consider it entirely unrealistic to look for a halving of the death rate by the end of the century, and to expect to see marked reductions in serious injuries and disabilities.

The knowledge of how to do it is already with us – now we need to put it all into practice.

USEFUL ADDRESSES

Action for Child Safety
BP Charity Base, The Chandlery, 50 Westminster Bridge Road, London, SE1 7QY.

Action for Sick Children (formerly NAWCH)
29–31 Euston Road, London, NW1 2SD.

Advertising Standards Authority (ASA)
Dept X, Brook House, Torrington Place, London, WC1E 7HN.

Alcohol Concern
305 Gray's Inn Road, London, WC7X 8QF.

Association for Consumer Research (Formerly Consumers Association)
2 Marylebone Road, London, NW1 4LB.

Association of Chief Police Officers
Room 311 Wellington House, 67–73 Buckingham Gate, London, SW1E 6BE.

BBC TV
London, W12 7RJ.

British Association for Accident and Emergency Medicine
c/o Royal College of Surgeons, 35-43 Lincoln's Inn Fields, London, WC2A 3PN.

British Association of Paediatric Surgeons
Royal College of Surgeons of Edinburgh, Nicolson Street, Edinburgh, EH8 9DW.

British Horse Society
Stoneleigh Park, Kenilworth, Warwickshire, CV8 2LR.

British Medical Journal (BMJ)
PO Box 295, London, WC1N 9TE.

British Paediatric Accident and Emergency Group
c/o Dr J Robson, Alder Hey Children's Hospital, Liverpool, L12 2AP.

British Paediatric Association (BPA)
5 St Andrews Place, London, NW1 4LB.

British Red Cross Society
9 Grosvenor Crescent, London, SW1X 7EJ.

British Standards Institute (BSI)
2 Park Street, London, W1A 2BS.

British Toy and Hobby Manufacturers Association
80 Camberwell Road, London, SE5 0EG.

British Waterways Board
Melbury House, Melbury Terrace, London, NW1 6JX.

Building Research Establishment
Building Research Station, Garston, Watford, Hertfordshire, WD2 7JR.

Campaign for Lead-free Air (CLEAR)
2 Northdown Street, London, N1 9BG.

Centre for Ethnic Minority Health Studies
Field House Teaching Centre, Duckmill Lane, Bradford, BD9 6RE.

Chief and Assistant Chief Fire Officers Association
10–11 Pebble Close, Amington, Tamworth, Staffordshire, B77 4RD.

Child Accident Prevention Trust (CAPT)
4th Floor, Clerk's Court, 18–20 Farringdon Lane, London, EC1R 3AU

Childline
Freepost 1111, London, EC4B 4BB.

Child Poverty Action Group
1–5 Bath Street, London, EC1V 9PY

Children Legal Centre
20 Compton Terrace, London, N1 2UN

Commission for Racial Equality
10–12 Allington Street, London, SW1E 5EH.

Community Education Development Centre
Lyng Hall, Blackberry Lane, Coventry.

Cot Death Research and Support for Bereaved Parents
8A Alexandra Parade, Weston-super-Mare, Avon, BS23 1TQ.

CRUSE
Cruse House, 126 Sheen Road, Richmond, Surrey, TW9 1UR.

Department of Health
Children's Division, Alexander Fleming House, Elephant and Castle, London, SE1 6BY.

Department of Trade and Industry
Consumer Safety Unit, 10–18 Victoria Street, London, SW1H 0NN.

Department of Transport
Road Safety Division, Room C17/08, 2 Marsham Street, London, SW1P 3EB.

Early Learning Centre
South Marston, Swindon, SN3 4TJ.

Electricity Council
30 Millbank, London, SW1P 4RD.

Faculty of Public Health Medicine
4 St Andrew's Place, London, NW1.

Fair Play for Children
137 Homerton High Street, London, E9.

Fire Protection Association
140 Aldergate Street, London, EC1A 4HX.

Fire Research Station
Melrose Avenue, Borehamwood, Hertfordshire, WD6 2BL.

Firework Makers' Guild
PO Box 29, Hove, East Sussex, BN3 5RP.

Foundation for the Study of Infant Deaths
35 Belgrave Square, London, SW1.

Friends of the Earth (FOE)
377 City Road, London, EC1V 1NA.

Glass and Glazing Federation
6 Mount Row, London, W1Y 6DY.

Health and Safety Executive (HSE)
Baynards House, 1 Chepstow Place, London, W2 4TF.

Health Education Authority (HEA)
Hamilton House, Mabledon Place, London, WC1H 9TX.

Health Education Board for Scotland (HEBS)
Health Education Centre, Woodburn House, Canaan Lane, Edinburgh, EH10 4SG.

Health Promotion Authority for Wales
8th Floor, 2 Fitzalan Road, Cardiff, CF2 1EB.

Health Service Economic Research Unit
University of York, York.

Health Visitors Association
50 Southwark Street, London, SE1 1UM.

HM Agricultural Inspectorate
St Hugh's House, Stanley Precinct, Bootle, Merseyside, L20 3QY.

Institute of Consumer Ergonomics
75 Swingbridge Road, Loughborough, Leicestershire, LE11 0JB.

Institute of Home Safety
132 North Road, Dartford, DA1 3NB.

Institute of Road Safety Officers
31 Heather Grove, Hollingsworth, Hyde, Cheshire, SK14 8JC.

Institute of Trading Standards Administration
4/5 Hadleigh Business Centre, 351 London Road, Hadleigh, Essex, SS7 2BT.

Institution of Environmental Health Officers
Chadwick House, Rushworth Street, London, SE1 0QT.

Low Pay Unit
9 Upper Berkeley Street, London, W1H 8BY.

Medical Commission on Accident Prevention (MCAP)
c/o Royal College of Surgeons of England, 35–43 Lincoln's Inn Fields, London, WC2A 3PN.

Mobility and Vehicle Information Service (MAVIS)
c/o Transport Research Laboratory, Old Wokingham Road, Crowthorne, Berkshire, RG11 6AH.

Mothercare (United Kingdom) Ltd
Cherry Tree Road, Watford, Hertfordshire, WD2 5SH.

National Association of Health Authorities and Trusts (NAHT)
Birmingham Research Park, Vincent Drive, Birmingham, B15 2SQ.

National Association of Young People's Counselling and Advisory Service (NAYPCAS)
17/23 Albion Street, Leicester, LE1 6GD.

National Campaign for Firework Reform
118 Long Acre, London, WC2E 9PA.

National Children's Bureau (NCB)
8 Wakley Street, Islington, London, EC1V 7QE.

National Children's Homes
85 Highbury Park, London, N5 1UD.

National Children's Play and Recreation Unit
359–361 Euston Road, London, NW1 3AL.

National Council for One Parent Families
255 Kentish Town Road, London, NW5 2LY.

National Council for Schools' Sports
Staddlestones, 1 Peartree Road, Herne, Kent, CT6 7EE.

National Curriculum Council
15–17 New Street, York, YO1 2RA.

National House Builders Federation (now Building Employers Federation)
82 New Cavendish Street, London, W1M 8AD.

National Playing Fields Association
25 Ovington Square, London, SW3.

National Poisons Information Service
(These addresses are for the use of health professionals only – not the general public)

1   New Cross Hospital, Avonley Road, London, SE14 5ER.
2   The Royal Infirmary, Lauriston Place, Edinburgh, E3.
3   Royal Victoria Hospital, Grosvenor Road, Belfast, B12 6BB.
4   Jervis Street Hospital, Dublin 1.
5   Ambulance Headquarters, Old Ty-Bronna, Fairwater Road, Fairwater, Cardiff, CF5 3XP.

National Society for the Prevention of Cruelty to Children (NSPCC)
67 Saffron Hill, London, EC1N 8RS

National Voluntary Council for Children's Play
c/o National Children's Bureau, 8 Wakley Street, Islington, London, EC1V 7QC.

Northern Ireland Office: Department of Health and Social Services
Dundonald House, Upper Newtonards Road,
Belfast, BT4 3SF.

Office of Population, Censuses and Surveys
St Catherine's House, 10 Kingsway, London, WC2B 6JP.

Parliamentary Advisory Council on Transport Safety (PACTS)
c/o St Thomas' Hospital, Lambeth Palace Road, London, SE1 7EH.

Pedestrians Association
1 Wandsworth Road, London, SW8 2LJ.

Policy Studies Institute
100 Park Village East, London, NW1 3SR.

Pre-School Playgroups Association
61–63 Kings Cross Road, London, WC1X 9LL.

Public Health Alliance
Room 204, Snow Hill House, 10–15 Livery Street, Birmingham, B3 2NU.

Resuscitation Council (United Kingdom)
Department of Anaesthetics, Royal Postgraduate Medical School, Du Cane
Road, London, W12 0HS.

Royal Institute of British Architects (RIBA)
66 Portland Place, London, W1N 4AD.

Royal Life Saving Society
Mountbatten House, Studley, Warwickshire, B80 7NN.

Royal Society for the Prevention of Accidents (RoSPA) (England and Wales)
Cannon House, The Priory Queensway, Birmingham, B4 6BS.

Royal Society for the Prevention of Accidents (Scotland)
Slateford House, Lanark Road, Edinburgh, EH14 1TL.

Royal Society for the Prevention of Accidents (Northern Ireland)
117 Lisburn Road, Belfast, BT9 7BS.

Royal Society of Medicine
1 Wimpole Street, London, W1M 8AE.

Scottish Home and Health Department
New St Andrew's House, Regent Road, Edinburgh, EH1 3OE.

Socialist Health Association
195 Walworth Road, London, SE17 1RP.

Sports Council
16 Upper Woburn Place, London, WC1H 0QP.

St Andrew's Ambulance Association
St Andrew's House, Milton Street, Glasgow, G4 0HR.

St John Ambulance Association
1 Grosvenor Crescent, London, SW1X 7EF,
and
Supplies Department, Priory House, St John's Lane, London, EC2M 4DA.

Standing Conference on Drug Abuse
1–4 Hatton Place, Hatton Gardens, London, EC1N 8NO.

Training in Health and Race
18 Victoria Park Square, Bethnal Green, London, E2 9PF.

Transport 2000
Walkden House, 10 Melton Street, London, NW1 2EJ.

Transport Research Laboratory (TRL)
Old Wokingham Road, Crowthorne, Berkshire, RG1 6AU.

UK Health for All Network
PO Box 101, Liverpool, L69 5BE.

UNICEF
United Kingdom Committee for UNICEF, 55 Lincolns Inn Fields, London, WC2A 3NB.

Welsh Office
Cathays Park, Cardiff, CF1 3NQ

INTERNATIONAL

Center for Disease Control (CDC)
Division of Injury, 1600 Clifton Road NE, Atlanta, Georgia GA 30333, United States of America.

Centre Internationale de l'enfance
Chateau de Longchamp, Bois de Boulogne, 75616, Paris, France.

Child Accident Prevention Foundation of Australia (CAPFA)
3/26 Liverpool Street, Melbourne, Victoria 3000, Australia.

Child Accident Prevention Foundation of New Zealand
PO Box 6101, Dunedin, New Zealand.

Children's Hospitals Injury Reporting and Prevention Program (CHIRPP)
Childhood Diseases and Injury Section, Room 602, Brooke-Claxton Building, Tunney's Pasture, Ottowa, Canada, K1A OK9.

European Consumer Safety Association (ECOSA)
c/o Consumer Safety Institute, Hobbemastraat 22, P O Box 75169, NL-1007 AD, Amsterdam, Netherlands.

Institut National de la Sante et de Recherche Medicale (INSERM)
U 149, 123 Boulevard de Port Royal, 75014 Paris, France.

Insurance Institute for Highway Safety
1005 North Glebe Road, Arlington, Virginia 22201, United States of America.

National Institute of Child Health and Human Development
9000 Rockville Pike, EPN Room 633, Bethesda, Maryland 20895, United States of America.

National Safe Kids Campaign
Children's National Medical Center, Michigan Avenue NW, Washington DC, 20010-2970, United States of America.

Royal New Zealand Plunkett Society
PO Box 642, Dunedin North, New Zealand.

Swedish National Child Environment Council
PO Box 22106, S-104 22 Stockholm, Sweden.

World Health Organization
Regional Office for Europe, Scherfigsvej 8, 2100 Copenhagen O, Denmark.

BIBLIOGRAPHY

Books and publications on general health and child health

Black J. *Child health in multicultural society* (2nd edn). London: British Medical Journal Publications, 1990.

Butler NR *et al*. *Britain's Five Year Olds*. London: Routledge and Kegan Paul, 1980.

Carstairs V, Morris R. *Deprivation and Health in Scotland*. Aberdeen: Aberdeen University Press, 1991.

Department of Education and Science. *The Health of the School Child 1966–1968*. London: HMSO, 1969.

Department of Health and Social Security (now Department of Health). *Fit for the Future* (Report of the committee on Child Health Services [The Court Report]). London: HMSO, 1976.

Department of Health and Social Security (now Department of Health)/OPCS. *Hospital In-Patient Enquiry (Table 14) 1965–85*. London: HMSO, 1987.

Department of Health. *Promoting Better Health – The Government's programme for improving primary health care* (CM 249). London: HMSO, 1987.

Department of Health. *Public health in England* (Acheson Report) CM289. London: HMSO, 1988.

Department of Health. *The health of the nation* (CM 1523). London: HMSO, 1990.

Department of Health. *The Health of the Nation; A Strategy for Health in England* (Cm 1986). London; HMSO, 1992.

Department of Health. *Working for patients*. London: HMSO, 1989.

Faculty of Community Medicine (now Faculty of Public Health Medicine). *Health for All by the year 2000. A management action pack*. London: Faculty of Community Medicine, 1986.

Faculty of Public Health Medicine. *Health Measurement Toolbox* (3rd edn). London: FPHM, 1991.

Faculty of Public Health Medicine. *UK levels of health*. London: Faculty of Public Health Medicine, 1991.

Hartunian NS, Smart CN, Thompson MS. *The incidence and economic cost of major health impairments: a comparative analysis of cancer, motor vehicle injuries, coronary heart disease and stroke.* Arlington, VA: Lexington Books, 1986.

Illingworth RS. *The normal child* (9th edn). London: Churchill Livingstone, 1987.

Kellmer Pringle M. *A fairer future for children.* London: Macmillan, 1980.

Kellmer Pringle M. *The needs of children* (3rd edn). London: Hutchinson, 1986.

Linthwaite P. *The health of travelling mothers and children in East Anglia.* London: Save the Children Fund, 1983.

Littlewood J, Tinker A. *Families in Flats.* London: HMSO, 1981.

Lowry S. *Housing and health.* London: British Medical Journal Publications, 1991.

Mares P, Henley A, Baxter C. *Health care and multi-racial Britain.* London: Health Education Council/National Extension College, 1985.

Medical Officers of Schools Association. *Handbook of school health* (16th edn). Lancaster: MTP Press, 1984.

Miller FJW, Court SDM, Knox EG, Brandon S. *The School years in Newcastle-upon-Tyne.* London: Oxford University Press, 1974.

Myers N (Ed). *The Gaia Atlas of Planet Management.* London: Pan Books, 1985.

National Children's Home. *Children in danger.* London: National Children's Home, 1988.

Office of Population, Censuses and Surveys. *Occupational Mortality 1970–1972* (Series DS no 1). London: HMSO, 1976.

Royal College of Physicians. *Preventive Medicine.* London: Royal College of Physicians, 1991.

Townsend A, Davidson N. *Inequalities in Health* (The Black Report). London: Penguin Books, 1982.

Willis M, McLachlan ME. *Medical Care in Schools.* London: Edward Arnold 1977.

World Health Organization. *Targets for health for all.* Geneva: WHO Publications, 1988.

Books and publications on general safety and accident prevention

Berfenstam R, Jackson RH, Eriksson B. *The Healthy Community. Child Safety as part of Health Promotion Activities.* Stockholm: Folksam Insurance Group, 1988.

Cliff KS. *Accidents: causes, prevention and services.* London: Croom Helm, 1984.

Department of Health. *Strategies for accident prevention* (Report of a colloquium of the Medical Royal Colleges of the UK). London: HMSO, 1988.

Gardner AW, Roylance PJ. *New Essential First Aid*. London: Pan Books, 1967.

Henry J, Volans G. ABC of poisoning. Part 1 Drugs. *Br Med J*. 1984; **289**: 20 articles.

National Association of Health Authorities/Royal Society for the Prevention of Accidents. *Action on accidents – the unique role of the health service*. Birmingham/London: NAHA/RoSPA, 1990.

National Maternal and Child Health Clearing House, Washington, DC. *US Injury Prevention: Meeting the Challenge*. Oxford: Oxford University Press, 1989.

Royal College of Surgeons. *Accident prevention: a social responsibility*. London: Royal College of Surgeons, 1989.

Royal College of Surgeons of England. *The management of patients with major injuries* (Irving Report). London: Royal College of Surgeons, 1988.

Spence MJ, Redmond AD, Edwards JD. *Trauma Audit – the use of TRISS*. *Health Trends*. 1988; **3**(20): 94–7.

St John's Ambulance Association. *The Essentials of First Aid* (3rd edn). London: Dorling Kindersley, 1983.

St John's Ambulance Association, The British Red Cross Society. *First Aid Manual* (5th edn). London: Dorling Kindersley, 1987.

Stanway A. *Family First Aid and Emergency Handbook*. London: Rainbird for Boots, 1980.

Trinca GW, *et al. Reducing traffic injury – a global challenge*. Royal Australian College of Surgeons, 1988.

Books and publications on child safety and accident prevention

Alpert JJ, Guyer B (Eds). Injuries and Injury Prevention. *Paediatr Clin North Am*. 1986; **32**(1): 1–270.

Asher J. *Keep your Baby Safe*. London: Penguin, 1988.

Baker SP. Childhood Injuries: the community approach to prevention. *J Pub Hlth Policy*. 1988; 2.3.

Berfenstam R, Gustafson LH, Peterson O (Eds). *Prevention of Accidents in Childhood*. Sweden: Uppsala University, 1977.

Bowman JA, Sanson-Fisher RW, Webb GR. Intervention in Pre-schools to increase their use of safety restraints by pre-school children. *Pediatrics*. 1987; **79**: 103–9.

Child Accident Prevention Trust. *Basic Principles of Accident Prevention: a guide to action*. London: CAPT, 1989.

Child Accident Prevention Trust. *Preventing accidents to children – a training resource for health visitors*. London: Community Education Development Centre, HEA, 1991.

Cohen D, Kilham H, Oates K. *The Complete Book of Child Safety*. Bromley: Harrap, 1991.

Constantinides P. *The Management Response to Childhood Accidents* (A guide to effective use of NHS information and resources to prevent accidental injuries in childhood). London: King's Fund Centre for Health Services Development, 1987.

Department of Trade and Industry, Health Education Authority. *Approaches to local child accident prevention*. London: CAPT, 1991.

Department of Transport. *Transport statistics, Great Britain, 1977–1987*. London: HMSO, 1989.

Haddon W Jr., Baker SP. Injury Control. *Preventive and Community Medicine*. 109–140. Clark D, MacMahon B (Eds). Boston, 1991.

Health Education Council and Scottish Health Education Group. *Play it Safe*, 1982.

Illingworth CM. *The Diagnosis and Primary Care of Accidents and Emergencies in Children*. Oxford: Blackwell Scientific Publications, 1978.

Jackson RH (Ed). *Children, the Environment and Accidents*. Tunbridge: Pitman Medical, 1977.

Jackson RH. *The basic principles of accident prevention in childhood*. Geneva: WHO, 1982.

Kempe RS, Kempe CH. *Child Abuse*. London: Fontana Open Books, 1982.

Kohler L, Jackson RH (Eds). *Traffic and Children's Health*. Stockholm: Nordic School of Public Health, 1987.

Laidman P. *The role of the health visitor in the prevention of accidents to children* (Research report No 12). London: HEA, 1987.

Levene S. *Play it Safe – The Complete Guide to Child Accident Prevention*. London: BBC Books, 1992.

Manciaux M, Romer CJ (Eds). *Accidents in childhood and adolescence – the role of research*. WHO/INSERM, 1991.

Office of Health Economics. *Accidents in childhood*. London: Office of Health Economics (briefing No 17), 1981.

Pearn J (Ed). *Accidents to Children – their Incidence, Causes and Effects*. Melbourne: Child Accident Prevention Foundation of Australia, 1983.

Pearn J (Ed). *The Prevention of Childhood Accidents – Design, Education and Legislation*. Melbourne: Child Accident Prevention Foundation of Australia, 1982.

Pless IB. *The Science and Art of Injury Prevention in Childhood: Perspectives from Britain and Abroad*. London: Child Accident Prevention Trust, 1992.

Poche C, Yode P, Miltenburger R. Teaching self-protection to children using television techniques. *J Appl Behav Anal*. 1988; **21**: 253–61.

Raymond S, Tatum S. *An evaluation of the effectiveness of the RAC/ACU motorcycle training scheme*. Salford: University of Salford Press, 1977.

Renaud L, Suissa S. Evaluation of the efficacy of simulation games in traffic safety education of kindergarten children. *Am J Public Health*. 1989; **79**: 307–9.

Research Institute for Consumer Affairs. *Disability – The long-term consequences of accidents to children* (Occasional Paper 4). London: CAPT, 1984.

Riding P. *Play it Safe! The Story of a Nationwide Child Accident Prevention Campaign.* London: BBC Education, 1983.

Sayer S. *Playing Safe.* Wellingborough: Thorsons, 1989.

Struckman-Johnson DL, Lund AK, Williams AF, Osborne DW. Comparative effects of driver improvement programs on crashes and violations. *Acc Anal Prev.* 1989; **21**: 203–15.

Taylor C. An Accident Prevention Intervention Programme. In Pearn J, *The Prevention of Childhood Accidents.* Melbourne: Child Accident Prevention Foundation of Australia, 1982.

Valman HB. *Accident and Emergency Paediatrics* (2nd edn). Oxford: Blackwell Scientific Publications, 1979.

Vince CJ (Ed). *Preventing Adolescent Injury: Roles for Health Professionals.* Newton, Mass: Education Development Centre, 1989.

Whalley J. *The National Health Service and Social Cost of Children's Accidents: A Pilot Study.* London: Child Accident Prevention Trust, 1992.

Wilson MH, Baker SP, Teret SP, *et al. Saving Children. A Guide to Injury Prevention.* New York: Oxford University Press, 1991.

World Health Organization. *Accidents in childhood – facts as a basis for prevention.* (Report of an Advisory Group, Technical Services Report Number 118.) Geneva: WHO, 1957.

Monographs, journal articles and scientific papers on social and environmental factors and children at work

Adelstein AM, White GC. Causes of children's deaths analysed by social class. In *Child Health, A collection of studies on medical and population subjects.* London: HMSO, 1976.

Alwash R, McCarthy M. Accidents in the home among children under five: ethnic differences or social disadvantage? *Br Med J.*, 1988; **296**: 1450–3.

Avery JG, Vaudin J, Watson JM. *Geographical and social variations in deaths from childhood accidents in England and Wales 1975–1984. Public Health.* 1990; **104**: 171–82.

Bijur PE, Stewart-Brown S, Butler N. Child Behaviour and Accidental Injury in 11,966 pre-school children. *Am J Dis Child.* 1986; **140**: 487–92.

British Medical Association. *Living with Risk.* Chichester: Wiley for the BMA, 1987.

Brown GW, Davidson S. Social class, psychiatric disorder of mother and accidents to children. *Lancet*, 1978; **1**: 378–81.

Cameron D, Bishop C, Sibert JR. Farm Accidents in Children. *Br Med J.* 1992; **305**: 23–5.

Children's Legal Centre Information Sheet. *Young people at work*. London: Children's Legal Centre, 1987.

Grieve R. Young children's perception of danger. *Br J Dev Psychol*. 1985; **3**: 385–92.

Health and Safety Commission. *Preventing accidents to children in agriculture – approved code of practice and guidance notes*. London: HMSO, 1988.

MacLennon E, Fitz J, Sullivan J. *Working Children* (Low Pay Pamphlet No 4). London: Low Pay Unit, 1985.

Klein D. Societal influences on childhood accidents. *Accid Anal Prev*. 1980; **12**: 275–81.

Lavalette M, McKechnie J, Hobbs S. *The Forgotten Workforce: Scottish Children at Work*. Glasgow: Scottish Low Pay Unit, 1991.

MacFarlane A. Child Deaths from Accidents: Place of Accidents. *Population Trends* 1979; **15**: 10–15.

MacFarlane A, Fox J. Child Deaths from Accidents and Violence. *Population Trends*. 1978; **12**: 22–7.

Marcusson H. Oehmisch W. Accident Mortality in Childhood in selected countries of different continents 1950–71. *WHO Statistics Report*. 1971; **30**(1): 57–92.

Marmot M, Adelstein A, Balushu L. Immigrant mortality in England and Wales. *Population Trends*, 1983.

Mitchell RG. Accidents in childhood. *Dev Med Child Neurol*. 1967; **9**: 767–8.

Norman L.E (Ed). *Road Traffic Accidents: Epidemiology, Control and Prevention*. Geneva: WHO, 1962.

Office of Population, Censuses and Surveys. *Occupational Mortality, decennial supplement 1970–72: England and Wales* (Series 23, No. 1). London: HMSO, 1978.

Pochin E.E. The acceptance of risk. *Br Med Bull*. 1975; **31**: 184–90.

Pond C, Searle A. *The Hidden Army. Children at Work in the 1990s*. London: Low Pay Unit Pamphlet No. 55 (undated).

Sharples PM, Storey A, Aynsley-Green A, Eyre JA. Causes of fatal accidents to children involving head injury in the Northern Region 1979–86. *Br Med J*. 1990; **301**: 1193–7.

Sibert JR. Accidents to children; the doctor's role. Education or environmental change? *Arch Dis Child*. 1991, **66**: 890–93.

Sibert JR, Maddocks GB, Brown BM. Childhood accidents – an endemic of epidemic proportions. *Arch Dis Child*. 1981; **56**: 225–7.

Sibert J.R. Stress in families of children who have ingested poisons. *Br Med J*. 1975; **3**: 87–9.

Taylor B, Wadsworth J, Butler NR. Teenage Mothering; admissions to hospital and accidents during the first five years. *Arch Dis Child*. 1983; **58**: 6–11.

Vipulendran V, Mason AR, Sunderland R. Cost to the NHS of accidents to children in the West Midlands. *Br Med J*. 1988; **296**: 611.

World Health Organization. The epidemiology of road traffic accidents. *WHO Regional Bulletin European Series No 2*. Geneva: WHO, 1976.

Road traffic accidents

Arnburg PW. The design and effect of child restraint systems in vehicles. *Ergonomics*. 1978; **21**: 681–90.

Avery JG, Avery PJ. Scandinavian and Dutch Lessons in Childhood Road Traffic Accident Prevention. *Br Med J*. 1982; **285**: 621–2.

Backett EM, Johnston AM. Social patterns of road accidents to children. *Br Med J*. 1959; **14**: 409–413.

Baker SP. Motor vehicle occupant deaths in young children. *Pediatrics*. 1979; **64**: 860–61.

Bodenham A, Newman RJ. Restraint of children in cars. *Br Med J*. 1991; **303**: 1283–4.

Chapman AJ, Wade FM, Foot HC (Eds). *Pedestrian Accidents*. Chichester: Wiley, 1982.

Child Accident Prevention Trust. *Every Ride a Safe Ride*. London: CAPT, 1992.

Child Accident Prevention Trust. *Guidance Notes on Child Car Seat Schemes* (2nd edn). London: CAPT, 1990.

Child Accident Prevention Trust. *Low Cost Cycle Helmets Schemes: Current Practice Guide No 2*. London: CAPT 1992.

Child Accident Prevention Trust. *The safety of children in cars*. London: CAPT, 1988.

County Road Safety Officers Association. *A Highway Code for Children*. London: CRSOA, 1984.

Department of Transport. *Compulsory seat-belt wearing*. London: HMSO, 1985.

Department of Transport. *Children and roads: A safer way*. London: HMSO, 1990.

Department of Transport. *Kill your speed, not a child*. London: HMSO, 1990.

Howarth CI, Routledge DA, Repetto-Wright R. An analysis of road accidents involving child pedestrians. *Ergonomics*. 1974; **17**: 319–30.

Howarth CI, Repetto-Wright R. The Measurement of Risk and Attribution of Responsibility for Child Pedestrian Accidents. (*Safety Education*). RoSPA, 1978; **144**: 10–13.

Illingworth CM. 227 Road Accidents to children. *Acta Paediatr Scand*. 1979; **68**: 869–73.

Jackson RH. Hazards to children in Traffic. *Arch Dis Child*. 1978; **53**: 807–813.

Lawson SD. *Accidents to young pedestrians: distribution, circumstances, consequences and scope for counter-measures*. AA Foundation for Road Safety research and Birmingham City Council, 1990.

Local Authority Associations. *Road Safety Code of Good Practice*. London: LAA, 1989.

Organization for Economic Cooperation and Development. *Traffic Safety of*

Children. Paris: OECD, 1983.

Pearn JH. Fatal motor vehicle accidents involving Australian children. *Aust Paediatr J*. 1978; **14**: 74–7.

Plowden S, Hillman M. *Danger on the road: The needless scourge*. Policy Studies Institute, 1984.

Preston B. Statistical Analysis of Child Pedestrian accidents in Manchester and Salford. *Acc Anal Prev*. 1972; **4**: 323–32.

Preston B. *Child pedestrian accidents in Manchester and Salford*. Manchester: Institute of Advanced Studies, 1976.

Robertson LG. Crash involvement of teenage drivers when driver education is eliminated from high school. *Am J Pub Hlth*. 1980; **70**: 599–603.

Sabey BE. *Road safety and value for money* (TRRS Supplementary Report No 581). Transport and Road Research Laboratory, 1980.

Sabey BE, Banbana E. Road accidents in childhood: the problem, In *Proceedings of a Conference on Road Accidents in Childhood*. London: Parliamentary Advisory Council for Transport Safety and the Child Accident Prevention Trust, 1987.

Sadler J. *Children and Road Safety: A survey amongst mothers*. London: Office of Population, Censuses and Surveys Social Survey Division, HMSO, 1972.

Sandels S. *Children in Traffic*. London: Elek, 1975.

Thompson RS, Rivara FP, Thompson FP. A Case Control Study of the Effectiveness of Bicycle Safety Helmets. *N Eng J Med*. 1989; **320**: 1361–7.

Ward H. *Preventing Road Accidents to Children: The role of the NHS*. London. HEA, 1991.

Williams AF, Zador P. Injuries to children in automobiles in relation to seating location and restraint use. *Accid Anal Prev*. 1977; **9**: 69–76.

World Health Organization. *The Epidemiology of Road Traffic Accidents*. Copenhagen: WHO Regional Office for Europe, 1976.

Home accidents

Backett EM (Ed). *Domestic Accidents*. Geneva: WHO, 1965.

British Association of Paediatric Surgeons. *Report of the Child Resistant Closures Working Party*. London: British Association of Paediatric Surgeons, 1983.

Burman S, Glen H. Accidents in the Home. London: Croom Helm, 1977.

Child Accident Prevention Trust. *Architectural glass accidents to children* (Occasional paper no 3). London: CAPT, 1982.

Child Accident Prevention Trust. *Burns and Scald Accidents to Children*. London: Bedford Square Press/NCVO, 1985.

Child Accident Prevention Trust. *Keep Them Safe*. London: CAPT, 1990.

Child Accident Prevention Trust. *Keep your Baby Safe*. London: CAPT, 1990.

Colver AF, Hutchison PJ, Judson EC. Promoting Children's Home Safety. *Br Med J*. 1982; **285**: 1177–80.

Committee on Accident and Poison Prevention. First aid for the choking child. *Am Acad Paediatr*. 1981; **67**: 744.

Craft AW, Lawson GR, Williams H, Sibert J. Accidental childhood poisoning with household products. *Br Med J*. 1984; **288**: 682.

Craft AW. Circumstances surrounding deaths from accidental poisonings 1974–1980. *Arch Dis Child*. 1983; **58**: 544–6.

Department of Prices and Consumer Protection. The Home Accident Surveillance System. *Analysis of Domestic Accidents to Children*. London: Department of Prices and Consumer Protection, 1982.

Department of Trade and Industry. *Child poisoning from household products*. London: HMSO, 1980.

Ewart N. *Unsafe as Houses: A Guide to Home Safety*. Poole: Blandford Press, 1981.

Fleming P, Gilbert R, Aza Y, *et al*. Interaction between bedding and sleeping position in the sudden death syndrome: a population-based case-control study. *Br Med J*. 1990; **301**: 85–9.

Fraser N.C. Accidental poisoning deaths in British children 1958–1977. *Br Med J*. 1980; **280**: 1595–8.

Goulding R. *Poisoning*. Oxford: Blackwell Scientific Publications, 1983.

Lawson GR, Craft AW, Jackson RH. Changing pattern of poisoning in children in Newcastle 1974–1981. *Br Med J*. 1983, **287**: 15–17.

MacQueen IAG. *A Study of Home Accidents in Aberdeen*. Edinburgh: Churchill Livingstone, 1960.

McLean W. Child poisoning in England and Wales – some statistics on admission to hospital 1964–1976. *Health Trends*. 1980; **12**: 9–12.

Mofenson HC, Greensher J. Management of the choking child. *Paediatr Clin North Am*. 1985. **32**: 183–92.

Office of Population, Censuses and Surveys. *Deaths by accidental poisonings 1962–1976*. London: HMSO 1978.

Page M. *Child Safety and Housing*. London: Child Accident Prevention Trust, 1985.

Pearn J, Nixon J, Ashford A, Corcoran A. Accidental poisoning in childhood – five year urban population study with 15 year analysis of fatality. *Br Med J*. 1984; **288**: 44–6.

Vale JA, Meredith TJ. *A concise guide to the management of poisoning*. London: Churchill Livingstone 1985.

School and play accidents

Bennett J. *School accidents*. London: Child Accident Prevention Trust, 1985.

Chilton T. *Children's play in Newcastle-upon-Tyne*. National Playing Fields Association, 1985.

Department of Education and Science (now Department of Education). *Guidelines to schools on First Aid*. London: DES, 19.

Department of Education and Science. *Safety in Education series*. London: DES, published between 1972/1983

Fair Play for Children. *Danger on the Playground*. London: FPC, 1978.

Fireworks involved in accidents in Great Britain 1981/85. Birmingham: RoSPA, 1986.

King K, Ball D. *A Holistic Approach to Accident and Injury Prevention in Children's Playgrounds*. London: LSS, 1989.

National Children's Play and Recreation Unit, (Department of Education and Science, Welsh Office Education Department). *Playground Safety Guidelines*. London: NCPRU, 1992.

Sport and leisure accidents

Avery JG, Harper P, Ackroyd S. Do we pay too dearly for our sport and leisure activities? *Public Health*. 1990; **104**: 417–23.

Firth JL. Equestrian injuries. In Schneider, *Sports injuries, mechanisms, prevention and treatment*. Philadelphia: Williams and Wilkins, 1985.

Gustafsson LH, Hammarström A, Linden K, *et al*. Child-environment supervisors – a new strategy for prevention of childhood accidents. *Acta Pediatr Scand*. 1979; suppl 275: 102–107.

Jackson RH, Craft AW. Injuries to Boys who Scramble. *Br Med J*. 1979; **i**: 1624.

Kemp A, Sibert JR. Drowning and Near-Drowning in Children in the United Kingdom: Lessons for Prevention. *Br Med J*. 1992; **304**: 1143–6.

Kemp AM, Sibert JR. Outcome in children who nearly drown: a British Isles study. *Br Med J*. 1991; **302**: 931–3.

Levene S. Dog bites to children. *Br Med J*. 1991; **303**: 466.

Mason MA. Children on motorcycles: a cause for concern. *Br Med J*. 1984; **289**: 854–5.

OPCS. *Fatal accidents during sporting and leisure activities*. London: HMSO, 1990.

Pearn JH, Nixon J. Prevention of childhood drowning accidents. *Med J Aust*. 1977; **1**: 616–8.

Pearn JH. The management of near-drowning. *Br Med J*. 1985; **291**: 1447–52.

Peterson R. Morbidity of childhood near-drowning. *Paediatrics*. 1977; **59**: 364–70.

Salzer E.M. *The child's right to play – the Swedish concept for better play facilities*. The Swedish Institute, paper No 220.

Shewell PC, Nancarrow JP. Dogs that Bite. *Br Med J*. 1991; **303**: 1912–3.

Smith RA, Ling S, Alexander FW. Golf related head injuries in children. *Br Med J*. 1991; **302**: 1505–506.

Regular publications on accidents

Annual Report of the Registrar General for Northern Ireland. London: HMSO, annually.

Annual Report of the Registrar General for Scotland. London: HMSO, annually.

Child Accident Prevention Trust: *Child Safety Review*. Published twice yearly.

Department of Transport. *Road Accidents Great Britain. The Casualty Report*. London: HMSO, annually.

Events of the year Accidents and Disasters. London: J Whitaker, annually.

Health and Safety Commission. *Child Safety on Farms*. London: HMSO, annually.

Health and Safety Executive Pamphlets on Agricultural Safety. London: HMSO, published annually/biannually.

Home Office. *Fire Statistics United Kingdom*. London: Home Office, annually.

Mortality Statistics Accidents and Violence. London: HMSO, quarterly.

Office of Population, Censuses and Surveys. *Death by Cause* (DHL series). London: HMSO, quarterly.

Royal Society for the Prevention of Accidents. Birmingham: RoSPA. *Care on the Road. Care in the Home. Safety Education*.

Royal Society for the Prevention of Accidents. *Road Accident Statistics* Birmingham: RoSPA, annually.

INDEX

Abuse 115–24
  physical 53, 60
    warning signs 117
  psychological 117–18
  sexual 118, 118–19
Accident and Emergency department,
    child abuse and 123
Accident and Emergency specialists 130
Accident and Emergency system,
    computerized 157
Accident proneness 17
Addresses, useful 186–94
Adolescents/teenagers 12
  driving by 133–4
Adults, pedestrian accidents and
    responsibility of 25, see also Parents
Advertising 164–5
Advertising Standards Association 164
Aerosols 54
Age 6–7
  bicycle riding and 29
  car safety devices and 37
  home accidents and 44, 45
    death from 49
  school accidents and 71
Aggression 13
Agricultural accidents see Farm
    accidents
Air travel 41–2
Apnoea monitors 69
Architects 131, 139
Area Child Protection Committee 120
Asian families 16
Assault 115–24
Attitudes
  changing 128, 174
  parental 12–13

Baby 6, 11
  home accidents 45, 66–7
  newborn, midwives and the 130

Baby bouncers 67
Baby walkers 66
Bath tub drowning 94
Behaviour, child's 13–14, 128–9
  changing 174
  pedestrian accidents and 25
  poisoning and 53
Bicycles 28–33, 135, 136
  accidents with 28–33, 136
  crash helmets 135
  state of 30
Bites 96–7
Black spots, accident 167–7
Boys see Gender
Bouncing castles 78
British Association of Paediatric
    Surgeons 163
British Medical Association 162
British Paediatric Accident and
    Emergency Medicine Group 163
British Paediatric Association 163
British Red Cross Society 187
British Safety Council 162
British Standards Institution (BSI) and
    their standards 145–7, 151–2, 163
  horse riding and 100–101
  playgrounds and 80–81
British Summer Time 167
Brittle bone disease 15
BSI see British Standards Institution
Builders 139
Building Research Establishment 153
Building safety 142, 154
Building sites 46
Bullying 73, 74, 123
Bureau European de Union
    Consumateurs 151
Burns 48–53
Buses, children in 39
Bye–laws, local 140–41

Car(s) 33–8, 180–81, *see also* Drivers;
    Road traffic; Vehicles
  future improvements 180–81
  occupants 33–8
    fires and 48
    law regarding 37, 143, 155
    safety devices 36, 37, 133, 143, 181
Care Order 120
CEN and CENELEC 150
Central Office of Information 159
Child abuse *see* Abuse
Child Accident Prevention Trust 139,
    162, 165
Child development 11–12, 129
Children Act 1989 119
Child resistant containers 56
Children's Hospitals Injury Reporting
    and Prevention Programme
    (CHIRPP) 157
CHIRPP 157
Choking 61–2
Coaches (sporting) 89, 132
Coaches (vehicle) 39
Committee European de Normalisation
    (CEN) and CENELEC 150
Community leaders, teaching 177
Community nurses 130
Computerized Accident and Emergency
    system 157
Consumer organizations, European
    150–51
Consumer Policy Committee in British
    Standards Institute 151–2
Consumer Services, local authority 160
Consumers' Association on product
    safety 145, 163
COPOLOC 150
Costing an accident 170–72
Cot death 67–70
Council Committee on Consumer Policy
    (COPOLOC) 150
Council Engineers and Surveyor's
    Departments 160
Cranfield Institute of Technology 152–53
Cumberledge report on community
    nursing 130
Cutting accidents 57–9
Cycles *see* Bicycles; Motorcycles

Death (accidental) 1–4
  age and 7
  causes 2, 8
  cot 67–70
  on farms 109–10

at home 49
  measurement of numbers of 172–3
  non–accidental 115–16, 122–4
  on roads 8, 166
Deliberate harm *see* Non–accidental
    injury
Department of Education 159
  school accidents and 74
Department of Employment 159
Department of Health 156–8
Department of the Environment 158
Department of Trade and Industry 158–9
Department of Transport 158, 165
Designers 131, 183
  home 52, 131, 180
  role 183
Development, child's 11–12
Disabilities, children with 14–15
Disadvantaged children 13
Disasters, natural and man–made
    113–14, 138–9
Doctors, child abuse and 121, 122, *see
    also* General practitioners
Dog bites 96, 97
Domestic accidents *see* Home
Down's syndrome 14
Drivers
  cycle accident prevention and 32
  horse riders and 100
  pedestrian accident prevention and 27
  teenage 133–4
Drowning 91–5
Drugs 56

EC *see* European Economic Community
Education 127, 128–35, 177–9, *see also*
    School; Teachers
  farm safety 111–12
  future directions 177–9
Education authorities and services 160
  child abuse reduction and 121
  school accident prevention and 74
Education programmes 173–5
  redesigning and modifying 174
EEC *see* European Economic
    Community
Electricity board 64
Electrocution 63–4
Emergency Protection Order 120
Employment of Children Act 1973 108
Engineers 131
Environment(s) 10–11, 126, 135–9,
    179–81
  accidents and 10–11

books and publications on 199–200
drowning 95–6
farm 112
home 50
safe, creating 3–4, 127, 135–9, 179–81
  future directions 179–81
Environmental Health Departments 160
Epilepsy 15
Ethnic minorities 15–16
  education of parents in 131
European Consumer Product Safety
  Association 151
European Economic Community
  product safety and the 149, 164
  road safety and the 168–9

Fairgrounds 80–81
Falls 43–7
  from horses 98, 99
Farm accidents 109–12, 138
  legislation preventing 108–9, 112, 143,
    154–5
Fat children 15
Fire(s) 52–3, 161
  car 48
Fire
  Fire Prevention Officers 161
  house 48–9, 52–3
    ethnic minorities and 16
    legislation concerning 141–2
Firearms 103–5
Fire authorities 161
Fire Research Station 153
Fireworks 81–4
First Aid 133
Foreign bodies, inhalation/ingestion of
  61–2
Fragilatas osseum 15
Furniture, nursery 67

Gender 5
  home accidents and 44
    death from 49
  pedestrian accidents and 25
  school accidents and 72
  sport accidents and 86
  suicide and 123
General practitioners 131
  child abuse and 122
Geographical factors 8–10
Girls see Gender
Glass injuries 57, 58
Glue sniffing 54
Government, accident prevention and

the 40, 131–2, 140, 156–61, 166–7
bicycle 33
burn 52
cutting/piercing 59
Guidelines on Child Safety in Housing
  139

Haddon's Principles 125
Handicapped children 14–15
Hanging 60
Hats see Helmets
Hazard reduction workshops 133
Headgear, protective see Helmets
Health and Safety at Work Act 1981
  108, 108–9
Health and Safety at Work etc. Act 1974
  76, 112
Health and Safety Commission 159
  Preventing Accidents to Children in
    Agriculture: Approved Code of
    Practice and Guidance notes 112
Health and Safety (First Aid)
  Regulations 1981 76
Health authorities, car occupant accident
  prevention and 38
Health Education 133–4
Health Education Authority 161
Health, general and child, books and
  publications on 195–6
Health of the Nation (Green Paper) 4
Health professionals/staff 129–31, 177–8
  active participation 177–8
  burn prevention and 51
  poisoning prevention and 56–7
Health region (in UK), costs of accidents
  to 171–2
Health visitors
  checklist 130
  child abuse and 122
Hearing 14
Helmets
  cycle crash 135
  horse riding 98, 99, 100–101
Home 43–70, 139, 145–7, 180
  books and publications on accidents at
    202–3
  deaths at 8
  designers and builders 52, 131, 180
  fires at see Fire
  fittings/equipment in, improving safety
    of 145–7
  future improvements 180
  legislation regarding safety at 141–2,
    153–4, 182

Home Accident Surveillance System 157
Home Office 158
Homicide 115–16
Horse riding 97–101
Hospitals, child abuse and 122–3
House *see* Home
Housing 13
Housing departments, fall prevention
    and 47
Hypothermia, drowning and 95

Ice sports 90–91
IEC 150
Independent Safety Organizations 161–3
Independent school, accident prevention
    75
Infants, pre–school 6, 11–12, *see also*
    Baby; Toddlers
Ingestion 61–2
Inhalation 61–2
Injury control 125
Institute for Consumer Ergonomics 152
Intelligence 13
International Electrical Commission 150
International organizations 149–51,
    163–4
    addresses 193–4
International Standards Organization
    150, 164
ISO 150, 164

Keep Them Safe 67
Keep Your Baby Safe 67
Kidsafe houses 131, 139
Knowledge, education increasing 128,
    174

Labelling 148–9
Law (and its enforcement) 127, 139–55,
    181–4
    car occupants and the 37, 143, 155
    child abuse and the 119–21
    farm accidents and the 108–9, 112,
        143, 154–5
    fireworks and the 83
    future changes 181
    school accidents and the 76, 142–3, 154
Lead poisoning, Asian families and 16
Legislation *see* Law
Leisure Accident Surveillance System
    157
Leisure and recreation 85–105, *see also*
    Play
    accidents associated with 85–105

books and publications on 204–5
    supervisors 132
Liability to accidents 17
Life years, loss of, measurement 173
Local authorities, preventive role of
    160–61
    burns and 52
    cycle accidents and 32
    falls and 47
    farm accidents and 112
    pedestrian accidents and 28
    playground accidents and 79–80
    poisoning and 56–7
    school accidents and 74
Local bye–laws 140–41
Local environment 139
Local government 160–61
Local groups, independent 163
Low Pay Unit, accidents with working
    children and the 106, 108

Man–made disasters 113–14
Manufacturers and retailers/traders 132,
    148
    cuts/piercing injuries and 59
    firework 83
    inhalation/ingestion of foreign bodies
        and 62
    motorcycle scrambling and 103
    of toxic substances 56
    toy 66
    vehicle *see* Vehicle
Media influences 164–6
Medical Commission on Accident
    Prevention 162
Medical officers, school 75
Medicine cupboards 56
Midwives 130
Minibuses 38–9
Ministry of Agriculture and Fisheries 159
Ministry of National Heritage 159
Mortalities *see* Death
Motorcycles 39–40, 101–3, 134
    sports involving 101–3
    training 134

National Association for Safety in the
    Home 163
National House Builders Federation 139
National Poisons Information Service 56,
    191
National Radiological Protection Board
    159
National Society for the Prevention of

Cruelty to Children 116
Natural disasters 113–14, 138–9
Natural environment 138–9
Newcastle-upon-Tyne health visitors
    study 134
    Head injury study 138
Non–accidental injury 53, 60, 115–24
    with firearms 104
Northern Ireland Office 159
NSPCC 116
Nurse(s)
    child abuse and 122
    community 130
    school 75
Nursery furniture 67

Obese children 15
OECD 149, 164
Office of Population, Censuses and
    Surveys 159
Organization of Economic Cooperation
    and Development 149, 164
Overactivity 13
Overweight children 15

Packaging, safety 159
Paediatricians 130
Parents 129, see also Adults
    attitudes 12–13
    burns and 50, 51
    car occupant accidents and 38
    child abuse and 116, 121
    cuts/piercing injuries and 58–9
    cycle accidents and 31
    drowning and 94, 96
    in ethnic minorities, education of 131
    falls and 46–7
    home accidents and 50, 55
    prevention of 46–7, 51, 56, 58–9
    horse riding and 100
    motorcycle scrambling accidents 102–3
    pedestrian accidents and 27
    playground accidents and 80
    poisoning and 55, 56
    school accidents and 75–6
    sport accidents and 89–90, 91
Parliament (British), law and 140
Parliamentary Advisory Council for
    Transport Safety 162–3
Pedestrian accidents 19–28
    ethnic minorities and 16
Pedestrian crossings 23, 24
Pelican crossings 22–3
Pharmacists 56

Physical abuse see Abuse
Piercing accidents 57–9
Plants 56
Play, accidents at 12, 76–84, 138, see
    also Leisure and recreation; Sport
    accidents; Toys
    books and publications on 203–4
Playgrounds 76–80, 138, 154, 181–2
Play it Safe 134, 165
Poisoning 9, 53–7
    ethnic minorities and 16
    legislation relating to 142, 153
    warnings preventing 148–9
Poisons, centres 56, 191
Police 161
    child abuse and 122
    cycle accident prevention and 32
Politicians see Government
Prevention/reduction (of accidents)
    125–55, 196–9
    in air travel 42
    books and publications on 196–9
    of burns/scalds 50–52
    to car occupants 35–7
    of child abuse 121–2
    of cot deaths 69
    of cuts/piercing injuries 58–9
    to cyclists 31–3
    of dog bites 97
    of drowning 95–6
    efficacy, evaluation 170
    of electrocution 63–4
    at fairgrounds 81
    of falls 46–7
    on farms 111–12
    of fire 52–3
    of firearm accidents 105–6
    with fireworks 83–4
    at home 46–7, 50–52, 52–3, 55–7, 58–9,
        60–61, 62, 63–4, 66, 67, 69–70
    of inhalation/ingestion of foreign
        bodies 62
    investment in 134–5
    of motorcycle scrambling accidents
        102–3
    to pedestrians 26–8
    at playgrounds 79–80
    of poisoning 55–7
    to railway users 41
    at school 74–6
    at sea 42
    of sport accidents 88–90, 91
    strategies 126
    of suffocation/strangulation 60–61

of suicide 124
of toy accidents 66
in workplace 108–9, 111–13
Producers *see* Manufacturers
Product safety *see* Safety
Proneness, accident 17
Psychiatric disorders, suicide and 123
Psychological abuse 117–18
Public utility companies 160–61

Race *see* Ethnic minorities
Railways 40–41
Recreation *see* Leisure; Play; Sport
Reducing accidents *see* Prevention
Referees in sport 89, 132
Regulations *see* Law
Reporting of Injuries, Diseases and
    Dangerous Occurrences Regulations
    1985 76
Responsibility 156–69
  of adults for child pedestrian accidents
    25
  for product safety 147
Restraints, child 36–7, 133, 143, 181
Retailers/traders *see* Manufacturers and
    retailers
Risk 17
  of burns 49–50
Risk taking 13
Road Safety Officer 160
Road traffic accidents 19–40, 136, 161,
    165, 166–7, 167–8, 171, 183
  books and publications on 201–2
  costs 171
  cycle accidents classed as 30–31
  death in 8, 166
  Down's syndrome and 14
  ethnic minorities and 16
  hearing and 14
  legislation concerning 37, 143, 155, 183
  safety campaigns/measures in
    prevention of 166–7, 167–8
Road Traffic Acts 161
RoSPA 162
Royal Institute of British Architects 139
Royal Life Saving Society 163
Royal Society for the Prevention of
    Accidents 162
Rugby, spinal injuries 87
Rural environments 138, *see also* Farm

Safe environment *see* Environment
Safety 196–9
  books and publications on 196–9

building 142, 154
product 142, 144–53, 154, 181
  improving 127, 144–53, 154, 156–64,
    181
  organizations involved in 149–50,
    156–64
  responsibility for 147
at school 142–3
Safety campaigns and measures, current
    166–7
Safety devices/equipment 182–3
  in cars 36, 37, 133, 143, 181
  legislation regarding 182–3
  in sport 87
Safety Education 12
Safety packaging 159
Scalds 48–53
School(s) 71–6, 142–3
  accidents at 71–6
    books and publications on 203–4
    legislation preventing 76, 142–3, 154
  cycle accident prevention and 32
School children 6, 12
  farm accidents 110
  home accidents 45–6
  pedestrian accidents 22
  in vehicles, accident prevention 39
School medical officers 75
School nurses 75
Schools Council 161
Schools programmes 178–9
Scottish Office 159
Sea accidents 41–2
Season
  cycle accidents and 29
  pedestrian accidents and 22
Seat belts 34, 36, 143, 181
  in public service vehicles 39
Sex *see* Gender
Sexual abuse/assault 118, 118–19
SIDS 67–70
Sight 14
Skiing 90–91
Snake bite 97
Social workers and social services 160
  burn prevention and 51
  child abuse and 120, 121
Social/socioeconomic factors 8–10,
    10–11, 12–13, 13–14, 15, 199–200
  behaviour and 13–14
  books and publications on 199–200
  environments and 10–11
  urban 137–8
  parental attitudes and 12–13

pedestrian accidents and 20–21, 24–5
Sound 14
Speed restriction and control 168
Spinal injury in rugby 87
Sport accidents 88–91, 97–103, 132, 179,
    see also Leisure and recreation
  books and publications on 204
St Andrew's Ambulance Association 192
Stings 97
St John Ambulance Association 192
Strangulation 59–61
Stress 13
Sudden infant death syndrome (SIDS)
    67–70
Suffocation 59–61
Suicide 122–4
Swimming 91–5 *passim*

Teachers, preventive role of 129, *see also*
    Education
  burns and 51, 52
  falls and 46
  pedestrian accidents and 27
  school accidents and 74–5
  teaching about 177
Teaching of teachers 177, *see also*
    Training
Teenagers *see* Adolescents
Television 165
That's Life 165
1000 Family Study 11, 13
Throttling 60
Time of day
  cycle accidents and 29
  pedestrian accidents and 21, 22
  road accidents (in general) and 167
Toddlers 6, 11
  home accidents 45
Top Gear 166
Town planners and planning 131, 136,
    see also Urban environments
Toxic substances *see* Poisoning
Toys 64–6, 142, 144–5, 182–3, *see also*
    Play
  safety 142, 144–5
    improving 144–5

legislation on 142, 154, 182–3
Traders *see* Manufacturers and
    retailers/traders
Traffic, road *see* Road traffic accidents
Train(s) 40–41
Trainers, sport 132
Training of child in safety practices/
    awareness 178
Transport Research Laboratory 153, 161
Transport, road *see* Road traffic
    accidents

Urban environments 136–8, 180
  safe, creating 136–7, 180

Vehicles *see also specific types of vehicle*
  design, bad 34
  drivers of *see* Drivers
  retailers/traders and manufacturers,
    preventive role of
    burns and 52
    car occupant accidents and 38
    cycle accidents and 33
    pedestrian accidents and 28
Violence against the person 117, 122
Visual function 14
Voluntary organizations/agencies 132,
    161–3
  child abuse and 122

Warfare 113
Warning labels 56
Warning notices 148–9
Watchdog 165
Weapons 103–5
Welsh Office 159
White paper 157
WHO 151, 163–4, 184
Woonerf system 136, 180
Work, accidents at 106–12
  books and publications on 199–200
  legislation preventing 143, 154–5
World Health Organization 151, 163–4,
    184

Youth leaders 132